P9-DDJ-688

PSYCHE, CULTURE
AND THE
NEW SCIENCE

E.W.F. TOMLIN

PSYCHE, CULTURE AND THE NEW SCIENCE: The role of PN

ROUTLEDGE & KEGAN PAUL
London, Boston, Melbourne and Henley

ST. PHILIP'S COLLEGE LIBRARY

901
T659 p

First published in 1985
by Routledge & Kegan Paul plc

14 Leicester Square, London WC2H 7PH, England

9 Park Street, Boston, Mass. 02108, USA

464 St Kilda Road, Melbourne,
Victoria 3004, Australia and

Broadway House, Newtown Road,
Henley-on-Thames, Oxon RG9 1EN, England

Set in 10/12 pt Sabon
by Ann Buchan (Typesetters), Surrey
and printed in Great Britain
by Billing & Sons Ltd, Worcester

©E.W.F. Tomlin 1985

No part of this book may be reproduced in
any form without permission from the publisher,
except for the quotation of brief passages
in criticism

Library of Congress Cataloging in Publication Data

Tomlin, Eric Walter Frederick, 1913–
Psyche, culture, and the new science.
Includes index.
1. Civilization, Modern – 20th century.   2. Need
(Psychology)   3. Art – Psychological aspects.
4. Religion and culture.   I. Title.
CB427.T63   1985   909.82   84–11645

British Library CIP Data also available

ISBN 0-7102-0199-0

ST. PHILIP'S COLLEGE LIBRARY

This book is dedicated
to the memory of
ROBIN GEORGE COLLINGWOOD
(1889–1943);
and to
RAYMOND RUYER
Professor Emeritus
University of Nancy

my philosophical masters

[81047

Contents

ST. PHILIP'S COLLEGE LIBRARY

Foreword

We are subjects as well as objects, and quite complicated subjects at that. The severe tabu long enforced in many academic circles against admitting this obvious fact is beginning to lift. But it has unfortunately left us with a great deal of leeway to make up in in trying to understand the matter. E. W. F. Tomlin has written a lively, stimulating, challenging book which can really help us here. As he points out, the idea that pretending to be soulless would save us from superstition was always mistaken. 'One cannot cast out myth by rationalism, because pure rationalism is itself a myth. . . . The rational intelligence must therefore fight on two fronts and against two kinds of superstition – superstition as conventionally known and that other form of superstition, reductionism.' There is nothing scientific about deciding to reduce away and ignore the complex, turbulent, problem-filled inner life which we all share, simply for the sake of intellectual tidiness. What words are we to use for it? Psyche, soul, emotion, mind and spirit all have their problems, yet we shall need all these and more if we are to do any sort of justice to our subject. And the starting dangers and confusions of our prosperous age make this a matter of public as well as private urgency. I am sure that Tomlin is right to treat the systematic neglect and starvation of the inner life as a central problem of our culture, and that his suggestions on how to remedy it can be very valuable.

Mary Midgley

ST. PHILIP'S COLLEGE LIBRARY

Preface

The first draft of this essay was made some years ago, when through the good offices of the British Council I was awarded a Fellowship at Wolfson (then University) College, Cambridge. I wish to record my thanks to both institutions for what proved for me a memorable year. Under pressure of other business, the work was then laid aside, until the approach of 1984 prompted me, with my publisher's encouragement, to explore the implications of an expression which had meanwhile gained currency in my own circle.

I call the work an essay, because it amounts to no more than an outline of a very wide subject. There are several topics here raised which, for reasons of economy, I have refrained from following up in detail. Some of these I may deal with later: others are thrown out for consideration by those better qualified to handle them. I have done my best to avoid the use of jargon. Had I invented a new terminology, my thesis would no doubt have acquired an air, however specious, of scientific sophistication. What I wanted to do, rather, was to invite the reader to dismiss his preconceptions, 'scientific' or otherwise, and to verify what I had to say from personal experience. It would be convenient also if, before starting to read, he would rid himself of another preconception, namely that philosophical discourse is beyond his grasp. This is a common assumption, which some philosophers, for reasons of their own, have gone out of their way to promote.

Since the argument applies for the most part to both men and women, I have endeavoured to make this clear in the context, even though one personal pronoun may be used. To seek to avoid sexist language by resorting to expressions which are ambiguous amounts to sexism in disguise.

Finally, if my main argument leads to conclusions which are unacceptable to the Establishment, all I need say is that this is not the first time I have skirmished with orthodoxy – and by orthodoxy I mean roughly the point of view which has crystallized round positivism (in biology, mechanism), and its more recent developments. Nor, given the nature of works I have in progress, will it presumably be the last. I still believe that the central point of this essay is one which had been unaccountably ignored, and which, if properly grasped, should modify our views on matters of crucial importance. To quote Suzanne Langer: 'Most new discoveries are suddenly-seen things that were always there.'

E. W. F. Tomlin
Morwenstow-London

Introduction
Myth, ideology and taboo

Anyone who has reached mature years is aware that his or her world has been undergoing a series of increasingly grave crises. Admittedly, in a world without media this impression would be greatly reduced. An historian of the French Revolution has pointed out that during the whole of the Terror – indeed, throughout the civil disturbances and the years of conflict that followed – a gardener's magazine appeared week by week in Paris without the smallest hint that anything unusual was taking place. Until the last decades of the twentieth century, the convulsions – political, economic, or military – could be called *external*. They happened in 'the outside world'. Bio-technology has now brought about a revolution of an *internal* kind. This is only now beginning to be realized. The possibility of cloning has affected the integrity and inviolability of the person. The contraceptive pill has had an influence on the family which may permanently alter, if not destroy, its traditional form. Dr Gregory Pincus, the expert on controlling human fertility, may prove to have exerted an effect on the population, and on the individual outlook, greater by far than did the Revd Thomas Malthus. Deeper and more extensive have been disturbances in the psychic field. Nothing has satisfactorily taken the place of traditional religion, save religion deprived of its traditional characteristics. All the sentiments that can be scooped up from an undoctrinal Christianity, from a variety of Hindu or Buddhist sects, a Sufism thoroughly westernized, and from the teaching of gurus of increasingly suspect credentials, are pressed into the service of the ghost of a religion. It is perhaps regrettable that another name for religion cannot be found, because for many people – no doubt understandably – the word calls up some of the least edifying traits of human nature: hypocrisy, deceit, and an apparently

1

limitless gullibility. As for the prospects of a 'revival of religion' in the old sense, the philospher T. E. Hulme, though a traditionalist, wrote many years back: 'I have none of the feeling of nostalgia . . . the desire to recapture the sentiment of Fra Angelico, which seems to animate most modern defenders of religion. All that seems to me to be bosh.'[1] He was surely right; but, oddly enough, the desire to recapture religious emotion, if not religious doctrine, is as intense as ever. The communal psyche is debauched to a degree quite unprecedented. There is a belief-explosion. Even militant humanists are found to favour ethical 'churches' which draw heavily on religious capital; and those who profess no religion at all are almost always those, as we shall show, to whom religious terminology comes most easily and in embarrassing surfeit of metaphor and symbol. They 'take leave of God', but they trail behind them a string of edifying clichés. Furthermore, those who claim to derive their values from something called Literature lean heavily on one or two figures – D. H. Lawrence is an obvious example – who have either manufactured a private religion of their own or who have been turned into pontiffs by their disciples, as F. R. Leavis turned Lawrence into a latter-day magus. This is to reverse the humanist treatment of Holy Writ. Recently we had 'The Bible to be read as Literature'. Now we have Literature (or a selection of it) to be read as the Bible. The crisis is a cultural crisis in every sense. And we, in the year 1984, are all involved.

To some members of the intelligentsia, the chief claim to distinction of our age is the expulsion of taboos. *Tabu*, a term of Polynesian origin, was familiar in Tonga when Captain Cook discovered the island in 1771. It covered not merely things revered for their sacredness but things dreaded for their supposed maleficence. Such ambivalence of meaning still attaches to the word. Our age is also one of demythologizing, of conflicting ideologies, of informational hypertrophy, and of *paradis artificiels* – subcultures based on drugs, witchcraft, etc.

What has become apparent, however, is that taboos, myths, and even ideologies have only to be expelled for others forthwith to take their place. If the taboo on certain forms of sex-life has been lifted, one has been clamped down on wild-life. Nothing disrespectful may be said about the whale or even the dinosaur. Indeed, the environment itself in its natural aspects had been declared sacred, in the sense that it must not be profaned. Nuclear fall-out, the 'greenhouse effect' due to excessive carbon dioxide in the atmosphere and consequent overheating, herbicidal defoliation, certain pesticides, the destruction of the Amazonian rainforest, and much else, are considered, and quite rightly, to be profanations similar to the sacrileges and impieties of the past. Furthermore, although religious traditions are sometimes subject to ridicule, the condemnation is neither uniform nor consistent: films and dramas guying Christianity are shown simultaneously with one so respectful to Islam as to omit the figure of the Prophet, for whom divinity, in fact, has never been claimed.

In other words, taboo and myth are not in themselves pathological phenomena, as the positivist thinkers – beginning with August Comte, continuing with Freud, and including the neo-behaviourists – tended to suppose. They are a necessary ingredient in human culture, only subject to the control of man's other great faculty, his rational intelligence. It was not for nothing that Margaret Mead, renowned for her study of primitive society (though possibly mistaken in some of her conclusions), declared that she was a believer in totem and taboo. The customs of what the pioneer anthropologist Edward Tylor called primitive culture – the initiations, rites of passage, etc. – are characteristic in some measure of all society. This is true not least of societies based upon 'scientific socialism', which differ from their forerunners in the exaggeration of their communal rites, the crudity of their mythologizing, and the fanaticism of their ideological propaganda. Whereas such political ideologies need demythologizing in the interests of social concord and world peace, the myths associated with some other spheres need to be revived. The difficulty is that myths, like the traditions that embody them, cannot yield to artificial rehabilitation. All that can be done is to create the conditions best suited to their steady, if necessary slow, emergence. That they will emerge is certain, for man cannot live without them. One cannot cast out myth by rationalism, because pure rationalism is itself a myth. In any case, myth and science have always been intimately associated. 'Science', as Sir Karl Popper observed, 'must begin with myth and with the criticism of myth: neither with the collection of observations, nor with the invention of experiments, but with the discussion of myths and of magical techniques and practices.'[2] The rational intelligence must therefore fight on two fronts and against two kinds of superstition – superstition as conventionally known and that other form of superstition, reductionism.

Introduction

The educational systems of the Western World – which are often held up to the rest as examples for emulation – need reform in so far as they have tried, and largely failed, to supply that ethico-affective education which the family and the churches used to provide. Nor are they to be blamed for a failure which stems from the short-comings of those two institutions. The first has lost its cohesion; the second has compromised so much of recent years that the faithful – a small band in any case – hardly know where they stand. As for the rest, they seem to take their ethical standards, such as they are, as well as some of their myths, from the pop world: a circumstance which leaves them scarcely better off. The crisis of culture today is most acute not so much at the level of organized education – though the semi-literate products of our schools and even of our institutions of higher learning afford sufficient cause for alarm – as at that deeper level where the individual, at an age much earlier than is commonly imagined, begins to acquire what may be called instinctive education. This is the first psychic stage. But here we need to ask: what is the psyche?

1
Psyche, religion and the new science

The concept of psyche

If we examine works on psychology, we tend to find a conspiracy of silence regarding the definition of its central concept. In order to convince himself of this, the reader is invited to visit a large library and to study the relevant literature. If, after scrutinizing a hundred or so volumes, he is able to discover a consistent and coherent definition of the psyche, he will be more fortunate than the author, who has undertaken this task at more than one seat of learning. There must be few sciences which have been pursued for so long in a conceptual void. Books with titles such as *The Intrapsychic Self* [1] run to great length without providing the necessary enlightenment. Indeed, to take this book as an example, we are confronted at the outset with the question: 'What is the psyche of man – this never finished, for ever unfolding entity, which in its complexity has no equal in the world known to science?' – a question which forthwith gives place to a broader one: 'What is man – this lonely spectator of all times and places and all existences, who in his biologico-historical finitude is "touched inside" by all times and all existences? There are many approaches to these timeless questions', etc., etc. All we are told, however, is that 'the central factor' is 'what I call the intra-psychic self, this inner world of man', which is 'the core from which whatever is human expands and irradiates' – and which is also, we must remember, 'touched inside' by 'all times and existences'. It is not a promising beginning. 'The trouble is that the psychologists themselves cannot agree on what their science is about.' [2]

Nor, with very few exceptions, are the introductory volumes, the handbooks, the dictionaries, the digests, of much greater help. To take two examples. In *A Critical Dictionary of Psychoanalysis*, by Charles Rycroft (1972), we read: 'Psyche. The Mind. The psychoanalytical literature, following Freud, uses psyche and Mind *(Seele)* synonymously. Its two adjectives, psychical and psychic, are also synonymous with "mental" '. In *A Hundred Years of Psychology* (third edition, 1964), by J. C. Flugel and D. J. West, we find in the Index no mention of 'psyche' at all, and only one allusion to 'mind'. Moreover, the latter refers to a paragraph dealing with 'Wittgenstein's school of logical positivism' and the 'logical positivist standpoint of Ryle's *Concept of Mind'*, both descriptions of doubtful accuracy.[3] Yet it is evident that when psychiatrists, and writers on psychiatry, talk of psyche, they do *not* mean simply mind. The concept of the psyche was introduced, and the science of psychology promoted, because the psyche was considered to form a particular, if vaguely demarcated, mental sphere.

Like most other sciences, the science of psychology was the invention of the Greeks. Perhaps it was the single-handed invention of Aristotle; but the meaning of psychological terms in early Greek literature, much of it fragmentary, is often difficult to determine. Perhaps the most successful attempt at interpretation was that made by R. B. Onions in his *Origins of European Thought* (1951).[4] According to Onions, the word *phrenes*, which eventually came to stand for intellectual thought, originally meant 'lungs', though by the time of Hippocrates and Plato it had come to signify 'diaphragm'.[5] In Homer, *thymos*, namely mind or consciousness, was contained in *phrenes*, and therefore meant 'breath'; but breath was related to the blood, and the two in combination gathered strength with the nourishment of the body, and diminished with the body's inanition. Thus, with the shedding of blood, *thymos* began to take its departure from the body and finally left it inanimate.

The seat of the emotions was the heart, since the blood was thought to be concentrated there. Emotion caused changes in breathing, and therefore affected the *thymos*.

In contrast to *thymos*, psyche meant originally the soul, which was immortal. It was associated with the head. As the cerebro-spinal fluid was identified with the seminal fluid – an identification which was to have a long history – *psyche* was transmitted in the act of procreation by the father. The importance of chastity lay in the fact that it served to maintain vitality or the divine spark.

In due course, the distinction between *thymos* and *psyche* became blurred; and thus in Aristotle's *De Anima*, the discussion of the soul or *psyche* was also the discussion of that which constituted a living being. A prolonged debate ensued concerning the location of the seat of consciousness. Was it in the heart, as the Egyptians had thought, or the head?

In *De Anima* Aristotle was concerned with the soul and in the *Metaphysics* with the intellect. Thus there grew up a distinction between intellect and soul whereby intellect was concerned with thinking and the soul with activities which, even in the theological sphere, were designated as feeling. Aristotle had given little attention to feeling in *De Anima*.[6]

No doubt because of a new attitude towards feeling, and because of the uprush of communal feelings of a particular kind, the science of psychology was reborn – though sometimes in unscientific guise – at the end of the fifteenth century. This stage was of great importance, though it is often neglected: the article on the History of Psychology in the *Encyclopaedia Britannica* (1963) jumps from St Augustine to the seventeenth century. In what does its importance consist?

In 1486 was published a volume entitled *Malleus Maleficarum*, or the 'Hammer of Witches', by the Dominican Heinrich Institor (Krämer) and Jakob Sprenger. This murky treatise became the bible of the organizers of a relentless witch-hunt. The authors sought to show 'how devils can enter the heads and other parts of the body of men, and move the inner mental images from place to place'. The operation is without pain because 'he [the devil] does not cause any actual physical change in the organs, but only moves the mental images'. Relying on this tenuous psychological explanation, they proceeded to examine the phenomena of witchcraft and demonology. These included sexual relations with the devil, possession by succubi and incubi, witches' ceremonial, and the influence of witches on the fortunes of both man and beast. The persecution which resulted was not, it must be emphasized, applied uniformly by the Church: there was a league, not for the last time, between the ignorant populace and certain 'intellectuals'. In his study *The European Witch-Craze of the 16th and 17th Centuries* (1967), Hugh Trevor-Roper points out that although the authors of the *Malleus* had been ordered by Innocent VIII in his Bull *Summis Desiderantes Affectibus* (1484) to put down witchcraft in Germany, they 'found themselves obstructed by the ecclesiastical establishment in that country', so much so that they were 'reduced to forging the approbation of the University of Cologne'. Even when the persecution of witches was at its height, with hundreds of unfortunate women confessing to be in league with the devil, the established Churches in France and England showed marked opposition to it; 'practically no witches were burnt in Rome during the whole period of the witch-craze'. Who, then, was behind it?

> The pressure throughout came from a lower level, from the mis-sionary orders who moved among the people. . . . The popes might authorize, but the pace was set by the tribunes of the people, and the tribunes in their turn responded to popular pressure, seeking a scapegoat for social frustration.

A century later, Jean Bodin (c. 1530-1596), reputedly one of the greatest humanists of his time and in some respects an advocate of religious tolerance, wrote a book, *De la Démonomanie des Sorciers* (1580), 'demanding death at the stake not only for witches but for all who do not believe every grotesque detail of the new demonology'.[7]

The social frustration referred to was the result of bitter religious conflict and consequent heresy-hunting. It was combined with the widespread belief in a variety of superstitious practices, of which the casting of horoscopes was one of the mildest. These stimulated communal fears and neuroses in such a way as to reinforce an already deeply-inculcated sense of sin.

Scholars courageous enough to oppose the prevailing hysteria were precisely those who were concerned to examine such tendencies objectively and to expose them as maladies of the soul. Among the foremost was Juan Luis Vives, born in Valencia in 1492, who became professor of humanities at Louvain, tutor to Princess Mary of England, and a friend of Erasmus and More. Vives's sincere attachment to the Church lent his work the more cogency. Although he edited St. Augustine's *City of God* and wrote much on education, his most important work bore the Aristotelian title of *De Anima*. This was a profound study of the emotions, perhaps the first treatise of its kind.

Another enlightened scholar was Johannis Weyer, born in Northern Brabant in 1515 or 1516 and trained as a doctor. In 1563, he published a book *De Praestigiis Daemonum*, which he translated into German in 1567. He argued, in a strikingly modern manner, that most so-called witches, whether through accident or systematic ill-treatment, were mentally disturbed. The people most deserving of punishment, he held, were the persecuting monks. Not merely was his book placed forthwith on the Index, but in 1590 his entire writings were banned, and they remained so until the beginning of the present century. Nor must we forget another enlightened man, Reginald Scott, whose *Discoveries of Witchcraft* (1584) was an attempt to explain away some aspects of witchcraft by demonstrating that they were due to sleight of hand. His book was thus 'virtually the first book to treat of conjuring as we know it to-day'.[8]

These two men well deserve to be called the fathers of modern psychology and psychiatry. Mankind owes them an immense debt.

With the increasing attention paid to the study of feeling and the emotions, the personality came to be regarded as a structure or architecture composed of more than one level, with a *psychic* level mediating between the organic and the spiritual. The science of the psyche, or psychology, was therefore the study of all the impulses which underlay or surrounded the sphere of thought or intellect. What had been implied ever since Plato wrote the *Republic* and the *Laws* and Aristotle wrote his *Rhetoric* and *Poetics* was that this intermediate sphere enjoyed a special importance. If all were right and healthy in *this* sphere, the personality as a whole would be balanced and, in the truest sense, sane. In the eighteenth century, two Germans elaborated this view into a new science, aesthetics: Baumgarten in his *Aesthetica* (1750) and Schiller in his treatise *On the Aesthetic Education of Man* (1793).

In speaking of the psyche, we do not of course refer to the capacity, authentic or not, for 'psychic experience'. The existence and authenticity of psychic phenomena, in the spiritualistic sense, and even of extra-sensory perception, are still far from proved, and may depend upon ambiguities of definition; but it is not our intention to pursue this line of enquiry. To the psychologist, the psyche and its field are a matter for rational investigation; the subject-matter of psychology can be called irrational only in the sense that it lies below the level of intellect. Nevertheless, the psyche is a form of intelligence; and to refuse to admit the claims of the psyche is to fail to give a proper account of the personality, which is an intelligent and intelligible whole. 'When the Intellect and Will . . . ignore the subconscious abyss of the Psyche, they do so at their peril; for, so far from being the whole of human nature, they are merely a spirit moving on the face of the waters – a feeble light cast by a wick that draws its faint luminosity from the opaque oil in the bowl of the lamp on whose surface the wick is floating.'[9]

The concept of mind

The sphere of the psyche has often been misconceived or ignored because it falls outside the conventional division of man into body, mind, and spirit. This remains the common 'dictionary' definition. It is a definition vaguely repeated in philosophical works of the idealist tradition, as well as in much theological literature. At the time of Descartes and throughout the Cartesian era, the body was regarded as a machine. Man differed from the animals in having a soul or mind attached to this machine, though the nature of the attachment gave rise to much argument. Descartes maintained that the connecting-link was the pineal gland, perhaps because he failed to perceive any other use for this organ, of which the function even today is by no means clear. Cartesian man, in Jacques Maritain's words, was 'un ange habitant une machine, dirigée par la glande pinéale'.[10] As a result, the mind or soul came to be regarded as a nebulous entity floating 'above' the body and at death separating from it, possibly to survive on its own. As to animals, they were, despite their name, regarded as mere bodies, that is, machines. On the analogy of the machines known at the time, their machinery consisted of levers and pulleys. Consequently, when animals were 'hurt', their 'sufferings' were due simply to the dislocation or grinding of machinery. Man's feelings, on the other hand, resulted from the temporary alliance between soul and body, whereby his organism was spiritualized, or, to use Aristotle's terminology, 'informed' by the soul. Whether there was a distinction between mind, soul and spirit was left unclear; Descartes seems to have identified all three. This ambiguity has affected all subsequent thought.

With the rise of the New Psychology – by which is meant the psychology arising from Freud's study of hysteria and of the interpretation of dreams – such difficulties, instead of being resolved, underwent a marked increase. The new concept of the unconscious posed a problem similar to that raised by the attached soul or spirit; for the unconscious, instead of floating 'above' the body, was conceived by the same spatial metaphor as inhabiting a nether realm. Furthermore, the concept of collective unconscious, as defined by Jung, raised even greater difficulties; for here was a mental realm trans-individual in scope, in which men's individual minds somehow had roots. A literature of prodigious proportions grew up, which, while claiming to explain many aspects of human behaviour, failed to answer the question how these mental spheres were related to the physical organism. Far-ranging studies of the connection between mind and body, such as Sherrington's *Man on his Nature* (1940), left the problem unsolved; for Sherrington seemed to regard the mind as 'outside' the body in a manner quite Cartesian.

From this state of affairs, it was but a step (in one direction) to the attempted liquidation of the whole problem of mind. This was accomplished by affirming that, on empirical evidence, the mind as a separate or independent entity did not exist. Such was the point of view of behaviourism, according to which thought was a 'laryngeal habit'.

In his *Concept of Mind* (1949), which made such a stir even outside the philosophical lecture rooms, Gilbert Ryle appeared to adopt a kind of behaviourism. The Italian translation of his book, presumably authorized, was entitled *Lo Spirito come comportamento*. Yet his liquidation of the mind as a concept, or more precisely his banishment of internal 'mental activities', was by no means successful. As C. W. K. Mundle pointed out, 'he unobtrusively admits by the back door the facts which he had ostentatiously kicked out of the front door'.[11] At the end of his book, however, Ryle implicitly renounced his overall reductionist position. He pointed out how the rise of the life sciences had disposed of the 'old' mechanism. He might have added that it had disposed of the new mechanism too. To that extent he may be regarded as an ally.

> The influence of the bogey of mechanism has for a century been dwindling because, among other reasons, during this period the biological sciences have established their title as 'sciences'. The Newtonian system is no longer the sole paradigm of natural science. Man need not be degraded to a machine by being denied to be a ghost in a machine. He might, after all, be a sort of animal, namely a higher animal. There has yet to be ventured the hazardous leap to the hypothesis that perhaps he is a man.[12]

In a sense we are back where we started, because some of us had taken that hazardous leap some time ago. Meanwhile, despite the arrival of a new behaviourism in the work of B. F. Skinner, biology and psychology have by now established diplomatic relations and even formed a condominium; and the old division between body, mind, and spirit has given place, except among intransigent physicalists like J. J. C. Smart and David Armstrong, to the organic, the

11

psychic and the spiritual, even if the last is often disguised under a variety of names.

The old division, originating with Descartes, implied a discontinuity between one stage and the next, or at least between the first stage and the other two. Whereas the body was merely *alive*, the mind and the spirit belonged to a higher and seemingly detached sphere – the sphere of mind proper. According to the new view, however, organism, psyche and spirit enjoy no such radical separation.

In this there is nothing recondite. Only consider the facts. Arriving as a structure in the spatio-temporal domain, an organism develops and forms itself from an embryo, stage by stage. (An animal organism is cited, but plants too are organisms, of which the seed is an embryo and the basic material protoplasm.) Now after the embryonic phase called gastrulation (literally 'stomach-forming') and the formation of the blastopore – a kind of proto-intestine – primitive organs develop, including the beginning of the neurula or neural plate, which is the forerunner of the brain and the nervous system. Mind is therefore not a ghost in the machine-embryo, nor a light suddenly and unaccountably switched on at the cerebral stage: first, because organic formation is inexplicable in purely physico-chemical terms, and secondly, because the neurula, though later to form brain and nervous system, is already a self-developing, self-possessing organ, derived from protoplasm which is itself self-possessed and engaged in self-formation. This protoplasm in turn depends upon a molecular basis with its own formative activity. Between the molecular level and the brain there is therefore no break but continuity. Molecular biology, far from demonstrating the truth of mechanism, as some molecular biologists have claimed, has vindicated what A. N. Whitehead called the philosophy of organism. Our brain or cortex thinks because the molecular level is engaged in the activity of self-formation. Cerebral self-consciousness must therefore issue from an anterior form of consciousness. This primary consciousness is not distinct from life but identical with it.

An organism is a unified domain, an individuality, self-possessing and, as it were, 'present to itself'. Another word for it is subject or being. Life is subjectivity or subjective being. As such, it is opposed to the non-living order of objects: that is to say, multiplicities or assemblages – rocks, chairs, machines, clouds, planets, etc. The world is therefore divided into subjects and objects: beings or unities on the one hand and statistical assemblages on the other.

Now let us go a stage further. If I, as an organism, am a being, subject, or individual, how do I appear to other beings, subjects or individuals? I appear to them, and they appear to me, as a body. This we know; but we also know that, as beings, subjects or individuals (persons), we are something else. The operative word here is 'appear'. Our bodies are the *appearance* in the spatio-temporal dimension of a *reality* which is consciousness. We are spatio-temporal structures for one another's perceptive faculties or senses only. We do not observe or perceive one another's consciousness; we infer them, and we can participate in them by cognition and communication. Nor do we see *ourselves* save as bodies, though we know by direct intuition that we are conscious selves. The conscious or subjective self, in fact, is the 'other side' of that which in the spatio-temporal dimension appears as the brain or the cortex. We cannot see this other side, because we can *see* only that which appears, the cerebral tissue. 'Le "corps" résulte, comme sous-produit, de la perception d'un être par un autre être.'[13]

It follows that, as thinking beings, we have an existence beyond the spatio-temporal dimension; but as perceptive beings we are at the meeting-place between the non-spatio-temporal and the domain of space-time. This is merely an account of our everyday experience; but it also reveals the human being as in tension between time and the timeless. Whereas abstract thought is indifferent to space and time, perceptive thought is always thought-here-and-now; or, to put it in another way, the hereness and the nowness, in unity, are the product of my thinking. In thinking, I create a *domain* of space-time.

Given in the barest outline, this view is of course in opposition to currently-held notions. It is called here 'the new science', because it liquidates the Cartesian division between body and mind, and provides a restatement of the age-old distinction between appearance and reality. The prevailing theory, which retains the division between life and consciousness, fails to account otherwise than by accident for the development of one from the other. As we are here concerned with the nature of the psyche, however, we shall dwell no longer on technical details. All we need stress is that the argument which follows presupposes a bio-psychical or psycho-biological view of reality. This is not to engage in some idealist or pseudo-mystical exercise; it is to take account of the new biology and the new physics at a time when philosophy, with certain exceptions, has tended to be linked to an out-of-date science. The new view is unfamilar only because of the long reign of another outlook, namely, materialism or positivism or mechanism, either explicit or in various forms of disguise. Edward Wilson's Sociobiology is both explicit and undisguised in its materialist approach.

Given the attention paid to religion and metaphysics in our argument, it is important to clarify at the outset their relationship to these new scientific views. Today, there are two main alternatives to the religio-metaphysical outlook, the Marxist and the humanist. It is naturally possible to adhere to both at once. Although these two philosophies are materialistic and positivistic, that is to say reductive, Marxism goes further than conventional humanism in that it lays down the pattern of society for the rest of time. Whether Marxians really believe that, through the next two billion years (the estimated duration of life on earth), a Marxist 'classless society' will persist unchanged seems scarcely credible. But they are supposed to believe it. In point of fact, despite their claim that Marxist socialism differs from any other kind of socialism in being *scientific*, they entertain at the same time a myth which runs counter to their scientific pretensions. This is the myth of the 'end of history'. It envisages a kind of day of judgment, or apocalyptic dénouement, when the dialectic will be wound up and the redeemed proletariat will come into its own. Meanwhile, the science to which Marxism officially adheres is the science or scientific *Weltanschauung* of the nineteenth century. According to this science, the world is composed not of subjects and objects but merely of objects. These objects, juxtaposed and externally related, function blindly – that is to say, without aim – in relation to other objects. The world is a kind of determinist charnel house, except that the bones never lived. So-called living things are no different from other things, in that their vital properties can be reduced to objects. This is likewise true of man. His so-called consciousness is merely a surface phenomenon, masking the machine which he really is. This follows from the fact that the basic reality is matter, and that everything can be reduced to it.

Nevertheless, the phenomenon of man (to use Teilhard de Chardin's expression) presents problems for both Marxism and humanism. According to Marxism, matter is *not* just inert; it is capable of dialectical movement. Thus the process which other people call life is merely a capacity of matter to originate states in

14

itself. According to Hegel, this dialectical process was characteristic of mind or what he called the Idea. Marx, turning the Hegelian idealism on its head – to use his own phase – maintained that the process was a purely material one, of which man was a part or product. Similarly, material processes, such as economic forces, explained the development of society, etc. That such material transcendence violates the first law of matter does not seem to worry Marxist theoreticians.

The humanist approach – or that form of humanism which has worked out a coherent philosophy – accepts the material, accidental, deterministic view of matter. What it denies, though not always explicitly, is that human consciousness, which originates science itself, is part of the inert 'world of science'. On the contrary, subjectivity, consciousness, and above all our liberty to think, are facts of which we are absolutely sure. To refuse to acknowledge them would be an absurdity, because it would be to reaffirm them at the same time. My liberty is a fact: determinism is a fact about the world. Since one cannot be born of the other, we are, so to speak, thrown into an alien world, alone and obliged to create our own nature. This is the point of view of existentialism, with its *en soi* and *pour soi* or their German equivalents.

The irony is that although existentialism separates the existential self from the materialistic world, the destiny of that self, once in the world, is as negative and pointless as its alien environment. Man, to quote J-P. Sartre, is 'une passion inutile'.

Although existentialism is no longer the battle-cry that it was immediately after the war, it represents, under whatever name it goes, the point of view next after dialectical materialism which emerges from accepting the mechanistic or materialistic philosophy of nature of the last century. These two philosophies are opposed not merely to what, for want of a better term, we have called the religio-metaphysical view, but to the new scientific outlook, of which they have failed to take account. In other words, the religio-metaphysical outlook, which is condemned as effete by the old science and by the philosophies based upon it, is in its essence, and rid of certain accretions, compatible with the new science. Hence the title of this book.

In referring to time and the timeless, it is important to bear in mind that space-time in this context signifies the space-time of *physics*, and that the timeless or 'eternal' strands for the whole dimension of the non-spatio-temporal, in which ideas and themes are progressively articulated. Every self is aware of a more or less successful penetration of the dimension, e.g., in a conversation between 'like minds' or in rare 'moments of vision'. There is a middle area in which, to quote Herder speaking of Schiller, we 'look down into the abyss of the human psyche to the point where the feelings of the animal turn into the feelings of the human being'. That psychic realm is our chief concern; but, to anticipate a later reference to the Logos, the sphere of the timeless or the eternal, though not supernatural in its immediate trans-spatio-temporal domain, leads to a realm beyond nature which ultimately confers on nature its meaning. It was therefore appropriate that Sir Thomas Browne in his *Religio Medici* (1643) should have called man 'that great and true amphibian', subsisting between a corporal and a spiritual essence.

2
Culture and the three nutritions

Instinct and psyche

According to child psychologists, instinctive education, or at least its basis, is acquired between the ages of nine to fifteen months. On the other hand, to say that 'children are not born with minds: they have to develop them by being initiated into the language, rules and purposes which constitute civilized society'[1] is surely misleading. They are born with instincts which are part of the psychic sphere of the mind. At that stage, it is obvious that we must talk of 'valencies' rather than values; and even when values are consciously grasped and apprehended, that grasp is always precarious. That is why men need to build up a cultural capital on which to draw for the conduct of life.

This instinctive stage is the primary stage of psychism. It achieves a higher stage when the organic instincts are overlaid by instincts which may be said to be acquired. Here again the ethologists have done some illuminating work. Lorenz and Tinbergen have used the word 'imprinting' (Prägung, a term originated in 1910 by the German ornithologist O. Heinroth, though the phenomenon was observed earlier) to explain the acquisition by the child of certain fundamental behaviour patterns. Lorenz's example in the animal world is the case in which the first creature observed by a young gosling becomes – and therefore remains – his 'mother'. These acquired patterns come to be dictated and controlled by memory-themes in the way that embryonic devolopment is controlled by formative themes. For instance, a habit that is acquired, and which remains thereafter under the control of memory-themes, is one's mother-tongue. Such a 'biological' interpretation of Chomsky's well-known theory of generative grammar would seem to be nearer to the facts than the reductionist interpretation given to it by some of

Chomsky's disciples, and sometimes implied by Chomsky himself. In a broadcast discussion with Stuart Hampshire, he remarked: 'Ultimately, I think that there will defintely some day be a physiological explanation for the mental processes we are discussing.'[2]

Included in the psychic realm are also the myths and beliefs which are seen now to constitute a preponderant element in all culture. Having examined the subject more thoroughly in the light of cultural anthropology, we know better than our forefathers did that sexuality is not a mere matter of physiological process or function; it is overlaid with a whole mythical palimpsest of the *erotic*. The Greeks showed their awareness of this by having a special Muse for the erotic (or erotic poetry), Erato. We have one too, however unofficial. The present, perhaps ephemeral, cult of sexuality is far from a reversion to plain physicality, as some of its champions claim, but rather a *culte*, an attempt to formulate a new myth in place of the old. Religion is the chief sphere in which cults, partly implicit and partly conscious, are ceaselessly issuing and undergoing modification. It is for this reason that we can describe the values or valencies of the psychic sphere as *opaque*.

> Psychic reality, and its structuring in terms of internal object
> relations, is made manifest in phantasy, of which day and night
> dreams and the play of children are the most clinically relevant
> examples. With these, however, we must link other forms of
> phantasy, the myths and legends of primitive peoples, folklore,
> and the imaginative creations of literature and art in all ages
> which together constitute a continuous revelation of the phantasy
> life of the human race, and throw a tremendous light on the
> workings of the unconscious.[3]

And, we might add, on the conscious too.

We are now in a better position to understand the nature of psychic reality in relation to culture in the conventional sense.

Culture and society

The twentieth century, or at least the first half of it, will be remembered for its two major wars, and for its clash of ideologies. It may also be remembered for another activity not altogether divorced from the ideological conflict. This is the export of cultures.

It is not for the first time that nations, taking pride in their cultural heritage, have engaged in cultural emulation or competition. The spread of Hellenism was perhaps the first instance in Europe of deliberate cultural dissemination, undertaken chiefly for reasons of prestige. In the Orient, the export of Chinese culture, especially to Japan, was another striking example. Although Hellenism was primarily a humanist culture, it was perhaps less divorced from religion than some scholars would have us believe. In the absence of Buddhism, it is doubtful whether Chinese cultural penetration would have assumed so dynamic a form. Today, those nations which seek to propagate their culture would without doubt resent the charge of religious proselytism. They claim to be disseminating culture pure and simple. This, if true, is perhaps the first time that such a thing has been attempted. And no doubt this attempt, made by so many countries simultaneously, reflects a particular view of the nature of culture. It may indeed mark the *end*, rather than the beginning, of a cultural tradition.

That this new attitude to culture should have given rise to a great debate on the nature of culture itself is not therefore an accident. Indeed the debate had been going on for some time. It began in the early nineteenth century. The Germans initiated it, with Fichte as its first articulate ideologue. His *Addresses to the German Nation* (1807-8) is primarily a eulogy and plea on behalf of German culture at a time when the nation itself was undergoing painful dismemberment by Napoleon. Matthew Arnold, himself a German scholar, continued the debate in such books as *Culture and Anarchy* (1869). But we have to jump the gap to our own times if we are to find a comparable preoccupation with the theme of culture. In our day, the debate has taken place against a background of speculation concerning the 'decline of civilization', which began with Max Nordau and Oswald Spengler. T. S. Eliot's *Notes Towards the Definition of Culture* (1947) proved a seminal work, and important comments upon it have been made by Raymond Williams and George Steiner.

Our primary purpose is to enquire what culture is at root and in its essence. This may enable us to understand better what is happening to our own culture. For the other important fact about Western culture is that it is the only one to have become world-wide. No 'developing' country has so far tried to turn its back upon Western culture and to adopt some other form. Western culture includes the culture of the communist world; for Marxism originated at the heart of European culture, and by becoming Marxist Russia has perhaps moved closer to Western civilization than it might otherwise have done. What is interesting and inevitable about the new world culture is that anything that happens in one part of the world affects every other part. Silenced by their own government, Soviet writers enjoy enormous prestige and sales outside the Soviet Union; and pop culture, of which some governments entertain the gravest suspicions, has it passionate youthful adherents everywhere. Ideas not immediately identifiable with Western civilization, such as Maoism, turn out to be derivatives of the Western tradition; for the anarchism and situationism of the young Maoists, while tenuously related to the Chinese form of communism, were directly derived from a certain Western tradition of radicalism. Hence there was a Western Maoism which Mao disavowed. Finally, those who seek to follow an 'alternative' culture, such as the inhabitants of hippy communes, are following practices and traditions which have appeared from time to time in the Western world. For there is an alternative to every society, namely, that which the society keeps in recess. Every now and then, as during the Cromwellian Commonwealth, they seek outlet. The limitation of the alternative society, like that of the alternative press, is that its schism can never be complete. A newspaper which denounces monopoly-capitalistic society cannot be initiated without a reserve of capital. A hippy commune exists *within* the social system it seeks to repudiate, and remains parasitic upon it, even to the extent of purchasing its goods at supermarkets and its exotic 'uniforms' at luxury boutiques. By contrast, it is the hard-up member of capitalistic society who patronizes the cheap department or co-operative store, which the hippies despise.

Why does every society pride itself on having some kind of culture, or at least the capacity to acquire it? We have only to ask this question to perceive that culture is conceived at more than one level. For the culture which a society (for example a 'developing' one) seeks to acquire, out of self-respect, is surplus to the one it has already, or there would be no society in any recognizable sense. A society is not merely a group of persons in relation; it is a group of persons wishing to maintain these relations, though no doubt also to modify them. There is no society on record, except perhaps some of which Malinowski wrote as having died of collective boredom, which has voluntarily elected to disband itself, though there have been many which have been forcibly dismembered. And there have been some, such as Japanese society after the Meiji restoration of 1868, which have voluntarily and deliberately transformed themselves. This tendency towards conservation is probably due to the fact that a society experiences such difficulty in constituting itself that its members, having established certain traditions, do not willingly entertain their abandonment. Only *force majeure* brings most societies to an end; and one of the subjects of debate among historians and anthropologists is how this dissolution comes about. (We must distinguish society from the state, which may easily be transformed.) Just as the human race has probably never had the impulse to commit collective suicide, so all human groups seem to possess an impulse to perpetuate themselves by an *élan* which is more than biological instinct. That is to say, men in their various groups *will* to go on living, and to perpetuate themselves, because, despite the misery to which they have often been reduced, they still consider the effort worth while. There is an authentic record of a baby born to a Jewish mother in a concentration camp grave and fed initially on her tears: who survived. Malinowski's bored societies probably died out for reasons over and above their communal accidie. He did not make out his case very convincingly: it was simply that he failed to descry any other reason for their extinction. It is probable that societies go on living precisely because of their *culture*, in a sense to be defined. One of the most important contentions in Eliot's book is that culture is that which makes life worth living;[4] but it is more than doubtful whether Eliot had in mind merely the widespread appreciation of the *fine arts*, for many people evidently find life worth living without any such appreciation, and in the total absence of artistic interests. And here 'many people' means most people for most of history; for most of history is prehistory. It would still seem true that this great number lived by culture of some kind; and it is our task to enquire what this culture, this irreducible minimum of worthwhileness, may be.

The achievement of the state of humanity itself may have been the step forward which first lent to existence that quality which, at our own level, expresses itself in cultural enjoyment. It is not an accident that anthropologists, from the beginnings of their science, should speak of 'primitive culture' (e.g., Tylor), even though the word was used to signify merely a social grouping rather than the distinctive quality of the life lived by the group: a distinctive quality exceedingly difficult, at this distance in time, to define.

Space and time in culture

Why do not animals possess culture? Admittedly, one animal does, and that is man himself. Then what happened to this animal that caused him to take the step permitted to no other creature of his kind? And do not other animals, the higher ones at least, possess what may be described as a kind of proto-culture, such as characterizes also some creatures not to be regarded as 'higher' at all? The elaborate dances of the bee, for example, though directly related to the location of the food supply, are a form of 'art' which has to be acquired. It is doubtful whether this remarkable ritual is purely functional, for it depends upon a form of symbolism. Such symbolism is employed by all creatures which demarcate a life-space for themselves, e.g., those which use urine or glandular secretions to define their territorial boundaries. In other words, many non-human creatures evidently possess an intuition regarding *space*, which, in its higher forms, resembles that entertained by man. The difference is in the degree of *mastery*. Certain creatures indeed may be said to possess a space-culture, however rudimentary; and one of the most complicated and mysterious problems is why this space-culture should be so unevenly developed. It has been argued that some creatures, termites for instance, appear to have undergone a regression; that 'instinct began as a reasoned act', later becoming 'automatic' or 'instinctive'[5]; and that 'in termites the amount of degeneration accompanying social evolution is . . . much greater than in the ants', probably on account of 'an increasing need for protection'.[6] The implications of this theory of degeneration are difficult to assess; but some of the societies displaying a remarkable degree of sophistication of space-culture exist so far down the evolutionary scale as to prompt the question whether there is a graduated scale at all.

Entomologists and zoologists have long been divided into those favouring a behaviourist standpoint and those designated, often derogatorily, as pan-psychists. On the one hand, the purely functional attitude implies a break at some point, which in turn presupposes a miraculous jump to freewill, or a jump, scarcely less extraordinary, from what Julian Huxley calls 'apparent purpose' to purpose proper. On the other hand, the attitude of pan-psychism ignores the obvious part played by reflex, even at the human level. What would seem true, and true without question of the higher animals, is that by exerting a measure of control over their environment, such creatures treat it as *more* than spatial in the strict geometrical sense. The environment rather is a 'field', to the various parts of which they assign 'meanings', because the marks which they deposit are perceived for what they represent. The animal is already a metaphysical being. Admittedly, animal instinct does not go beyond typical representations, just as animal language does not go beyond a limited range of typical meanings. The space-culture of such creatures is therefore 'frozen'.

What would seem to distinguish man from the animals, in this sphere, is his special perception of *time*. To say that the animals have no sense of temporal passage would be risky, because we cannot know as much as that about animal psychology; but animals clearly do not behave towards time as the human being does. Man organizes time on his own behalf, exploiting or cultivating it in a manner similar to his exploitation and cultivation of space. Primitive man must soon have learnt how to prepare for coming storms, to take measures based upon past experience, and to devise new ways of physical protection. True, the animal can also react to a future storm, but, so far as we can tell, only as a present sensation or complex of sensations, just as his mating behaviour depends upon immediate reactions to stimuli. He can presumably read the atmospheric 'signs', just as he can read the 'signs' of his territory; what he cannot do is to entertain the concept of 'danger'. Nor can he react to a symbol which depends for its efficacy upon temporality: he could not, for example, respond to a signal comparable to a 'no waiting' notice valid only between certain hours. 'You cannot make any communication to him that is not taken as a signal of something immediately forthcoming.'[7]

In short, the animal appears to have no time-culture. Unlike man, he cannot dominate time. There is naturally a limit to man's temporal domination; but this is because he has, in Jacques Barzun's expression, a 'shared zoology'. If man were a pure spirit, he could exert total temporal mastery; but just as he seems capable of exploiting his spatial environment up to the limit of the possible, including the conquest of gravity, so he has turned the limitations of his temporal environment to his cultural advantage, making the idea of transience and of *lacrimae rerum* into great art. Indeed the sense of time would seem to have set man on the path of creation, for it is in the teeth of time that he has done anything creatively worth while. As long as the human race lasts, his culture will be above all a time-culture. Hence tragedy is the highest of the arts, with comedy next in rank, because at heart man knows that in his world of time nothing is ultimately serious. The vauntings of Ronsard and Shakespeare about the timelessness of their productions are a kind of supreme cheek, mocking destiny; but if we know Ronsard and Shakespeare, and especially Shakespeare, we also know that they had their tongue in it.

To say that animals lack time-culture is the same as to say that they have no history. The moment man began organizing himself into societies – and this meant to organize his already existing societies better, because in addition to a 'shared zoology', man had 'a shared society', and he still has, even though some of his partners are for the most part noxious and invisible to the naked eye – he set about deliberately creating an historic past. Depending for millennia on oral tradition, and practising a food-gathering economy until only comparatively recently, man embodied his history in what we should today call myth, with gods and heroes engaged in stupendous deeds. In point of fact, this form of history is still being written, even by historians who are under the impression that they have put myth altogether behind them. The pattern of almost all history books is divided into 'heroic epochs' or 'reigns'; and a 'tale' is told, with the 'marvels' given due prominence. Indeed, it is the academic historians, practising the traditional form of history, who tend to frown upon those who, repudiating this style of writing, approach the past with a more synoptic historical vision, seeking to isolate intelligible fields of study in civilizations or cultures. In his book *The Death of the Past* (1971), J. H. Plumb dismisses historians such as Toynbee as 'journalists', and, while impugning the *content* of most past histories, seems to approve their *form*. Rational history, which began to emerge in the eighteenth century, must employ both the microscopic and the telescopic method – a series of monographs or a series of interpretations by themselves are not enough – and in fact history has always moved between these two extremes.

Whatever the dispute between historians, man must seek to understand who he is. To undertake this enquiry is part of that culture by which, at the 'spiritual' level, he lives. History proper could not have arisen at the stage anterior to the Neolithic revolution, whereby man became a food-producing instead of a food-gathering animal, because he was so much a part of nature. There were naturally technical reasons why the new history could not exist; the important point is that the need for it was absent. What existed, in oral form, was the old history, designed primarily to reinforce the sense of community: and this it still does, as a comparison of national histories will amply confirm. It is interesting that Marxism, which is declared by its adherents to reflect the truly scientific view of society, should have been the occasion for the most frequent rewriting of history, as one myth has been exposed and given place to another. What existed, too, was a kind of permanent sacred history, united to the passage of the seasons and to events of crucial importance, such as individual birth, death and mating. This sacred history is still enacted; and there are special reasons, as we shall see, why such history is a permanent human necessity.

Signs and symbols

In speaking of animals and of creatures more primitive still, we have referred to the use to which symbolism has been put; but symbolism is a broad term, and we must distinguish within it at least two kinds. The first is that which biologists describe as the stimulus-signal. It is to such stimuli that the animal responds; and it is to comparable signals that *all* organic response is made, even at the level of embryonic development, where the signals may be chemical inductors. To describe the operation of stimulus-signals in this way is not to fall into Behaviourism, for the signal evokes an active response, not a passive one. It is doubtful whether the famous experiments of Behaviourism – e.g., the case of the dogs salivating at the ringing of a bell – prove what they claim to do. The dances of bees act as signals which, once perceived, elicit active response from the workers. And there are human responses, if relatively few, of the same order.

In general, human response differs radically from that occasioned by the stimulus-signal. It is human to 'stand back' from the object, to practise detachment, to say No; for, as Max Scheler said, the animal always says Yes to life even when fleeing from it. Consequently, the progress towards humanity would seem to have depended upon the stimulus-signal giving place, or rather precedence, to what is now generally called a sign or sign-symbol. With the development of the sign, it was possible to *entertain the object in its absence*, which is another way of affirming its idea or conception. A sign of this kind is a symbol properly so called.

How can this development of the sign have come about? Although the question is admittedly difficult, its difficulty has been exaggerated. It is often assumed that the transition from stimulus-signals to sign-symbols marked the origin of language, and in a sense this must be true; *but the use of stimulus-signals and the response to them was itself a form of language.* Unfortunately, the word language usually conveys the restricted notion of linguistic speech; but linguistic speech is a secondary development or specialization of language. Communication by gestures and cries must have antedated by a great stretch of time the development of linguistic speech. Similarly, the development of signs that were understood as such must have long preceded the refinement of vocal speech permitting the utterance of precise sign-symbols; and there is reason to think that this refinement was not achieved solely for the sake of practical communication. Describing her experience of learning language whereby her teacher splashed water over one hand and wrote the word water on the palm of the other, Helen Keller referred to water as a 'wonderful something'. Although this was reporting an experience long after it had taken place, the account rings true; the experience was partly aesthetic.

Language as symbolism

Helen Keller's experience of learning language as symbolism was accelerated because she had a teacher. Man or sub-man had to teach himself. Helen Keller did not succeed in grasping the nature of language (her actual speech was difficult to follow save through an 'interpreter') until she had perceived that the word water was not necessarily a means to the immediate gratification of drinking. She understood what language was when she realized that the *word* was the means to bringing the *idea* of water before her in memory or reflection or allusion, and finally when she grasped that all things had a name, with a particular significance, by which these operations could be initiated. The comparable transition in the case of pre-human creatures took place without the occurrence of any new mutation, organic or spiritual; but there must have been a new cerebral development, a modification of intelligence, whereby the transition was effected.

Before a society of truly human beings grew up, beginning perhaps with one consisting of a 'new' man and a woman who mated, there may have been isolated human creatures who, endowed with the new capacity, died without knowing what had happened to them. They may have assumed that they were either ill or deranged; and the view still lingers that those with particular powers of speech or verbal persuasion are different from their fellows, perhaps slightly odd or even a little mad, but in the more impressive cases 'charismatic'.

When language proper was developed, even at the most elementary stage, the world must have assumed a wholly new guise. Those who could name objects found that the world possessed a 'sheen' or 'glitter' which before was absent. This acquisition of a new dimension of significance added to purely aesthetic appreciation a heightening of value. And this is true of all objects, not simply the objects of nature. Technical knowledge of an industrial process, however elementary, adds significance to that process. When it was discovered that everything had a name, or was at least nameable, a new order was established. The world became a world of symbols. It was the world, nature, and man within nature, that the poet celebrated; and this provided him with a new environment, magical, sometimes benevolent, sometimes baleful. The earliest poetry, which contained the first history and the first science, was in due course recorded in 'sacred writing' or hieroglyphics. Hence there grew up the notion, which still persists, that if a word were employed for something non-empirical, or even invented, a corresponding object must exist. For the magical symbol could, it seemed, summon up the sacred object. And this no doubt came to be an important element in the origin of writing itself. In ancient Egypt, sacred writing was originally a medium confined to the priesthood, and the priests strove to maintain a monopoly of it. It was held to be of such efficacy as to be inscribed inside tombs for the benefit of the Pharaoh. These funerary inscriptions were supposed somehow to 'read themselves', because they were conjurations designed to bring the Pharaoh to the world hereafter and to preserve him in eternal health and prosperity.

Not only were various objects endowed with symbolism, but so also were the seasons. Unless they had been charged with prior symbolism, these events would not have been integrated later into the liturgical year. Thus spring became symbolic not merely of the emergence of new growth but of the love of man for woman; and this lent a significance to spring beyond anything biological, even though

27

biological forces provided its drive and basis. Nor was the symbolism of spring limited to the coming together of the sexes in mating. It was the symbol of renewal in general, even for those more advanced in years to whom the renewal of the earth signified the promise, however precarious, of another year in the flesh. The point is that this renewal of spirits is not simply dictated by pleasurable sensations. Spring is the season, but also the symbol, of growth; summer of maturity; winter of death. The passage from one to the other typifies the life of man. All culture is basically linked to the passage of the seasons. The Christian church wisely based its liturgy upon the pagan cults associated with the climaxes of the year; for paganism, still perhaps the natural religion of most men, has its own spirituality with which ecclesiastical dogma has shown remarkable powers of compromise, especially in countries where its basis remained intact. Pope Gregory the Great enjoined the Abbot Melitus, who travelled to Britain in 601, not to destroy the pagan temples, so that the converts 'may the more familiarly resort to the places to which they are accustomed'. Where, as in parts of Africa, the discrepancy between the two has seemed excessive, both cults have probably suffered. Missionary activity has made scant progress where the infrastructure has been deliberately demolished, because the alien spirituality has proved too abstract to grasp.

Primitive society and values

In a well-known learned magazine, there appeared some time ago a picture representing 'primitive man' engaged in quarrelling over an animal carcass. The scene was one of total confusion. The carcass was being hacked at indiscriminately; individuals were angrily disputing their rights to various portions; the stronger were dominating the weaker. That our ancestors conducted themselves in this unruly fashion, except at moments of crisis, is more than doubtful. (The picture was more nearly a symbolic representation of modern man overtaken by a crisis in international relations.) The idea of primitive anarchy, which was evoked so often in the eighteenth century, was probably derived from the fact that modern man had begun only recently to make contact with primitive peoples, *who were themselves in a late or decadent state*. This is not to suggest that, at the 'dawn of humanity', conditions were uniformly peaceful: the picture of early man in William Golding's novel *The Inheritors* (1955) probably owes something to R. B. Perry's *Children of the Sun* (1923). But there is no more need to attribute permanent anarchy, confusion and predatoriness to early human society than to attribute them to animal society. We need to go back in imagination to the time when a few men and women *discovered* that they were human; and while this may have engendered mutual suspicion, it would more likely have promoted, in the long run, a sense of solidarity. The earliest human beings would have been social animals by reason of their 'shared zoology'; and in this society there were specific roles and tasks to fulfil to which they became habituated. The idea that man is distinguished above all by being a gregarious animal is an error of which modern anthropologists have successfully disposed. Animal roles are determined by means of stimulus-signals, whereas in human society, despite the degree to which certain roles are biologically determined (in the family, for example), the majority are allocated according to a tradition of justice which depends upon a grasp of values. And even where fraud and contrivance are practised, as they always have been, the values are still honoured; for without the honour ascribed to values, their attempted undermining by a minority would be of no avail.

Being half an animal, man knows *what* he is, even though he may not know precisely *who* he is. By contrast, an animal does not know that it is one. It takes an effort of imagination to realize that the creatures who dominated the earth for much longer than man can never have known their own nature, except by direct primary knowledge, let alone the possibility of their death. Their inter-individual relations were likewise dictated by the adjustment of instinct, whereas those of human beings have been worked out, over and above that, in custom and legal systems. Indeed, it is the existence of custom and law which has permitted much of human conduct to revert to the 'automatic' character which is a feature of animal life. We need to be more like the animal in its instinctive acquiescence in order to be more human in our everyday behaviour.

Living in a psychological present, the animal cannot envisage ends, and is unable, even in his construction of nests, hives, or lairs, to create an institution. Nor are his 'ceremonies' akin to human ones, save in superficial appearance. The reason why animal behaviour assumes a stereotyped character is that the animal is not trying to be anything else, whereas man has an impulsion to transcend himself. His institutions are for that reason never static, or, if they are, they soon degenerate. The impulse in man is to endeavour to preserve an institution for as long as he can, because 'a community of individuals has to be kept going, has to be protected against disintegration just as much as an organism'.[8] Apart from anything else, it is wasteful to destroy the work of experienced people, to abandon archives and records, and even to evacuate buildings long associated with a particular activity. Man is even anxious to preserve ruins, for these are symbolic of the endeavours of his ancestors; it is surprising how much emotion can be engendered by the attempt to tamper with such remains. If a new institution be created, it is usually, if not always, established on the model of the old. It is remarkable how universities tend to resemble one another; the type of university building, Gothic and ecclesiastical, was until recently everywhere much the same, and this did much to convey what a university claimed to be. Based on secular principles, the 'new' universities have correspondingly altered their external appearances; and technical institutions, lacking traditional religious links, have assumed an aspect much like the machines which are their primary concern.

It is not an accident, however, that, even in the most up-to-date institutions, ceremonial has by subtle inertia lagged behind in respect of modernity. This is another proof of innate human conservatism. For the impulse towards self-discovery expresses itself as much in conserving and hallowing the past as in reaching out to the future. To anticipate the future is often to let loose the instinct for iconoclasm and destruction. 'Conserver et protéger ce qui existe déja est fade, difficile, laborieux. Détruire est amusant et exaltant.'[9] Aristotle said that man is the only animal who can 'join his end to his beginning'. There is no satisfaction in living solely with an eye on the future. In institutions dedicated to the most modern experimentation, the degree-giving ceremonies would be considered incomplete and inappropriate without ritual conducted partly in extinct languages and with the aid of caps and gowns designed by mediaeval schoolmen. Even in those institutions which have sought to break with tradition altogether, some form of ceremony is preserved at appropriate moments, as if a powerful instinct were still in play. In societies dedicated to ends different from those of the past, vast parades are held, incantations chanted, and forms of initiation practised which resemble those of a tribal era which have been abandoned, not least in countries where such an era is still a recent memory.

The cultural heritage and culture deprivation

Here we come round again to our central theme. What is preserved in the traditional ceremonies, etc. of which we have spoken is precisely a cultural heritage. Civilization is a matter of technical accomplishment; it is cumulative.[10] Culture, as its name implies, is a growth, if a slow growth, which each generation must choose whether or not to tend. The achievements of civilization are made in a logical order: certain processes could not have been evolved without prior discoveries. Maxwell's theory needed to be elaborated before radio was possible. We are *necessarily* more civilized than our ancestors; we are as cultured as we care to make ourselves. Hence the progress of civilization, though it has abolished many evils and lightened human labour, has not necessarily made for the greater happiness for which some reformers had confidently hoped. Indeed, there has been an increase in ailments of which previous generations knew nothing. More than half the hospital beds in Britain, as we write, are occupied by those suffering from mental illness. When Goethe said that classicism makes for health and romanticism for disease, he was referring to the natural and healthful capacity of culture. We cannot aim at happiness: it is a by-product of cultural growth. During the millennia before the rise of technological civilization – i.e. during the greater period of man's life on earth – the ordinary existence of people was rendered supportable by such cultural heritage as they had been able to preserve.

Admittedly, existence is scarcely tolerable, and finally impossible, without the enjoyment of the basic animal requisites of life: food, warmth, and human contact. But it is not necessarily true to say that cultural enjoyment begins only when these basic needs have been satisfied. *The true satisfaction of such needs assumes a cultural form.* The preparation of food is a cultural act, culminating in shared consumption, which is the origin of so much ceremony and ritual. Lack of attention to the preparation and serving of food entails a serious cultural loss.[11] The reason is that the preparation itself is a cultural, as well as a culinary act.

Watch a woman – a woman who really knows how to cook, I

31

mean – rolling dough. She's got a peculiar, solemn, indrawn air, a satisfied kind of air, like a priestess celebrating a sacred rite. And in her own mind, of course that's exactly what she is.[12]

It is hardly necessary to stress the importance of shelter in the cultural life of a people. Until recently, the focus of the house was the hearth, round which the family gathered, and which, apart from the dining table, was the focus of ceremony. Thirdly, the human individual needs the proximity of his kind, whether friend or partner or even acquaintance. We grow uneasy and sometimes even dejected when a post office clerk, shop assistant, or janitor, known for years through a few verbal exchanges, is suddenly no longer there. This is not true all the time, since solitude is no less urgent a need: but in the course of domestic life and of routine work, man needs company. In a sense his solitude can be provided only within a *community*. He creates best when there is a proper balance between solitude and gregariousness. 'Digging by oneself is drudgery, but shared with three others with only elbow-room between them it can be joy.'[13] Throughout much of history, the poor suffered as much from enforced overcrowding as from material privation, so that the equilibrium was seriously disturbed. In the Western world, a surprising number of people, even young people, live alone, but there are few without access to others or who lack the company of a pet or the solace of a patch of ground. The most tragic cases are elderly people living in isolation, where there can be cultural as well as material deprivation at its most extreme.

Alternatively, there may be cultural deprivation in a life of opulence, especially if recently acquired. A win at the Pools, after the first euphoria, is not always a blessing. Possessions and excessive addiction to comfort can bring about a form of accidie which deprives life of its flavour, simply because the taste is blunted. The spiritual poverty of the plutocrat, and even more of his wife, drifting round the world in search of pleasure, is usually written on their faces. Some people in this situation have struggled to escape from the toils of their riches by adopting, at moments, the 'simple life', like Marie Antoinette in the *hameau* at Versailles; but the diversion has proved as artificial as that to which it was meant to form an antidote. Tolstoy remarked how many of the rich people of his acquaintance were permanantly indisposed.[14] The ailments of the rich are often a consequence not only of an unnatural mode of life but also of a state which, in however wry a fashion, they have come to enjoy. For when we are ill we are obliged to suffer abstentions, so that illness in the case of a rich man or woman can afford a measure of physical and mental relief. Proust's aunt Léonie, so admirably drawn a character from his own aunt Elizabeth Amiot, was living the only life which her ample means made endurable. Had she not feigned permanent indisposition, her existence would no doubt have been prematurely cut short. The history of society – or Society – seems to suggest that, in every generation, certain illnesses have to be invented in order to render the daily round of the plutocracy supportable; and the resources , not to say the ingenuity, of the medical profession have often been taxed to the limit to minister to their needs. This is especially so today, when medicine has tended to create its own environment, and 'on a world scale, but particularly in the USA, medical care [has] concentrated in breeding a human stock that was fit only for domesticated life within an increasingly more costly, man-made, scientifically controlled environment.'[15]

By contrast, those who are genuinely ill, or who suffer grievous physical incapacity, are often those who are genuinely happy. Everyone must know or have known paraplegics or those suffering from incurable diseases who display a lightness of heart usually associated with the carefreeness of youth. This carefreeness may characterize also those who suffer from certain forms of mild insanity, such as the Mr Dicks of this world, who often arouse a reluctant envy in those regarding themselves as perfectly sane. The more likely explanation is the existence of health at a level distinct from the physiological; and it is to the examination of this that we now turn.

The three nutritions

One of the basic facts about the organism is that it sustains itself by selecting nourishment from its environment. The mechanism of this process, together with that of elimination, is very remarkable: as a result, the organism is infused with energy, voided of waste, and enabled to conserve its form. Now if the organism needs nutriment, so presumably do the other components of the personality, namely, the psyche and the spirit, though the manner in which such nutriment is furnished and assimilated at these levels may be very different.

At this point, it is important to guard against misunderstanding. The suggestion that the psyche or the spirit require nourishment (by which we mean structurizing energy) may be dismissed as a fanciful exercise in metaphor. On the contrary, we shall adopt a point of view nearly the reverse and contend that organic nutrition, instead of being the typical or most authentic form of nutrition, is nutrition in its crudest, grossest and most elementary form. Reflection will suggest that a scale of refinement in nutrition is compatible with what we know of organic, psychic, and spiritual activity.

What, then, is the nutrition or 'food' of the psyche? To plunge in *medias res*, the food of the psyche is *art*. By art, we do not mean merely the 'fine arts': these are specializations of art. Art is here understood in its broadest and most comprehensive sense as that which approximates to culture in general. Indeed, to provide the definition which we have been anticipating, culture, in its essence, is *psychic nutrition*.[16]

The nature of psychic nutrition

If culture is defined in this manner, two points already made are shown to be compatible. It was argued, following Eliot, that culture was that which made life 'worth living'. It was also maintained that if a measure of psychic health were achieved, the personality as a whole tended towards stability and balance. If culture and psychic nutrition are identical, the consistency of these claims is thereby confirmed.

Today, much is heard, especially in the Western world, about the 'crisis in the arts'; but this is chiefly a crisis among practitioners of a certain kind of art, namely, minority art. Meanwhile, many thinking people, including some artists, are uncertain whether art has a proper place or function in society: at best it tends to be regarded as an expensive ornament of life, and at worst a game. Nevertheless, the average man, though aware that art has something to do with culture, tends to regard culture as a kind of epiphenomenon, or what the Marxians called an ideology. This is perhaps because the official culture of our society is often out of touch with the culture or psychic nutrition which, at heart, we really relish and enjoy.

The word culture, though much abused and vulgarized, is an apt one, because almost all cultures are associated with what is called a *cult*. Here again the word must be understood in its widest sense. It refers to activities involving not merely a core of beliefs, but ritual, ceremony, drama, and myth, whereby that belief is symbolically represented. Ritual, manifesting a rite, involves thematism and rhythm: there is reason to believe that such rhythm and thematism, though greatly formalized and stereotyped, are prolongations of organic rhythms, as in the dance. Jung has stressed the two poles between which psychic energy flows. Of the therapeutic or nutritional value of such ritualistic activities, there is no doubt: dancing is taught as a social grace but also as affording emotional expression. Nor, to resume a point made earlier, is it accidental that all forms of culture, from the most primitive to the most sophisticated, adopt special ritual practices and observances in connection with the fundamental biological 'crises' of life: birth, puberty, mating, and death. A psychological crisis supervenes upon each biological one, and at such moments, as we all know, the psyche needs special fortification. The entry into the world of new life, the arrival at adulthood, the taking of a mate, and, for the mourners, the death of kindred and companions, require in each case a special emotional response, designed to promote a renewal of morale. Hence, too, the ceremonies that accompany all important appointments at the level of the state: coronations, the bestowal of honours, and the swearing in of ministers, whereby a new responsibility is assumed. Even when we 'give our word', we usually enact a simple ritual, be it but a gesture. The liturgies of the great religions, like the mass ceremonies of political cults, are carefully devised means to the purification and canalization of feeling; and where such liturgy is absent, or has fallen into disuse, substitutes must speedily be found.

In place of the 'initiation cults' associated with adolescence, especially in early societies, there is today an elaborate teenage cult, to which all the resources of the mass media are harnessed, with appropriate ecstasies and the carefully induced trance. Indeed, it is difficult to effect an adjustment of feelings, or to give social authorization to feelings already modified by a major biological crisis, without moments of suspension of consciousness. Psychic anaesthesia, which may take many forms, is a recurrent need, especially among the young.

In other words, ritualization and dramatization are psychic necessities for man; and whatever may be the ultimate aim of religion, its beginnings remain at the psychic level. The drama sprang from religious ritual; and it is to the impoverishment of drama when the religious connection, even in comedy and farce, is wholly severed.

Nor is it the big or crucial events only that require a measure of ritualization. The same is true of the ordinary events, the moments of life which, because of their regularity, form part of the cyclic process of living. There is a peculiar satisfaction, which is more than organic, in eating and drinking in compatible company. Meals must not merely be eaten; they must be seen to be eaten. When it is said that man is a gregarious animal, what is really meant is that he is an animal whose very togetherness provides a form of psychic nourishment. Social conversation, or mere *bavardage*, is required not merely for the exchange of information but for the satisfaction of a deeper need – stronger perhaps in women than in men – for the sharing and pooling of psychic experience. Moreover, the feeding of the organism has generated its own art, that of gastronomy. If cooking belongs to civilization, gastronomy belongs to culture.

Cultural sickness and cultural health

Here, perhaps, we have a clue to that problem which has for so long exercised the minds of educators, religious leaders, historians, and artists: the problem of the so-called 'sickness' of our culture. Admittedly, the subject encourages generalities, but possibly the explanation is simpler than we think. Although man is acquiring increasing material benefits (the 'affluent society' is a popular phrase), there is evidence that he is failing to get the proper kind of psychic nutrition. Modern man is obsessed with the desirability of an ever higher standard of living; it may be that this higher standard of living (which is never high enough) reflects a low standard of psychic nutrition. 'It is possible to feel "real" even when poor, and deficient in all that the "better living" of the politician offers us. It is even possible to find affluence a threat to one's sense of being human.'[17] Much sentiment has been outpoured on the joys of pastoral or bucolic existence; but it remains true that when the average man was a countryman or peasant – this means the majority of men until quite recently – the intimate contact with nature, and with other living creatures, provided a kind of permanent solace and satisfaction denied to the modern city-dweller. To live, to *thrive*, implies the maximum, if discriminating, contact with other beings, an inter-subjectivity that reaches down as well as up the scale of life. The rose-bed and the rockery, the kitchen garden and the window-box, the refreshing stream, even a view over the hills, provide their own particular psychic satisfaction. 'Oh, I could spend whole days and moonlight nights,' wrote Cowper, 'in feeding upon a lovely prospect! Mine eyes drink the rivers as they flow',[18] where the act of psychic nourishment is conveyed in the use of words 'feeding' and 'drink'. And there are special forms of psychic nutrition for particular occasions: the bouquet of flowers sent to the patient in hospital is a recognition that while everything is being done to repair the internal circuit of the organism, the needs of the psyche, especially at such a time, must not be neglected.

To take another ordinary example: the keeping of pets, like the keeping of children (which is a higher form of the same thing), is a way in which men obtain psychic satisfaction of a particular kind; for there is an obvious mystery about children, as about animals and birds, which helps to slake man's insatiable appetite for wonder and innocence. There is a mystery about forests and mountains too; but whereas one may domesticate children, animals, birds and plants, one cannot, unless one is very wealthy, domesticate forests and mountains; but that is where the state steps in, with its provision for National Parks, Reserves, and Nature Conservancy areas. Mountains and grandiose scenery in general are supposed not to have been appreciated before the Romantic Revival; but it was at this period that Nature was first *explored*, which was not so much to deprive it of mystery as to take up a different attitude to the mysterious. Nature can thus be included within Art because the Nature amid which we live has been fashioned by Art. To that extent, and including the 'wild' areas, all Nature is artificial.[19]

Needless to say, the existence of psychic nutrition has always been implicitly recognized, though apart from Aristotle few of the ancients drew attention to it. In our own civilization, one of the first men to perceive its nature and efficacy was Thomas More. In *Utopia* (1516), he speaks of 'pleasures which satisfy no organic need, and relieve no previous discomfort. *They merely act, in a mysterious but quite unmistakable way,* directly in our senses, and monopolize their reactions. Such is the pleasure of music.' And of the Utopians he says:

> They are also keen on the pleasures of sight, hearing and smell, which are peculiar to human beings – for no other species admires the beauty of the world, enjoys any sort of scent, except as a

method of locating food, or can tell the difference between a harmony and a discord. *They say these things give a sort of relish to life.*[20]

Psychic nutrition: true and false

One lesson to be learnt from the present cultural crisis is that it is better to make one's own culture than to absorb it passively and ready-made. Every day, and almost every hour of the day, powerful television and radio stations pour forth a steady stream of what is, in most cases, *ersatz* or pseudo-psychic nutrition. Anyone who has, by submitting to a test of endurance, listened for some hours to music programmes featuring listeners' choices or requests, often made on the occasion of a birthday or a wedding anniversary, must have arrived at the conclusion that psychic needs, themselves legitimate, are being satisfied at a very low nutritional level.

With the cinema, which fed the communal psyche for so long from a suburb of Los Angeles, and television which promises to feed it a good deal longer, and now video-cassettes which promise to turn us into a race of vidiots (to use Seymour Betsky's word), a world composed largely of unreality is held with a kind of permanence in front of the eyes of millions of people. Nothing comparable has ever happened before. The *attention* of mankind is coming to be permanently *distracted*. An *ersatz* dream life has been imposed upon it. Deprived of this form of distraction, the community must suffer the pains of the addict whose narcotics have been withdrawn. A popular newspaper once offered £10 to families to refrain from watching television for a week. At the end of that period, one of the recipients declared:

> I found Sharon [aged 8] telling me about her school and I discovered things about her I didn't know. But I'm glad we can turn on the TV again. Frankly, the week has put the greatest strain on us since we were married. I was so fed up one night I went to bed at 6.30 p.m.[21]

Since culture tends towards conservatism, the past itself can provide psychic nutrition. To 'live in the past' may be more satisfactory, more enriching, than to 'live in the future', and we can obtain a particular satisfaction from entering into an historical period and making it imaginatively our own. No doubt some profound dissatisfaction with contemporary life, or disillusion with political prospects, is at the root of the intense interest taken by the public, as never before, in both archaeological investigation and accounts of early civilizations. Part of this interest may be due to a fascination with social structures different from ours, especially those with a marked hierarchical basis. Naturally, such a view of the past, as Plumb has pointed out, is often highly romanticized; but the public must project its feelings somewhere, and where better than on a past which, as investigation advances, reveals increasing interest? By entering into the spirit of another epoch, we add something to ourselves, and the world acquires a new dimension. For what we are doing is seeking to enter into the feelings of our forebears. History continues to be written, and written with increasing confidence, both because we need to know how we have come to be what we are and because the idea of a 'before' and of 'forerunners' affords solace and comfort in our position of exposure to an unknown future. And no exposure is greater than that suffered at the present time, when technology, for all its benefits, has removed so many landmarks by which we were formerly guided. The past, as Simone Weil said, is 'a need of the spirit' (i.e. the psyche).

Thus those on holiday, who would never think of visiting their local church, swarm into the cathedral, or scramble over ruins, peer down at the archaeological site, and send postcards home to prove the discharge of their duty to the past; for it is the unfamiliar past which charms most, perhaps because it affords greater scope to the hungry imagination.

To say that man needs the company of the beings with whom he necessarily shares his world, and particularly that of his own kind, is not to go far enough. Man needs, so to speak, not merely himself: he needs the celebrity, the hero, the leader, the star. The presence of 'great' men or women affords a powerful psychic satisfaction, because such a person is surrounded with an aura of glamour, and we like to share in his glory. As most people are physically and mentally of moderate endowment, and few are really brave, they accord special veneration and applause to the hero or heroine, acquiring by their recognition the illusion, but also sometimes the reality, of fortitude, just as by their frenetic reaction to the presence of a star they experience the sensation of possessing something of his talent.

Desmond Morris in *The Naked Ape* (1967) argues that the shrill greetings accorded by young girls to a pop star are directed not so much at the hero as at one another, in order to demonstrate their sexual maturity. This would seem to be partly true; but it is also likely that they are seeking to indicate by their enthusiasm and competitive shrillness an individual claim to special understanding of their idol, in the hope that the message will get through to him.

Although for many years sociologists and political scientists, together with a few demagogues, claimed that man had a passion for equality, it is equally obvious that he (and he, here as well as elsewhere, implies she) desires ardently to see certain select persons exalted above himself. In fact, the two passions are not in conflict; they can co-exist, like other antithetical human passions. Man, assured of fair treatment by the state, forthwith goes in search of subjects for his emulation. He derives particular satisfaction from observing at a distance – if not too great a distance – the rites and customs of those whom he supposes his superiors. The look of unfeigned ecstasy on the face of strangers, especially women, drawn to the church door at the conclusion of a wedding – any wedding, but preferably a society or 'posh' one – or even watching a revered public figure emerge from his house and dive swiftly into his car, testifies to the emotional solace that fame provides. What is especially satisfying is fame or eminence sanctified by custom, which is for that reason often called 'hallowed'. A familiar face on TV is a source of psychic satisfaction. The reason why newsreaders attain this status is that, provided they have sufficient competence in other respects, they satisfy the common desire for reassuring routine. Theorists have drawn attention to the fact that man's psychic nature is inherently conservative; 'psychic reality, the inner constitution and organisation of each individual mind, is highly resistant to change'.[22] Most potent a focus of nutrition is therefore a figure who combines satisfaction of the desire for permanence and stability with the promise of seemingly infinite revelations of glamour, such as only youth and beauty and a certain 'undefiled' quality can provide. Thus a girl scarcely out of her teens, lifted to heights without parallel or precedent, and learning in a few months to command those heights, becomes a focus of psychic attention, through the media, to hundreds of millions. And in order to satisfy the public hunger which her new status as Princess and future Queen has generated, every popular periodical (save perhaps those of the Communist world and the openly pornographic) thereafter repeatedly reproduces that face, distinguished as it is from those habitually featured by reason of its transcendence of the erotic. And when the public is not gazing at her, they are reading about her. And when not reading, dreaming.

There is, however, one form of great man that no society can do without, though many societies have ignored him, and even on occasion recommended his expulsion. This is the artist himself. Whether writer, musician or painter, the artist, unless he be of mediocre talent or a mere *poseur*, is not a hanger-on of society, a misfit, an 'outsider', but someone as important as the priest and the healer, and perhaps a figure partaking of their gifts, and, as a 'cultural' figure, older than these. For he is *society's professional purveyor of psychic nutrition*.

There is a special reason why the artist, as thus defined, can provoke public hostility, especially at the outset of his career. For he is often concerned to change the community's feelings about itself, even if he does not do this consciously. Whether we like it or no, we *feel* differently as the result of a Shakespeare, a Blake, a Scott, a Byron, a Wordsworth, a Tennyson, an Eliot; but even so, the change of feeling affects initially only a small part of the community. Sometimes an artist destined to modify the public sensibility lives on the outskirts of society, receiving acclaim only after his death. Meanwhile, it remains true that the *professional* depends, as always, upon the amateur, and not the other way round; and the fine arts, being highly specialized accomplishments, depend upon that more diffused art which we have defined as affording psychic nutrition in general. The poet, being a specialist, deals in specialized feelings. Wordsworth's sensitivity to the countryside was that of a highly intellectual man. The countryman himself, inhabitant of the 'pastoral republic' which Wordsworth called the Lake District, was not less sensitive to the country, but merely less articulate. Articulateness means both loss and gain: for to articulate is to select but also to refine, and sometimes to etiolate. A society which deems itself cultured will display a refinement of manners and of sensibility far beyond anything achieved by the 'common people'; but minority culture, which is today often regarded as the only form of culture, will become ingrown and arid unless periodically refreshed by nutrition of a kind which, in the past, came from a 'lower' part of society. Wordsworth's 'Resolution and Independence' is a great poem because the leech-gatherer whom it eulogizes is a leech-gatherer. The position at present, especially in the United States, is that, except in the case of certain regional traditions, *poetry* is being written chiefly by university personnel for other university personnel, who also supply the critics.

The post-industrial epoch and psychic nutrition

The subsistence of minority culture today is due to a change in the provenance and quality of psychic nutrition, which reflects a change in the organization of society. In Britain, and in most Western countries, with the partial exception of France, there is no longer a social reservoir of health and potential creativity in the form of a peasantry. In 1800, as many as eighty-five people in Britain out of a hundred were engaged in agriculture: today, the number is three, and declining. Instead, the *media* are providing a very low quality of psychic nutrition, and those who control or dominate the media are in many cases members of the new Establishment which has grown up with the emergence of pop culture. Thus in the 1960s members of pop groups became arbiters of taste and opinion, issuing periodically political statements (e.g., on the war in Vietnam) of a predictably radical slant. That all psychic nutrition provided by the media is not necessarily *ersatz* must be stressed; it is the growing discrepancy between high quality and inferior material which gives ground for disquiet. The general level of popular entertainment has undergone, by any standards, a marked decline. And the press is in no better condition.

In fact, the reorganization of society has amounted to something like a revolution. If we regard agriculture as the primary social activity, and industry as the secondary, it is evident that just as industry has succeeded agriculture in importance, so the importance of industry itself is giving way to that of a group of activities best designated as tertiary. These activities are roughly concerned with 'information' (the French *informatique* is a useful word) and services. In short, we are already in the post-industrial age. The sources of our psychic nutrition are affected accordingly, though the conception of media put forward by McLuhan must be accepted with reservations. Media by themselves have no 'message'; they are by definition 'means' to conveying ideas, and the technical apparatus used for their conveyance has nothing like the effect McLuhan ascribes to them. Difficult otherwise to account for, the prestige of

McLuhan was due to the fact that he emphasized the role of media, and especially of the image, and therefore by implication the new role of tertiary activities. What McLuhan implicitly conveyed, though without overtly dealing with the subject, was the existence of *a crisis in psychic nutrition*. For in many cases the media are conveying 'packaged' psychic nutrition as far from being nutritive as some of our packaged food. Never has there been so much technical know-how at the service of psychic nutrition, and so little genuine psychic nutrition to be purveyed.

It is no part of our task to examine detailed 'mechanism' whereby the psyche is fed: this is a matter for the neurologist. We can merely draw attention to certain basic considerations. The part played by rhythm in energizing or toning up the psyche is evident. 'The moment the drum stops beating,' wrote Wyndham Lewis, 'the appeal of art weakens.'[23] Conceivably this dependence upon a regular beat is due to our uterine experience of the mother's heartbeat at seventy-five times per minute. What is in fact 'the major sound-signal of life in the womb'[24] is bound to have an important influence upon our later psycho-physical make-up.

Secondly, a great deal of psychic refreshment would seem to be due to the operation of evocative signals and sign-symbols which exercise a *thematic* effect – that is to say, the signals and symbols set going themes at the psychic level. A work of art can 'release' several themes at once, thereby forming a constellation, as can a work of nature: and this thematic movement constitutes the life of the psychic 'organism'. The ritualistic nature of some cultures, particularly of the Orient, is due to the response to regular stimuli, some from nature but most from the established cultural institutions.

Thirdly, nutrition at the psychic level, and probably more so at the spiritual level, is not merely energizing; it is constitutive. The psyche and the spirit are *modified* by a new experience, so that a man or woman who has acquired a measure of psychic or spiritual enrichment can legitimately be called 'cultivated' or 'cultured', even when lacking in formal education. This is a respect in which the psycho-spiritual nature of man differs from his organic nature.

Fourthly, the psyche's normal condition resembles that of repose or sleep. Pythagoras and Plato spoke of the soul as asleep in the body. This is understandable, because the continuous assimilation of nutrition would be injurious and perhaps ultimately fatal. There is psychic surfeit as well as psychic starvation. There is also psychic

43

intoxication. In fact, just as we limit our consumption of physical food, so as a matter of everyday prudence we instinctively ration our absorption of psychic nutrition. The individual or the family has its carefully-spaced 'days out', its celebrations, its anniversaries, its dances, its parties. These are occasions on which physical and psychic nutrition are combined. For such special occasions we are prepared, if necessary, to pay rather more than usual, and the extra money is normally to meet the cost of psychic nutrition. After a successful outing of this kind, the psycho-physical being is perceptibly refreshed. This is far from the case with substitutes for psychic nutrition, which lead often to excess in both consumption and expenditure (see chapter 3). It will be immediately obvious that while some may deride the whole idea of psychic nutrition, or dismiss it as based on mere analogy, the controllers of the entertainment and catering industry – practical, hard-headed people – make no such mistake. Providing the public with nutrition in ever more subtle forms, they charge for it accordingly.

At the same time, just as the physical organism needs not merely to feed intermittently but to breathe continuously through its pores, so the psyche in its dormant state must continue to breathe a nutritive 'atmosphere'. To that extent it is active. This 'atmosphere' is precisely the environment about which we hear so much and without which no psycho-physical organism can exist.

The environment, natural and social

Environment, a vague word in itself, is a compound of the organic, the psycho-organic, and the social (the idea of a dead inorganic world is now generally discarded by the new science). Therefore it yields not merely organic nourishment but a great variety of psychic nutrition. Our bodies too are part of the environment, which is why we decorate them. Only within the last decade or so have we come to realize the efficacy and potency of environmental psychic stimulation. In bringing up to date his *Anatomy of Britain*, published originally in 1962, Anthony Sampson found himself obliged in 1971 to introduce an entirely new category of social phenomena. This was concerned with the environment and with the conservation of resources, energy, forests, wildlife. The problem was not simply a physiographical one; for, as a writer in *The Times* (19 September

1983) pointed out, recreation and contemplation were involved too. In short, it was a matter of psychic renewal and a new category of profanation and taboo.

Edward Carpenter once wrote an essay entitled 'The Simplication of Life'.[25] Although the world it described seems remote to us, his message was a valuable one. Such an essay needs to be issued at regular intervals. This is not because life is getting more and more complicated. In some ways, life – or living – is a good deal simpler than it was when Carpenter first wrote. If it is complicated, the reason is that the range of choice is much wider. Technology has made this possible. Consequently, we have to make more decisions. In business, in public administration, and in the political domain, this is evident. But it is true also of private life. Even persons of no great wealth or possessions find it necessary to employ an accountant to cope with their tax-affairs. Before we can begin to have any private life, we have to call upon the help of a variety of public services. As for enjoyment of life, this is where simplication is most needed: for the most satisfactory of pleasures are the simple pleasures. Almost it might be said that all true pleasures are simple pleasures. That is why books on the 'joys of sex' are not always so satisfactory as they appear. In recommending so many complicated practices, they instil anxiety and discontent rather than satisfaction. Sex *is* perhaps the one sphere in which simplicity and moderation come near to providing the 'joys' that so often elude the sensualist.

This raises two matters of fundamental importance. First of all, there is a delicate, fragile quality about the psychic life which is often overlooked. A gentle upbringing is the best introduction to life – 'from quiet homes and first beginnings. . . .' Those who need a regular dose of violence – or who are given to understand that they do – are psychically impoverished. There is a psychic vacuum into which these forces rush. And by violence is not meant merely shooting or the buffeting of the person in films, novels and TV programmes, or in the private fantasies in which most people would seem to indulge, but excess of any kind. In a well-known essay on Pascal (of all subjects),[26] Aldous Huxley advocated a regime of what he called 'balanced excess' – an excess of chastity and an excess of indulgence, etc. But, like most exercises in excess, this was palpably absurd. You do not maintain balance by breaking the scales at both ends. This is drastically to disturb the psychic equilibrium. The Buddha, that moderate man, soon abandoned the regime of macerations in which, before his enlightenment under the Boh tree, he indulged. All the higher religions have established Orders in which asceses of varying severity have been prescribed; but the ones which have proved most successful, like the Benedictines and the Franciscans, have practised a remarkable degree of moderation. In fact, with one exception, that of sexuality, the Rule of St Benedict shows an understanding of human nature which may help to explain the remarkable achievements of that Order in reconstructing Western civilization after the fall of the Roman Empire. A day devoted to prayer, study, and agricultural labour, satisfied spirit, psyche and organism, in balanced moderation, better than a regime more consistently 'intellectual' or 'spiritual'. The latter type of Rule is obviously beyond the capacity of all but a minority. So is the total denial of sex, which, even in conditions which did not, as today, stimulate the appetite, nevertheless presented serious problems to monastic authorities. This St. Boniface (680-754) openly acknowledged, while his near contemporary, St. Aldhelm, showed that denial, supposing that it were genuine, did not prevent an unhealthy obsession with the subject, if his treatise on Virginity is to be taken in evidence.

This brings us to the second point. It is not suggested that monastic rules, even of the most temperate kind, are the ideal to which ordinary people should seek to conform; but a study of religious Orders in both West and East provides a valuable lesson in what, at that level, affords the best psychic nourishment. The 'idleness' of which at the Reformation many monks and nuns were accused (though a work such as *Piers Plowman*, written 1370-80, was equally accusatory) was a distorted reflection of that mixture of quietness, tranquillity and absorption in the beauty of nature (for most builders of monasteries were careful to lay on a permanent supply of psychic nutrition from the environment) which was thought conducive to the practice of piety. Monasteries in wild places 'were also seen as restoring paradise'.[27] Even given the other side of the picture – the winter chill, the dull insipid food, the foul diseases – it seems obvious that such solace was superior to the perpetual rhythmic stabbing of pop music which many workpeople today are prepared to endure as their environment throughout both work and leisure. Indeed, the effect of this iteration is to numb the psyche rather than to feed it.

Until well into the nineteenth century, the church or the churches provided for most people all the entertainment there was to be had. That is to say, except for church festivals, Sunday school treats, etc., the common people had no entertainment at all. Nor, except for saints' days and the great ecclesiastical festivals, did they have any holidays. (With regard to holidays, the ordinary Japanese had none until fairly recently, and the habit of not having them survives in the reluctance of many workpeople even now to claim their full entitlement.) Unable to conceive regular diversion or distraction, except the simple home pastimes, they did not feel the lack of it. To us, who sense the lack the moment it is withheld, their lives would have seemed insufferably boring.

The spread of universal education in England after 1870, together with the general rise in the standard of living, made the aspiring classes vaguely discontented with their lot. Consequently, they did not object to being told that their habits and pursuits were in need of reform. Even so, the attempt by well-meaning persons to 'raise the tone' of popular psychic nutrition was often misconceived. Parallel to the revival of folk music at the beginning of this century – the names of Cecil Sharp, Vaughan Williams and Gustav Holst come to mind – was a movement to rid the Church of all the 'bad music' which the Hymnody provided. There was a similar movement to get rid of the 'bad verse'. But the substitution of 'good music' for the old familiar settings, like the substitution of sophisticated jazz for the ragtime ('ragged time') originated by Scott Joplin around 1900, and – needless to say – the supersession of the bicycle ride for a spin in the car, did not always make for greater contentment. For one thing, the bicycle played a part in the emancipation of women which the car (that made them to some extent dependent again) never did. This was admirably brought out in that remarkable account of social change, Flora Thompson's *Lark Rise to Candleford*. Even today, when the pop industry is one of the most flourishing and the Top Twenty have an influence spanning national frontiers, and the private lives of pop singers are a matter of personal concern to millions, a rendering of 'Daisy, Daisy' (a bicycling song, as some perhaps need to be reminded) or 'Alexander's Ragtime Band', 'If you were the only girl in the world', or even 'The Bells of St. Mary's', strikes a chord, at least in the Anglo-Saxon psyche (but what about 'La Vie en Rose' in France?), which echoes more powerfully than the latest Eurovision hit. The author belongs to the last generation which sang in childhood, as a natural part of its repertoire, certain songs

47

dating from the Restoration period. And before the first 'Wireless Christmas' of 1920 or 1921 – depending on when the set was first obtained – the family would play ritualistic games of which the meaning of some had become unintelligible ('Here we go Looby Loo, Here we go Looby Lie . . .').

For certain ceremonial occasions, the most suitable music is not necessarily 'art' in the refined sense. It could be argued that for Armistice Day, Elgar's *For the Fallen* is more appropriate than Britten's *War Requiem*. In fact, the *Requiem*, though claiming to transmute grief into art, may turn out to be a more propagandist work than Elgar's setting of Lawrence Binyon's fine poem. We shall revert to this subject in the next chapter.

The same applies, after a couple of decades of erotica, to the simple Love Story. This is another proof of the conservatism of the psyche, which its adaptibility only serves to confirm ('Let my people be thy people . . .'). For millions in the West, Christmas is still the great annual festival, and it is becoming so in Japan. Even the Soviet Union has its 'Winter Festival', which everyone knows is Christmas in disguise. The significance of Christmas for psychic nutrition was brought out precisely by the young lady who said that, since it was such an enjoyable occasion, she did not see why religion should be brought into it. To cap that, we may quote the TV administrator who in 1977 remarked that, as Christmas Day fell on a Sunday for the first time for several years, 'we had to have a bit of religion in the evening'.

Conceive – if such a thing be possible – a life without provision for the psyche at all. It would not be worth living; indeed, it would not be livable. What the Americans call 'raw feels' are not enough, any more than raw food is enough. But nor is a perfectly fed, warmed, sexually-satisfied organism enough, though some behavioural psychologists have claimed that, given such organic contentment all round, religions and philosophies, lacking a role to play, would disappear. The survival of man as a dissatisfied, exploring, enquiring, aspiring creature proves them wrong. Why is it true, as John Stuart Mill felt obliged to admit, that 'Socrates dissatisfied is better than a pig satisfied' (he later substituted 'man' for 'Socrates')? Because Socrates is a dissatisfied man and not a satisfied pig-man. It is as simple and as complicated as that.

Hence, certain forms of imprisonment, especially of young people lacking mental resources, can be demoralizing to a degree which must defeat the whole purpose of custodial sentencing. True, there are other forms of confinement, such as prolonged hospitalization, which are markedly psycho-sensory depriving; but this is relieved by nurses, who minister as much to the psyche as to the organism, and whose devotion anyone who has been so confined must extol. Even if imprisonment may serve to protect society from the criminally vicious (which it does), the fact remains that because such an environment erodes their human qualities, it constitutes an unacceptable form of psychic deprivation. We need to work out a new custodial policy; for if we are prepared to keep the criminal alive, we must not render him psychically all but dead. Extreme psychical impoverishment was precisely the aim of *la vie concentrationnaire*, as it is of the Gulag. The twentieth century has exhibited the first systematic experiments, in both war and peace, in the prolonged, if not permanent, application to a section of society of psychic starvation. That a creed based on the ideal of universal brotherhood should have brought about the most monstrous example of man's inhumanity to man is one of history's grimmest ironies. A rule of the Nazi concentration camps was that no prisoner might touch another, save for purely utilitarian purposes. Women prisoners in particular have testified to the extreme cruelty of this prohibition. Given the constant psychic signalling from mother to child, or lover to lover, or friend to friend for that matter (though more evident perhaps in the Mediterranean than the Nordic cultures), the horror is only too apparent. Certains forms of anguish, as we know, are due to the lack or removal of this form of reassurance. The psychiatrist would do better to search for evidence of individual psychic deprivation than to try to plumb psychic depths where individuality has ceased to have a meaning. Apart from reassurance, insurance itself is in large part concerned with helping to preserve or to restore those sources of nutrition on which we rely for our psycho-organic wellbeing. Everyone knows that a sum of money, paid out by an insurance company on the morrow of some disaster, is not in itself compensation; but it can go towards that initial raising of psychological morale which, in the organic sphere, is effected by some medical restorative or even, temporarily, the 'stiff drink'. The insurance premium is thus a regular outlay designed to buy off, or to minimize, future anxiety regarding sudden psychic deprivation.

3
Positive and negative nutrition

PN the essence of culture

Now that the expression psychic nutrition has been sufficiently employed to remove its unfamiliarity, we propose henceforth to use the letters PN for short. There are many precedents for this: ESP, IQ, and a host of acronyms. PN is the essence of culture, and culture without PN is a husk without a kernel. It is to this aspect of culture that we shall chiefly pay attention. The problem of an age dominated by tertiary activities is the problem of preserving culture not for prestige reasons but for basic social health. This was a point repeatedly made by that perceptive psychologist D. W. Winnicott. One of the objections to a situation in which minority culture exists in a hot-house condition is that such culture is itself largely prefabricated and packaged, so that minority culture and mass culture are equally inefficacious in providing PN. And so often *ersatz* PN is subsidized by official funds, whereas it is no more possible to produce PN by direct policy than it is to cultivate happiness by the award of grants.

At this stage, it will be useful to provide additional notes on the examples of PN that have been given, and to add a few others, so that the reader may obtain a rather better idea of that which is intended. This list is followed by some examples of negative PN, and finally of substitutes for it.

Examples of positive PN

(a) Ritual and drama

Modern life provides little opportunity for psychically satisfying ritual, which is perhaps the reason why pop festivals have enjoyed so

51

great a vogue. On such occasions, young people feel that they 'belong'. They also have a feeling that they belong to each other: the film *Woodstock* emphasized the degree to which the participants fell in love or reached a new stage in their love-life. The music does not have to be particularly good. In fact, it may not be good at all.

> An outdoor concert by the Rolling Stones is an interesting piece of large-scale theatre; the fact that it has no musical value whatever is cancelled first by the evident pleasure of the spectators, who simply enjoy the massiveness and the sense of occasion.[1]

By contrast, the ritual associated with the church, even the Catholic Church and High Church Anglicanism, had been losing its appeal. Officiants and congregation had been undergoing increasing separation, until in some services the ritual seemed to be going on regardless of the presence of the congregation, and the interspersed hymns served only to emphasize the distance between the two. Attempts have been made to remedy this situation, but not always with the success anticipated. In continental cathedrals, where the congregation stands and moves about, devotion may be less – or less overtly – intense, but the psychic benefit may be greater. So far as we know, the early Christian rituals, especially the Eucharist, approximated more to this type of function. In certain Buddhist countries, Thailand for example, attendance in the temples takes the form of family or friendly gatherings, with everyone seated on the ground and feeling 'at home', instead of, as so often in the Anglo-Saxon countries, 'in church'.

Drama continues to thrive because the actors, if skilled, communicate directly with the audience. The drama, at its best, is therefore a form of collaboration,[2] and the audience leaving the theatre feels that it has undergone a therapeutic cure. The therapy acts chiefly on the psyche. As a psychic power-house, neither the cinema nor TV will ever supersede the theatre. A great dramatic performance is one that gives the impression of being designed for that particular occasion, and an actor is a master in so far as he can sustain that impression. In the cinema and on television one performance must suffice: and to sit through the repeat of a film never fails to arouse faint surprise that the showings should turn out to be identical. That the cinema can produce therapeutic effects is not in dispute; but until recently its hold was due to psychic effects of another kind. There was the Dionysiac cult of the star, with its resultant fantasies, which many people embraced more assiduously than is commonly admitted: a fact demonstrated by the ready sale of meretricious supporting literature of a kind which the theatre cannot match. Of what other figure than a film star could it be said that he 'drove a generation of women frantic and men to drink' (of Omar Sharif)?[3] Now television has outmatched the cinema at this level. The TV 'personality', haunting the home of millions, has enjoyed a new kind of fame.

Yet the true reason why the drama retains its appeal is that it provides a microcosm of life itself. The drama is life *in parvo*. But it is life which we can see out to the end, whereas the life of the spectators is still being enacted. Those who leave the theatre are obliged to proceed with the *business* of life; the *play* is left behind. But precisely because it is a play we have seen from start to finish, the result is nourishing, as is a melody by reason of its return to its starting-point.

Fire, the supposed outward manifestation of the pure, invisible fire or *pur spermantikos*, which is an adjunct of so much ritual, must have been one of the earliest sources of psychic nutrition, and the camp fire or hearth fire the place where PN was most often generated. Until fairly recently, the family, seated round the hearth, derived a certain amount of self-hypnosis by gazing into the blaze or embers and seeing 'pictures in the fire'. This was perhaps the first example of non-participatory drama, save in respect of the imaginative freedom to project the action. A new ritualistic stage was reached when it was found possible to carry fire about, and to employ various focuses of fire for ceremonial purposes: the altar fire gave place to ceremonial lamps and candles. Despite the diverse coquetry of lampshades, electric light has never provided so satisfactory an ambience for PN. In the 1950s, the perennial need to see 'pictures in the fire' was catered for by the most sophisticated (and also quasi-hypnotizing) peep-show yet devised. The TV screen is likely to remain the chief fount of PN for most people for the rest of history – supplemented, as it is bound to be, by the next development whereby it will be possible, under strict government control, to 'plug in' to any part of space and to view what is happening there.

(b) The hero cult

Even before the growth of the media there were stars of a kind. Muriel Bradbrook has pointed out that the clown Tarlton in the Elizabethan Age was virtually the first star in England, perhaps 'the first man to be known . . . simply in terms of his personality'.[4] It is a commonplace that everyone needs a father-figure, but the hero is more than that. Not many people particularly want to assume the role of a father-figure, but everyone would like to be a hero. In default of being one, the ordinary man or woman seeks to 'borrow' some of his allure. In our age, however, hero-worship has taken a new turn. Pop stars and sportsmen have exceeded in fame and glamour the traditional purveyors of PN, royalty. This is partly because royalty of recent years has shown, or has been made to show, its common humanity (the attempts by film and other methods to demonstrate that royalty are 'people like ourselves' have the opposite effect to that intended, because a hero or star has to be, as stated, a better or greater self), and partly because pop stars and sportsmen can be seen as masters of sexual prowess, and sex is modern man's substitute for true PN. Indeed, in some cases, such as that of the late Marilyn Monroe, the qualifications for being a film-star were openly acknowledged to consist exclusively of sex-appeal; and there was something pathetic in the wish, expressed by this sensitive creature not long before her death, that she might one day 'become an actress'. Similarly, there is at least one football star today whose achievements on the field are accorded second place to his achievements in another sphere.

Nevertheless, pop stars come and go; but a monarchy, or a president endowed with monarchical attributes, such as President Kennedy or General de Gaulle, enjoys a certain permanence of esteem which PN requires. The British monarchy, and to some extent that of Japan, of which we shall speak, has been the most successful in maintaining its hold, even after its prerogatives have been removed by slow constitutional evolution. This deprivation of political power has not reduced, but merely laid bare, that other potency which authority of any kind needs in some degree in order effectively to maintain itself; and it is this potency or prepotency which, because of training as well as of natural charm, has raised the British monarch's prestige higher – in some respects, and given the adverse forces at play – than it has ever been. It is laid down in textbooks that the monarch reigns but does not rule, but the present Queen certainly exercises rule in one sphere, only now outshone by her daughter-in-law. As a political commentator has written: 'Whole books have been filled with dreams that enchant her subjects – and not only by night. . . . Do Americans dream of President Carter, Russians of

President Podgorny, Frenchmen of President Giscard d'Estaing? I doubt it.'[5]

(c) Children and pets

Of all natural activities, reproduction is the most shrouded in mystery, and to reproduce one's own kind rarely fails to arouse excitement and wonder. 'An interesting condition', a 'happy event', the announcement of the 'cancellation of engagements': such phrases testify to the atmosphere of excitement and mystery surrounding parturition and childbirth. Naturally, the chief satisfaction from the birth of a child is obtained by the parents and their other children; but everybody feels he has a right to take an interest in a baby, whatever the circumstances:

> Lorsque l'enfant paraît, le cercle de famille
> Applaudit à grands cris. Son doux regard qui brille
>   Fait briller tous les yeux.
> Et les plus tristes fronts, les plus souillés peut-être,
>   Se dérident soudain à voir l'enfant paraître,
> Innocent et joyeux.[6]

It is not simply that the creature represents new life: the impulse of every adult, save one who 'cannot stand children', is to enter into communication with the child, employing a language which the latter usually tolerates rather than understands. This communion, if effective, affords extreme pleasure, and the result is psychic alleviation. Communication of a similar kind is conducted also with certain animals, especially those we have adopted. Much of the conversation is clearly unintelligible to the creature addressed; but a domestic animal may afford satisfaction by the mere fact of 'belonging' to his master or mistress or to the whole family, and by being displayed as such, so that the loss of a favourite pet is a severe psychic deprivation. Hence the trouble taken to ensure the safety of animals or birds when the family has to move or to travel, and the revulsion felt against negligent owners. In many cases, the creatures are worth nothing save in a psychic sense, but this is for some people their supreme importance. Needless to say, the attachment to pets is merely a positive example of that attachment to living nature which human beings today need as much as their ancestors did: that is to say, an attachment to their 'world', or a world they have made their own. There is also a part of nature which arouses fear and dread, and this provides its own specialized kind of PN, of which we shall speak.

Just as children provide a particular form of PN, without which no community can be counted stable, so the child requires for its welfare an education which must have PN for its foundation, and for a time its chief constituent. There are parents who wish to give their children an exclusively 'rational' upbringing, but the attempt always breaks down. This is because the child himself envelops what he is taught with make-believe, and cannot be brought to discontinue the practice until he has reached the stage at which it ceases to be necessary. For whatever education we are given, we bend it to our own purposes; to this extent we always educate ourselves. The child may therefore instinctively resist that for which he is not ready; and this is a reason for refraining from giving him prematurely too 'progressive' a training – a point to which zealous sex-educators might usefully pay attention. The present attempt to 'abolish child-hood' may cause a psychic lesion of incalculable harm.

(d) Women

We have pointed out that glamour is an authentic form of PN, whereas sex in the raw, being largely physiological in its appeal, fails to be psychically nutritive, or is at best productive of *ersatz* PN.[7] Throughout history there has been a campaign, waged usually by men, to keep woman psychically 'incandescent': by dressing her up, by subtly revealing – by concealing – her erogenous zones, and, at certain moments, by putting her 'on a pedestal'. This movement has been countered by a different sort of campaign, aided and abetted by women themselves, to throw off and abolish the 'female mystery'. 'Women's liberation groups attack all forms of mystification of women in modern society.'[8] The photograph of a woman on another sort of pedestal in the defunct magazine *Nova* was an extreme example of such demythologizing. The movement towards total female emancipation, which is of recent origin, may be said to have run parallel to the movement of secularization, of which indeed it is a part. In the past, woman, as mother or mistress or both, has fulfilled a social role which, though subordinate, has exerted great power in the world. At the upper levels of society, she has provided a milieu or setting for men's activities. She has generated a psychic ambiance which the male has found peculiarly congenial for the deployment of his inventive powers, his talents for negotiation and business, and his need for relaxation. The virtual disappearance of the salon has resulted in the impoverishment of social life, which has meanwhile witnessed the emerged of the technocrat at the expense of the statesman. Yet, in their time, a Lady Blessington or a Lady Radnor, or even a Lady Astor (to confine ourselves to Britain), has exercised an influence far greater than that of many 'free' or 'liberated' women. The apostrophes and paeans of praise of woman, scattered throughout Disraeli's novels, but especially *Coningsby* (1844) represent celebrations of her crucial psychic importance in social life.

At the lower levels of society, woman's influence has been equally important, if somewhat more confined. But here again, her power has been that of a focus or fount of psychic energy, as much as that of home manageress. All activities are deployed round her. Consequently, the death of a mother has something particularly tragic about it, as if a tribal goddess had suddenly vanished. Hence the speed with which a motherless (young) family may acquire a new guardian of the home, and the extraordinary adaptability of the woman in such circumstances, moving into the distraught little society which, with tact and understanding, she quickly binds and moulds to her will.

Although some women are genuinely intellectual and can easily compete with men in the academic field, the *typical* woman remains a non-intellectual or psychic figure, for whom instinct and feeling are all-important. 'As a woman,' writes Ann Oakley, 'in the first place, my emotions rule my life. From them I derive the pleasure and pain of my existence. My thoughts are directed by them. There is nothing that I do or think which is not inspired by feeling.'[9] The psychic energy she generates is eminently fortifying, which is why for most men it is a necessity to have a woman 'behind' them. The propaganda put out by so many organs, but above all by women's magazines, implying that sex-appeal is the over-riding necessity for women, is a gross simplication of woman's basic needs – and men's. Clothes are assessed according to their sexual allure; every woman is invited to engage in what the cosmetic experts call 'the struggle for beauty'; and from an early age she is possessed with mounting anxiety as to whether she can possibly win through in this relentless contest.

The truth is that sex which is always 'appealing' is a wasting asset, especially as the sexuality in question is usually of a purely physical kind. Glamour is sexuality combined and supplemented with PN; it is this which constitutes Eros. And if it is a question of sexuality versus PN, it is PN that nearly always wins. The 'can't-see-what-he-sees-in-her' type of woman, carried off in marriage, abundantly demonstrates this truth. We refer to marriage deliberately, for a man is able literally to feed off such psychic provision, which can increase with the passage of years. Sex is for affairs: PN is for matrimony. And possibly the serious crisis in the institution of marriage is due partly to the quality of the sex-information and counselling disseminated, especially in the popular press. Yet well-meaning people, panicking at the sight of so much marital failure, urge more and more 'education' of the kind which almost totally ignores the psychological side, and thus speeds the disasters which it is supposed to forestall. Those who advocate 'free' sex, on the other hand, and who logically stress the physiological aspect, incur the wrath of certain advocates of Women's Lib (as well as more moderate persons), who denounce the use of women as pure sex-objects, to which, in consequence of their own propaganda for the elimination of the female mystery, they may themselves have helped to reduce them.

Given the 'law of diminishing returns' which applies to sex-appeal in particular, it follows that the recent cult of nudity for its own sake is not so much a throwing open of women's charms to an appreciative public as a desacralization of the female form. The result is that she furnishes no longer true but *ersatz* PN. This is to the impoverishment of culture. Fortunately, there are signs that the tide is turning. Indeed, apart from the rise of new venereal diseases, a swing back to former standards may be necessary in order that genuine PN may be provided again by the female. These changes cannot be deliberately contrived, or the result too will be *ersatz*; but human nature has a way of readjusting itself according to an inner law. This of course is not incompatible with movements to the redress of obvious inequalities – political, economic, and social – any more than it is incompatible with women occupying the highest posts.

The existence of a limited number of exclusively male societies, clubs, etc., with their highly formalized organisation, testifies to the extent to which society in general depends upon that powerful, sustaining influence of women which we have mentioned. It might even be argued that women are more genuinely social beings than men, focuses of social concourse, which would explain the slightly unnatural atmosphere prevailing in women's clubs, staff-rooms, etc.

(e) Darkness and light

From women to darkness there is a natural transition, because darkness and the female principle are closely related. The female womb is 'dark', the female mystery is a 'dark' mystery, and

> The Night was made for loving
> And the Day returns too soon.[10]

D. H. Lawrence was preoccupied with the 'dark gods' of sex, which, contrasted with 'sex in the head', implied an emphasis on the psychic realm. Hence the particular glamour of twilight, 'le moment crépusculaire', the hour for lovers, the hour of expectancy:

> At the violet hour, when the eyes and back
> Turn upward from the desk, when the human engine waits
> Like a taxi throbbing waiting.[11]

In those regions of the world where the climate can be harshly torrid, such as parts of California, darkness is 'laid on' long before it is night, not merely as a physical relief but as a psychic aid. Broad daylight is the climate of reason and commonsense, whereas the realm of instinct is spontaneously thought of as dark. Similarly, the night club is the place where the 'nether' feelings are stimulated; and until recently the performances in such places were slightly 'daring' in their semi-nudity, whereas, with total strip-tease, the secret and mystery are gone, and the shows therefore take place as much during the day as the night, and sometimes in the morning, which until recently was considered the hour least appropriate for entertainment of a sexual kind.

As night conceals and hides, so it symbolizes not merely the darkness of the psyche but its opacity. Hence the mystery and romance traditionally associated with woods and forests, where outlaws such as Robin Hood traditionally had their haunts, where 'mysterious' men such as charcoal-burners plied their trade, where 'little people' dwelt, and where special rites were performed ('the sacred wood'). With the virtual disappearance of forests, and the advent of Forestry Commissions, the woods have been desacralized, and with them a potent source of PN. For the 'primaeval forest' symbolized not merely psychic depths but those realms from which man or his precursors emerged. Consequently, the depths of the sea, which is the original source of life, has sometimes been represented as a vast forest, full of mystery and the macabre, silent and inchoate.

Hence also the attraction of caves, and cave exploration, partly no doubt because these places still subconsciously serve to remind us of the homes of our first ancestors, and partly because their exploration, by the expert speleologist or by the amateur, symbolizes the urge to plumb the ultimate mystery, that which is to be disclosed 'where the darkness ends' or which is itself a preternatural darkness, total oblivion, the 'heavy, sealing darkness, silent, all immovable' of D. H. Lawrence.

In a certain measure, darkness is a necessary feature of certain social functions. This is true above all of the ceremonial dinner party. All meals, even breakfast, demand a certain amount of ritual; but of the chief meals of the day, dinner is that which requires not merely the highest quality of physical nutrition but the maximum of PN. Hence it may be highly ritualized. When the working day was differently arranged, lunch was a meal capable of providing a degree of PN, and there have been breakfasts with the same dual provision, such as the famous literary meals given by Samuel Rogers or those presided over by Oliver Wendell Holmes. Then there is the 'wedding breakfast' – held early (it is said) so that the bridegroom should not have time to get drunk – which is a farewell meal, since it is an occasion following which the two chief participants take their leave. Here the toasts and presents are symbolic of the PN which the guests wish the married pair to give each other as part of the meaning of 'to love and to cherish'. Nevertheless, the dinner party, being the meal most conducive to the generation of PN, needs special attention given to its arrangement; the decking of the table as of an altar, the display of flowers, the elaborate dress of the guests, the ordered seating, the libations, and, even now, the special function and movement of the womenfolk. The ritual darkness will receive greater emphasis by being penetrated by candlelight, or sometimes this darkness will be 'suggested' by candles burning while lights are still on, a curious but significant custom. Both breakfast and lunch are eaten in the knowledge that the working day, or part of it, is still ahead. Distractions at such a time, e.g., breakfast television, may for some prove irksome. The invasion of yet another part of the day by entertainment may seem an inappropriate way of feeding the psyche, which is braced for plainer fare. At such a time even the cheerfulness of the winsome presenters may grate on the feelings. By contrast, dinner and its aftermath evoke a special solemnity, since they are to be followed by the sleep suggestive of death. Moreover, there should be a special quality about the talk at dinner; the decline of the art of conversation has undoubtedly robbed this meal of much of its significance and enjoyment. Listening half-asleep in bed to the rise and fall of the adult voices below, the child believes that the talk bears upon ultimate things, and so it may do. If the meal is a success, the guests will have absorbed PN as well as physical food. And as the guests go out in the dark, they are able to face life, and therefore death, with renewed resolution and serenity. It is not an accident that Novalis's *Hymns to the Night* (1800) contain a mystical exaltation of death. Granted, the PN provided on such occasions may be of an *ersatz* kind, the product of sustained tittle-tattle and frivolity, and then the result is boredom and exhaustion. This, alas, is true of many an official gathering, as it may be true of the ordinary cocktail party with its forced clamour.

The whole history of lighting affords insight into changes in the taste for PN. Light is both an illuminator and a hypnotic. The fire which once lit and warmed the cave, though only fitfully, was also the focus of rapt communal attention. Similarly, the flickering candle, and even the incandescent gas-mantle, provided more potent psychic pleasure than the bland electric light bulb. The installation in some Catholic churches of electric bulbs which, for the requisite sum, may be illuminated for such time as the devotee wishes, cannot replace, as a votive offering, the candle stuck on a prong, which as it furls and dribbles grease will resemble nothing so much as a perservering but fragile spirit. So important a part have candles played in social life that the candlestick and candelabra have themselves become vested with PN. In the first chapter of the *Book of Revelation*, it is the candlesticks ('lampstands', *Jerusalem Bible*) which represent the Seven Churches of Asia. Indeed, the silver and golden candlesticks as ornaments have a beauty that takes precedence over their primary utilitarian function.

(f) Fear

Darkness can inspire fear as much as excitement; but there is a kind of fear, not too exaggerated, which serves to provide a form of PN. Up to a point, people like to court danger, to experience thrills, to 'dare' themselves and others, to make each other's flesh creep. This is especially the case with young people, who derive psychic exhilara-

61

tion from going a little farther than normal and in tempting fate. In Jane Austen's *Northanger Abbey* (1797), the heroine, Catherine Morland, approaches the 'romantic' abbey 'resolved on alarm' and 'craving to be frightened'. At its extreme point, this object is achieved in games or contests such as Chicken, when cars are driven directly at each other and the idea is to determine who swerves out of the way first. (This game, for game it is, is used often in illustration of certain aspects of Conflict Research.) Or it can be obtained by a ride on a 'thrill machine' such as the Big Dipper. It is significant that Jeff Nuttall in his *Bomb Culture* (1970) speaks of the mods and rockers riots of the early 1960s as part of an 'excitement game'. In activities less extreme but inducing a mood of calculated tension, the result is still psychically exhilarating, and a higher state of morale may be achieved. As life goes on, the need for such flirtation with danger normally decreases, because the adult has either proved his mettle or has sought out ways in which his latent fears can be sublimated. An old man who persistently went in for thrills would be considered immature.

In certain aspects, nature remains a source of fear and dread, though less so than formerly. The human race still huddles together round the fire (or the 'box'), in order to shut out the terrors which surround us all the time. And there can be few people who, lost in a remote stretch of countryside or at sea or on a mountain enveloped in mist, fail to suffer a moment of *frisson*, which is not simply a fear of exposure but a dread of the unknown. On the other hand, as life and nature become progressively desacralized, the need to go in search of danger, to raid the unexplored, increases; and so we witness more and more calculated feats of daring – crossing seas solo in light craft, tubs or even baths, being a current favourite. For now that the land is practically all explored, the sea, with its uncertain 'temperament', remains the only part of nature, save for outer space, which has preserved its mystery. (Space exploration is barred to individual initiative on account of the expensive equipment needed; otherwise interplanetary travel would already, we may be sure, have been attempted by thousands of 'privateers'.) And the great enthusiasm inspired by such expeditions shows how keenly the ordinary man seeks to share in the resulting psychic satisfaction: indeed, such satisfaction is their chief end, since the scientific benefits are usually negligible. The honours often bestowed on the participants, who are amateurs in the true sense, are society's reward for affording it a vicarious supply of PN. The *Guinness Book of Records* is a compendium of feats which, undertaken largely for their own sake, have provided psychic stimulus to thousands who, from one end of their lives to the other, may never undergo an experience the least degree out of the common.

(g) Games and sport

In feats of prowess or daring such as those described, there is always an element of action for its own sake. This is, or should be, the essence of sport. Games are played for the love of them, but the indirect result is the provision of PN. Everybody who has engaged in sport knows that the result is not merely a physical but a psychic satisfaction. Although some people play games purportedly to 'keep fit', this does not explain the 'cult' of sport, which has always possessed vague religious associations, as in the case of the funeral games of Ancient Greece and of the Maya civilization. A game is a contest, but a contest of a particular kind, involving strict rules governing behaviour 'on the field'. Thus every game forms a kind of rehearsal for the 'real thing'; and it is this make-believe element in games which causes the PN they provide to be comparatively mild, for the *esprit de corps* involved is a short-lived affair. Nevertheless, it is a PN particularly well-adapted to children and young people, whose instincts are in process of growth and in need of training and control. Middle-aged people who participate in communal games are therefore still at heart 'boys'. Older people usually play games, such as golf or bowls, for exercise rather than for competition, since their instinctive life is less compulsive. If games were always played according to the rules, however, the cult of sport would be different from what it has now become. In fact, sport is involved with the hero cult; and the *victor ludorum*, or supreme winner, provides an enormous fund of PN, so much so that the feelings of both players and spectators may be raised to a pitch of frenzy which the game itself is insufficient to absorb. Hence the rowdiness of much modern sport; the fouling, the insulting of the umpire, the absurd self-adulation of the player who scores a goal, followed by frenetic hugging and embracing, and the total neglect of some of the traditional sporting ideals, such as 'fair play' or 'let the best man win'. Of the World Cup Final in 1982 *The Times* (12 July 1982) commented on 'the series of fouls that littered the whole evening'. Of the Australian cricketer,

Dennis Lillee, *Now!* Magazine wrote (2 July 1979): 'He works himself up into a mood of hatred by listening to the crowd chanting "kill, kill, kill".' This must suggest a lack of balance in communal culture. For the behaviour of spectators, with their hostility to the opposing side, the running fights that follow the match, the wanton destruction of property, and even the attacks on persons wholly unconnected with the game, indicate that the rules originally worked out mainly by (in Britain) public school boys are not adapted to the psyche of the new middle classes. What this section of the community is cultivating is not sport in the sublimated sense at all, but an up-dated version of that orgiastic religion to which most societies have given periodical outlet, as in the Roman Saturnalia and Lupercalia. Football itself was played originally on feast days, and for years hymns were sung after matches; now sporting events themselves determine holidays, the songs are often ribald, and the outcome violence.

(h) War

Closely related in its psychic influence to (f) and (g), but over the 'brink', is the hazardous game of war. War, too, is played on a 'field', a battlefield. There are also winners and losers (or there used to be). A great deal of research has been undertaken, especially since the dropping of the atom bomb in 1945, into the origins of war and the means to its prevention; and Conflict Research, which we have mentioned, has tried to reduce the whole problem to formulae, or to an aspect of the theory of games. Although the theory of games is not the same as gaming, the idea that war is a kind of game is by no means preposterous, for this is the best way to make war tolerable, and often how, between conflicts, it is presented. (A curious example of the nature of war as a game, at least in so far as its rehearsals are concerned, was the case of the calling off of manoeuvres by the American army in Germany on 13th April 1952, because of a number of fatal accidents. Here the rehearsal was too authentic, so it was abandoned.) In war, psychic satisfaction is obtainable at the greatest risk of all; but it is a price which, until recently, people were still prepared to pay, even if reluctantly and after much grumbling. The inconvenience and the great suffering involved did not prevent peoples in the past from engaging in prolonged rivalries – vendettas, wars for prestige, religious conflicts, and even totalitarian wars:

which suggests that some deep satisfaction must be derived from such collective action. The satisfaction is that obtained, at least in retrospect, on the psychic plane, its keenness and relish being due precisely to the fact that it is sought and exacted at great risk. After all, war is 'the real thing'. Those who suffer maiming in the process are regarded as the victims of ill-luck; and while those thought likely to recover are given considerable publicity, the badly injured are kept judiciously out of sight. In general, however, except at the great moments when, in Churchill's words, it is 'equally good to live or to die', the actual course of war has often been boring and uncomfortable. The chief satisfaction of war is having taken part in it and survived it, for it provides a form of camaraderie or *esprit de corps* difficult to achieve in peacetime, and this is a rich source of PN. That is why a defeated nation can still regard war as having been worthwhile, and why reunions of combatants take place with as much enthusiasm among the vanquished as among the victors.

In peacetime, but in war above all, an especial glamour is associated with those who engage in the risky business of espionage. This is because, though there are vague laws of war affecting normal combat, espionage involves breaking as many rules as possible. To engage in such covert activity is therefore to participate in the most exhilarating game of all, pitting one's daring and ingenuity against extreme odds. Ian Fleming, who exploited this aspect of war (hot and cold) to great profit, put the case in all its stark and grim excitement when he said of espionage, and the torture to be expected and applied, 'it is a tremendous game' (sic).[12] Because it is so 'tremendous' a game, not many people have been prepared to play it; but the vicarious thrills are such that the successful spy, with a few exceptions, remains a glamour-figure second to none. No doubt this is because war has otherwise been desacralized; and, apart from successful generals, the spy is the only charismatic figure left. Hence, although people endeavour to work up indignation against traitors such as Kim Philby or Anthony Blunt, there is a sneaking admiration for men who could have acted for two intelligence services at once over a period of forty years.

With the arrival of the nuclear age, the nature of war has undergone radical change. If, as seems likely, the conflicts of the future are to consist in the summary massacre of entire populations, the game of war will hardly be worth playing. For war by its nature has ceased to be a game, which is always played to some extent 'for fun'. The massive campaigns against nuclear war are therefore different in kind from the pacifist agitations of the past; and the support given to movements such as CND by women, who were not preponderant in the old pacifist movements, may be due not to hatred of war as such but to an obscure feeling that the new sort of war is unsatisfactory, since it destroys non-combatants as indiscriminately as fighting men, and it no longer provides that opportunity for the exercise of male prowess which, despite the contribution of the women's services, was the chief point of fighting. It is not an original remark to say that women, from the time of the Spartans onwards, have always covertly approved of war, at least in the conventional sense, because in the end war is the defence of house and home and therefore of the woman's physical and psychic domain. The problem for the future is how to find a substitute for war which will engage the same instinctive 'valencies'. Admittedly, there are other fruitful sources of PN in war: the uniforms, the parades, the martial music, the campaign medals. These and other pageantry, which former wars provided more plentifully than modern wars (a cavalry charge is a more inspiring sight than a tank attack, as the cinema has demonstrated), contribute to that 'sense of glory' which is productive of psychic exhilaration. Consequently, although the nuclear age is supposed to frown on war as a means to the settlement of national disputes, the fact remains that films, television programmes, exhibitions, and books on war, lavishly illustrated and lauding victor and vanquished, enjoy an enormous and mounting popularity. 'War has become trendy.'[13] Moreover, although certain films are apparently designed to underline the evils of war, the ordinary film-goer does not always view them in this light and may misunderstand their purpose. He regards the violence and slaughter as part of the excitement of this unique game, deriving the more gusto from it in that the hero manages always to survive the dangers, and concluding that it is, after all, a game eminently worth playing.

(i) Memory, recollection and nostalgia

Memory, or rather ideas capable of recollection, implies the existence not just of one self but of many. I can 'consult myself', that is to say, one of my past selves. To do so is to obtain nourishment, and there can be few, if any, human beings who do not enrich themselves from time to time in this way. Our memories are part of our personal capital of PN; and this capital can be 'worked'. We have only to think of the hundreds of poems evocative of memories, as well as much 'haunting' music. Samuel Rogers's poem 'The Pleasures of Memory' (1792) is a treatise in polished verse on memory as a source of PN. The role of scents in providing stimulus-signals for memory was first stressed by Schopenhauer. In short, memory as nutriment at the psychic level is one of the most convincing proofs of the existence and function of PN.

(j) The Grand Inquisitor's Trinity

The passage in *The Brothers Karamazov* (book V, ch.5) about the Grand Inquisitor is justly famous. In maintaining that human beings need a perpetual diet of 'miracle, mystery, and authority', the Inquisitor was making a pronouncement upon the needs of the human psyche. We would prefer a quadri-partite series, namely, *myth*, miracle, mystery, and authority.

To some, this will seem to suggest that the psyche needs to be fed upon falsity and lies; but, at the *psychic* level, the question of truth does not arise. What appeals to the psyche is image, not idea. The sphere of art is imagination, which is indifferent to the distinction between truth and falsehood. While seeing the play, we do not ask whether Hamlet did or did not live. If it could be demonstrated that there was never any such person, this would make no difference to the merits of Shakespeare's drama. The psychic appetite for 'myth, mystery, miracle, and authority' results from the fact that we are part of nature, and that we originate from it. Our origin is – and will probably always remain – a mystery to us, seeming to constitute a perpetual miracle, expressible only in myth, and claiming authority over us, since we are all subject to nature's sentence of death. 'Mysteries are the food of the mind, and all the fundamental mysteries are necessary to sanity. In asylums you meet people who have the answers: sane people never have the answers.' Interviewed in his eightieth year,[14] I. A. Richards was indulging in the hyperbole of old age; but he was unquestionably right about ultimate matters. Admittedly, it could be argued that the world of nature may one day be proved to be a machine and ourselves as cogs in it (though how the proof could be arrived at is not clear); and indeed the universe of Newton and Einstein is more 'rationalist' than the universe of Ptolemy or that of the mediaeval cosmologists. But that is not how our psyche reacts to the world. As Jung and Guntrip have stressed, our instinctive life is older and more 'conservative' than our intellectual life; and it is stimulated by the old and 'conservative' objects and activities we have already described. Not for nothing do we refer to eternal youth, to the 'eternal woman', or to 'age-old instincts'. Although science may be able to explain the physico-chemical constitution of the earth, and the neuro-physiological make-up of humans beings, the psyche will still derive its nutrition from nature and man and woman as psycho-biological entities, capable of activating instinctive themes. Despite the marvels related in science fiction, and the prophesies of futurologists concerning human mutation, man's psychic life is implicitly recognized as a constant,[15] or men would stop reading such fantasies. No one is interested in creatures which do not *feel* as we do, whatever the superiority of their intellectual faculties; nor would we consider experimental embryology worth while, or even ethical, if it were to produce creatures fundamentally different from us. Indeed, the possibility of cloning raises these matters in acute form.

If changes in our make-up were considered likely to result in the extinction of emotions such as love, most people would regard the future with undisguised horror. Only if the future were to permit the continuance of culture in our habitual sense of the word would it be regarded as tolerable. This culture must provide outlet for instincts which are not merely gregarious but isolating, not merely authoritarian but submissive. Psychic life is healthy if these contending instincts are balanced and polarized; and such equilibrium, which must characterize the higher emotions too, is the equivalent to the criterion of truth and falsity on the plane of intellect. 'Myth, mystery, miracle, and authority' evoke the *emotions* which constitute psychic life; and the fundamental part played by women in society is that they may furnish all these psychic expressions together. Although Lévi-Strauss's theories about the 'exchange of women' seem to be concerned solely with the avoidance of incest and the ensuring of the birth-rate, the circulating of women, and their occasional capture by other tribes, may also have been in the interests of a satisfactory psychic life. The great Sabine rape was due to the Roman need not just for women but for woman. This role of woman as purveyor of PN is confirmed in homosexual communities, where the 'woman' is not absent but present in the form of the female-type pathic. How often do apologists for homosexuality insist that the homosexual displays an emotional difference from his fellows, even though this contradicts the claim that he is by nature fundamentally the same.

It will be clear that when we refer to the psyche, and the reactions which it displays to its environment, we mean always man *at the psychic level*. It is the whole man that feels, just as it is the whole man that perceives and thinks. But sometimes feeling takes command, just as sometimes the brain turns itself into a calculating-machine, or a group of people transform themselves into another kind of machine by forming a human chain in order to effect a rescue. It is this predominance, or temporary increase, of psychic activity to which we refer when we speak of the psyche in isolation. To take a historical example: the British people as a whole still entertain, though less than in the past, a latent fear of Popery. This originated in events, not all of them connected with religion, which took place in the sixteenth and seventeenth centuries. The mild phobia in question has not gone into the average man's intellect; it has not gone into his bloodstream: it has gone into that part of his nature where phobias and other such feelings lurk. In short, it is a psychic phenomenon. Similar though more positive phenomena were movements such as Methodism in the eighteenth century, and, more restricted in scope, the Oxford Movement in the early nineteenth.

(k) Humour

This is among the most potent forms of PN. Humour is one of the ways, and for some people the chief way, in which the imperfections of the human condition, their own and other peoples, are rendered supportable. Indeed, the radical imperfection of that condition – for an apparent contradiction at the heart of reality has been recognized by all philosophies as the ground of the philosophical impulse itself – is implicit in all but the most superficial humour. Hence the Utopias conceived by idealists have no more place for the humorist or the comedian than for the shaman or the priest. To look into the evil of the human heart requires rare spiritual courage. Those possessed of it in abundance include the author of the Book of Job (and before him the author of the *Epic of Gilgamesh*), Sophocles, Langland, Shakespeare, and a fine spirit like Tolstoy, at moments Ibsen, with Goethe rarely. But there is another way of coping with evil and the weakness on which it battens: the authors of the miracle and mystery plays adopted it by turning the Devil into a figure of fun. Chaucer did it by viewing many of his pilgrims in the spirit of levity.

As a tradition of polite society develops, the role of humour is increasingly taken over by wit; but no culture is so stable as to dispense with humour altogether, because no society is uniformly cultured. If the wit of the refined or educated elite can prove a defence against vulgarization, so a corrupt elite may precipitate by way of reaction the uprush of a savage humour on the part of the oppressed. Orwell pointed out, with reference to Dickens, that all genuine humour has something subversive about it. The eighteenth century, in particular, exhibited both extremes. On the other hand, neither wit nor humour, but merely rancour or invective or at best persiflage, is at the disposal of the governing class of a totalitarian state. Hence the daily atmosphere of such societies is one of un-relieved solemnity and hebetude. But of course no totalitarian state is totalitarian throughout; in all sections, save perhaps the upper bureaucracy, there circulates the breath, however faint, of liberty. This may be mirrored in that black ghoulish humour which other oppressed peoples, such as the Jews, have used to redress the miseries of their existence.

Court ritual as elaborate as that practised at Versailles under Louis XIV cannot be sustained without periodical release. The horseplay familiar at the Sun King's court, as chronicled by Saint-Simon (which included urinating on one another's beds), contrasts markedly with the chaste Cartesian poetry of Racine. Every rigid society has had its Lord of Misrule. The social fabric can hold together only by a slight bursting at the seams. Even the Bolshevik tyranny, in its earliest phase, was palliated by the two licensed clowns, Bim and Bom. Although forbidden in the inner sanctum, humour lurks in corners of the corridors of power. How else would the structure of absolute authority endure?

Humour has its correlative solemnity, which it cunningly exploits, as the technique of every comedian proves. But there are professions which are uniformly solemn in character, like diplomacy. Between Foreign Offices, communication is invariably grave and slightly pompous in tone. This is partly because the relations between nations are still to some extent in a state of nature, so that the extreme formality associated with the conduct of foreign affairs is in some degree a façade. In this sphere, every slight or presumed insult has to be registered, noted, chronicled, and, so far as possible, repaid by studied 'protests'. An extreme example of recent years has been the meetings at Panmunjom between North Korea and the UN (chiefly American) officials – 'the longest armistice' – where even a slightly higher flag placed on the negotiating table has to be 'answered' by an equivalent gesture on the other side. A solemn farce is being conducted, and both sides know it. But the humour of it all has to be suppressed.

Such diplomatic solemnity is a survival or offshoot of that fervent patriotism which provided so much PN, especially for the upper classes, from the time of the Victorian imperial hegemony until almost the other day. The Fatherland cult may have been an even stronger source of PN; but being associated with continental *Sturm und Drang*, it was of a less serene kind. The residual appeal of British patriotism, however, was shown during the Falklands conflict of 1982, where it emerged spontaneously from the heart of the people. As letters to *The Times* made clear, the intelligentsia was largely against such an exploit, though often for surprisingly superficial reasons. By contrast, post-Vietnam America is still demonstrating a PN void in this sphere. The 'new' countries continue to draw upon a source of chauvinistic PN, manufactured at the time of the liberation movements: hence the danger run by anyone, especially if he be a member of the former master nation, who indulges in flippancy in countries recently 'freed'. Nationalism provides the necessary PN in states which secularism has otherwise voided of the *sensus numinis*.

Whereas diplomacy wears a solemn face, politics, as publicly conducted, is 'all smiles'. The diplomat must act as if he were the embodiment of secrecy and confidentiality; the politician needs to convey the impression of absolute candour. He must demonstrate that he has nothing up his sleeve, that he can be trusted implicitly, that he is 'one of us'. Hence the reassuring grin which irradiates his face whenever he emerges, or as soon as the cameras are trained on him. Most anthropologists now agree that the bared teeth, without which no smile is complete, are meant to demonstrate that predatoriness and menace are in abeyance. Royalty also must maintain this 'all smiles' attitude, because the monarch symbolizes the anonymous citizen raised to the highest eminence. The Ottoman sultans signified this by marrying a slave, usually a Circassian, a race renowned for beauty. He showed thereby that he was at one with his heterogeneous flock. Especially is this true of monarchy in the age of the 'common man'. Not pretending to be a magnified version of the mill girl or the match girl, Queen Victoria could afford to be solemn.

She rarely smiled in public, though, as we know from a few surviving photographs, she had a charming smile. The bland smile of the public man – which is as requisite as much in opening a fête as in presiding over a commission – partly conveys condescension and may on occasion signify contempt. In such a case it tends to fade into a smirk. Mussolini's smile was of that kind; Hitler, at least on the job, never smiled at all.

The smile of the old-fashioned high-kicking chorus-girl, beaming over the footlights, was a direct provision of the PN for which the audience craved. It was an assurance that 'all shall be well', and is well. The patrons of the music hall attended for psychic recharging. There was a certain classlessness about them, even about the few affluent dudes at the stage door. By contrast, the sultry sex-scowl of TV ballerinas, crouching animal-like before the cameras, conveys a lower form of PN, depending for its efficacy on the stimulation of mild sexual excitement. It leaves the audience or viewer in a condition less than euphoric; for desire, as Somerset Maugham remarked in his story *Rain*, 'is sad'.

The strained, obligatory toothy smile of the beauty queen is by its symmetrical curvature intended to sum up and complete the perfection of her bodily curves; but by thus proclaiming a perfection unattained or unattainable by her sisters, she exudes a measure of disdain. Her perpetual hovering smile may momentarily turn into a simper. D. H. Lawrence, who knew what he was talking about, said that nothing was more repellent than a really pretty woman. Even when art had approached naturalism, as during the Italian Renaissance, painters were careful, or moved by instinct, not to paint the Virgin as if she were a beauty queen. Indeed, none of the celebrated Virgins have been in the conventional sense beautiful, still less pretty. When Catholic iconography has veered towards an exaggerated sentimentality, as towards the end of the Counter-Reformation baroque, there has usually been a reaction towards the hieratic, austere beauty of Byzantium. Naturally, the ideal of beauty varies with the degree to which the psychic palate has become jaded. The current ideal of erotic beauty is unlikely to persist. A society needs a type of female excellence, slightly withdrawn and inaccessible. Some of us are old enough to remember the black and white or tinted photographs of 'soulful' young ladies on sale at haberdashery shops, which were purchased more by women than by men. They represented the current ideal of female charm. Although a reversion to such virginal beauty is scarcely conceivable, a study of some female pop stars suggests that a change in that direction might attract both sexes, sated with the deliberate attempt of models to look like expensive – or not so expensive – whores.

Powerfully nutritious is the humour which raises a hearty laugh. Laughter is an explosion, and therefore a relief, whereby we may break out of a situation of unease. It enables us to cross the embarrassment barrier, which may otherwise give rise to agonies of discomfort. Indeed, the history of laughter and the history of embarrassment (for both undergo modification with changing circumstance) may turn out to be closely linked. In his *Keats and Embarrassment* (p.3), Christopher Ricks has argued that an alternative to embarrassment is indignation: 'one hot flush drives out another'. But indignation, as a rule, causes renewed embarrassment, which is catching anyway; it does not deflect it like laughter, which turns the flush of unease to one of 'good humour', an expression recalling mediaeval physiology. There is a marked contrast with wit, which can leave the subject wounded. Those who, on account of their dramatic gifts, have 'filled many lands with laughter' – an Aristophanes, a Molière, an Oscar Wilde, a Shaw – may be counted among the great human liberators. No doubt the caves of the earliest hominids echoed with a laughter which kept at bay fear and loneliness, and may have played a part in that slow humanization of man which is still far from complete. On the other hand, laughter is at the secular end of the scale of PN. The Virgin – talking of the Virgin in Western art – is rarely represented as laughing (an exception is the 'Laughing Madonna' on the west front of Rheims cathedral); and laughter plays no part in religious ritual, though the laughter of demons – 'the chuckle spread from ear to ear' – is sometimes heard offstage. The smile, on the other hand, even if only faint, conveys an impression of ineffable mystery and benevolence: hence the reputation of the Sphinx and the Mona Lisa. In the *Paradiso*, where light is so powerful a symbol, and where the Empyrean (heaven) is represented as being composed of

> pura luce:
> luce intellettual, piena d'amore,

Dante's guide is St Bernard, the theologian who came nearest, in the poet's view, to an intellectual understanding of Divinity. But it is Beatrice who has conducted him up to the Crystalline Heaven, the abode of the angels; and it is upon the light of her *smile*, as he sees her transfigured there, that his soul feeds (Canto XXX, 19-33). This is perhaps the point in poetry, if not in all art, in which psychic and spiritual nutrition are most perfectly blended. And as Dante rightly says, no poet can venture further.

Like any other form of nutrition, humour, to be effective, must be fresh. A joke or quip, repeated, almost always falls flat. You cannot detonate the same explosion. To suppose otherwise would be to fall into that embarrassment from which you had been delivered. As Jean Cocteau remarked, 'Astonishment only works once.' So does the genuine pleasantry, and even more the prank and the practical joke, which is a kind of flirting with embarrassment. No one is more tiresome than the raconteur, propping up the bar and going through his repertoire of 'the one about. . . .' He produces in his audience a state worse than embarrassment – psychic enervation.

This raises the delicate subject of the differing appeal of humour to men and women. Bawdry, until recently a male preserve, was resorted to in the absence of the PN conferred by female company. It was a way of 'earthing' the sex instinct. It stressed the cruder aspects of genito-urinary function, just as monkish theologians like Tertullian sought to keep sex at bay by describing women as excremental vessels. Many of the riddles circulating in mediaeval monasteries were, as surviving texts witness, coprological.[16] The 'dirty' jokes current among boys approaching adolescence are a defence against the frightening and distressing nature of that change; and the taste for them vanishes with the ecstasy of first love, if only to be resumed at first disillusionment. The invasion of entertainment by bawdry is part of that demystification of the female ethos of which we have spoken, and partly the result of the attempt by the media to cater for what it believes to be the tastes of a mass audience. Yet there is evidence to suggest that the practice of innuendo, accompanied by the lewd gesture (the word innuendo itself literally means 'to convey by a nod') in the typical TV 'comedy show' is a protest, however subconscious, against that very defeminization which initially permitted its acceptability as 'family entertainment'. The most successful practitioners of innuendo are male; a Marie Lloyd is a *rara avis*. Moreover, a delicate, attractive young girl, uttering obscenities from the stage, though not unknown, is unusual, and to most people offensive even today. All the more interesting that the radical feminist should campaign more against the strip-tease artist than against the level of TV comedy, though the latter is far more damaging and subversive to the female ethos. Woman as sex-object may cheapen the sex: woman as object of scatological ridicule negates it. For as long as we mildly shock, we recognize an intractible sensitivity which, on pain of stymieing the whole operation, we are careful not to crush. Whereas 'to do dirt to sex', in Lawrence's phrase, is somehow to uncouple the instinct from its affective complement. That the vogue for coarse *badinage* will pass, as the extremes of female radicalism themselves diminish, seems probable. Meanwhile, throughout the so-called Sexual Revolution, there has been little diminution, according to reliable statistics, in the sale of romantic literature, the readership of which is almost wholly female. And even the most liberated of women, who may go so far as to deny the existence of love and even of the maternal instinct, is sometimes found to guard a secret *cache* of romantic sentiment. To such a woman, hardbitten in the extreme, the author once read that remarkable passage in *Lady Chatterley's Lover* (chapter 7) describing the sensations experienced by women in sexual intimacy – which is effective precisely because it is not clinical – and found, on concluding, that his listener had been reduced to tears.

(1) The role of wine, sweets and spices

The psychic and organic are intimately connected. Even the most naive idealist must acknowledge that thoughts and feelings are somehow involved with the physiological mechanism of the organism. The materialist goes a stage further: he explains this involvement by asserting that the whole system is physiological, thereby espousing a thoroughgoing behaviourism. But such abolition of thought fails to explain how Behaviourists came up with the idea of behaviourism. Above all the organic and the psychic enjoy an interplay which can be of extreme fruitfulness. The interplay can be the result of what may be called an evocative signal: e.g., Schopenhauer's instance of the evocation of memories by scents. A good dinner is not merely one which stimulates the gastric juices; it *evokes* a particular psychic mood, within which ideas can grow. In other words, all forms of nutrition are linked and mutually sustaining. A certain creative amplitude – that of a Villon, a Chaucer, a Shakespeare, a Rabelais, a Goethe, a Dickens, a Victor Hugo, a Tolstoy – would seem to derive from a prodigious appetite at the physical, the psychic and the intellectual level. No doubt the sexual powers can be involved too, though the cases of Carlyle and Ruskin – men endowed with remarkable imaginative gifts – might seem exceptions. On the other hand, sexual expression may, as Frank Harris remarked in the second half of *My Life and Loves* (and he should have known), dissipate rather than create energies. Of this Balzac and perhaps Zola were also aware. Although organic health is obviously desirable, certain forms of asceticism are not incompatible with psychic health and intellectual vigour. The pursuit of value may entail the control of 'valencies': an athlete in training needs to discipline his appetites. Nevertheless, there is good reason to believe that every mature culture needs the support of a developed and refined gastronomy; Brillat-Savarin (1755-1826), the great master of taste and apostle of *la gastronomie transcendante*, was one of the first to perceive this fact. Wine and the art of living have from the earliest times gone together. It is not for nothing that one of the greatest of philosophical discussions was called the *Symposium*, a 'drinking together', over which Socrates presided. Here we see illustrated an important truth. Wine can indeed 'with logic absolute The seventy-seven jarring sects confute'; but this is because the temperate consumption of wine makes for a mood of benignity. Here you have your evocative signal again. Despite problems of alcoholism, France remains the land of logic and reason, as well as the land of wine. Wine, too, has always been associated with religion, except in the case of certain extremist sects, as it has, to the cultivated mind, always been associated with love: that is to say, with the meaning of life and with that which, in Hardy's line, 'lures life on'. Indeed, the *Symposium* treats of the nature of love in its two forms, sexual and divine. Without love, life is indeed 'a poor thing at best' – as that Puritan utilitarian, James Mill, conceived it to be, according to his son, who, in consequence of the emptiness of the paternal training, suffered a breakdown in early manhood.

Few philosophers have drawn attention to another pleasurable, though easily abused, adjunct to the art of living, namely the whole category of foodstuffs known as sweets or, more correctly, sweetmeats. For the greater part of history, indeed until the import of sugar from the West Indies in the sixteenth century, the prototype of all sweet things, apart from fruit, was honey. The use of the adjective 'sweet' in such mystical writings as *The Fire of Love* by Richard Rolle (1300-49) was due to the rarity of the sweetening agent.

Around honey, and consequently the honeycomb and its inhabitants, a mythology grew up. And where there is mythology there is an element of culture. Every recognizable society has devised its particular form of confectionery; and at one time the proliferation of sweetshops (American candystores) paralleled that of taverns. In this development, the product of the cacao seed played a major part. In fact, the word chocolate comes from the Aztec word *xocalatl* (borrowed by the Spaniards in the seventeenth century), which meant 'sour'. Thus chocolate itself had to be sweetened and flavoured. The chemistry of the sweetening process – the breaking down of sugar into glucose and fructose, and the excess being converted in the liver to glycogen – is not our concern: all we would indicate is the evident need for 'sweetness' at the psychic as well as at the physical level. (In the Islamic world, on the occasion of the great *Bayrams* or religious festivals, sweets take the place of the forbidden alcohol, especially at that which follows Ramadan, appropriately called in Turkish Şeker or Sugar Bayram.) And this need is apparent from the earliest years. Children sucking sweets, lollipops, ice-cream, etc., continue the early comforting experience of the dummy; for the habit – with which the adult world was until recently only too willing to conspire – has more to do with sustaining morale than with plain nutrition. Hence, formerly, the never-misplaced presents of sweets to children; the liberal sweet-ration during the last war (another morale sustainer); and the custom, though less fashionable than heretofore, of presenting beribboned boxes of chocolate or candy to lady-loves at assignations, or theatres, etc., for the purpose of moving the heart rather than of stimulating the luteinizing hormones. Indeed, the wrapping of sweets and particularly the use of sparkling foils are not merely a protection but an evocative signal. Packaging, to which so much attention has recently been given, itself provides a PN stimulus.

The other need, also catered for effectively only from the sixteenth century – the East India Company was started by the London grocers in 1599 – was for the correlative of sweets, namely spices, especially pepper, nutmeg, ginger and cinnamon; hence such names as the Spice Islands. These gastronomic auxiliaries, which include the more mature cheeses, may not be necessities of life, but they are desirable adjuncts to good living. Their influence is organo-psychic. Only when they are cultivated for their own sake do they become inimical to culture in the true sense. The wine-snob or the wine-bibber, like the gourmandizer, makes as an end what should be only a means.

Even so, the importance and significance of sweetmeats in particular is demonstrated by the designation of 'nice' people as sweet, or sweet-natured. Similarly, the Sanskrit root of the word reminds us that it is also at the origin of the word 'suave', and therefore of 'persuasive'. Hence the current and slightly pejorative meaning of 'sweetener'. The business lunch or entertainment is an attempt to create the kind of PN *ambiance* in which the client can be put in the frame of mind conducive to satisfactory bargaining. According to Tacitus, the Germans never signed a treaty, political or commercial, unless they were in a state of mild intoxication. The habit has now received wider application. This is another example where the expense of providing PN is, in most countries, tax-deductible. The receipted bill, duly submitted, is for psychic, not physical, fare. As such it is allowable. Firms are not in the business of feeding their clients' stomachs but rather their psyches.

Over the last few years, the consumption of sweetmeats, and indeed the taste for them, have undergone marked decrease, at least in the West. This is because, however much they may have met a social and therefore psychic need, they can prove physically deleterious. For a variety of reasons, but chiefly for aesthetic ones, the young have modified, though not reversed, a trend which was producing an overweight generation. Substitutes are bound to be found. Perhaps, in tobacco and/or drugs, they have been found for some: the increase in the consumption of alcohol testifies to the fact that they have been found for others. Human nature has a way of working out its psychic salvation; and an equivalent of something to 'hand round' for the purpose of gently stimulating morale and promoting fellowship, will undoubtedly be devised, possibly in rituals akin to the Japanese Tea Ceremony.

(m) Islands

It is because 'no man is an island', to quote from Donne's famous sermon, that islands, especially remote ones, have always acquired a certain numinousness and glamour. Not without reason have many Utopias, above all that of Thomas More, to which most of them owe their inspiration, been situated on islands. Bacon's New Atlantis was an island. Aldous Huxley's final Utopia was in fact called *Island* (1962). Some of the 'island universes', recently discovered, have been invested by Science Fiction writers with the qualities of Utopia. And if the Christian paradise is not sufficiently defined as to take insular form, the Paradises of the Ancient World were typified as 'islands of the blest'. Moreover, when the aged Ulysses in Tennyson's poem sets out on his last voyage ('old men should be explorers', as Tennyson's successor in the twentieth century said), he declared:

> It may be we shall touch the Happy Isles
> And see the great Achilles. . . .

And so, in our own lives, a visit to 'the island' satisfies a psychic hunger, which even the exhilaration of mountain-climbing fails to match. For all islands, because of their approximations to the perfect figure of the circle, are invested with some measure or hint of perfection, and their very boundaries appear to render them immune to change, which is another Utopian characteristic. Many – such as Iona, or Lindisfarne, or Patmos – are known as Holy Islands, to visit which is to be spiritually uplifted. Their numinousness is reflected in the practice, which dates from the time when many such islands were discovered, of giving them directly religious names: Trinidad, Ascension, Christmas, Easter, Espiritu Santo (in the SW Pacific).

In a sense, therefore, there are no ugly islands. All islands are beautiful – Belle Ile, Fair Isle, Isola Bella, Formosa ('beautiful island') – by virtue of the PN they are deemed to provide. With islands are linked the particular spell of *horizons* – the 'volupté melancolique des horizons', as Chateaubriand put it. Hence we derive a particular pleasure from reading or hearing about islands: *The Mysterious Island* of Jules Verne (one of the best of his books, perhaps for that reason), *To the Lighthouse* of Virginia Woolf, even Bahai, the 'special island' of *South Pacific*, or the Hebridean 'Road to the Isles', especially as we may never take it.

Naturally, the attraction of islands does not extend to every piece of land surrounded by water. Whereas many islands are places to escape to, even if only in imagination, some are so designed as to preclude escape – as formerly Devil's Island or Alcatraz; but these are deliberate parodies of Utopia, and consequently the nutritional features have been purposely excluded or reduced to a minimum. Thus Robinson Crusoe on Juan Fernandez was at once in paradise and in prison. His 'prison' was to be deprived, until contact was established with Man Friday, of human company; which deprivation, unless voluntary as in the case of the monks of the Thebaid or Thoreau at Walden, no amount of impersonal PN can compensate for. The entubbed Diogenes – that 'ungainly product of luxury', as Hegel called him – or St Simon on his pillar in fifth century Constantinople were by contrast crowd-drawers and popular entertainers, provoking that gaping and gawping which keeps a mob occupied and sustained in default of more violent enjoyments.

(n) Holy Cities

The idea of pilgrimage is very ancient. Human life used to be likened to a pilgrimage, on which everyone had embarked at birth: the simile is still used in sermons and school addresses. Derived from *peregrinus*, the word originally signified a stranger or sometimes a wanderer. It was used in particular for the wandering Celtic missionaries of the fifth and sixth centuries. During the Middle Ages, the pilgrimage was an activity which attracted merit. In the Islamic world the journey to Mecca remains quasi-obligatory for the devout Moslem. Pilgrimages were undertaken to places of primordial sanctity or to those made sacred either by visions of the Virgin (for example) or by spectacular martyrdoms. Such was Thomas-à-Becket's Canterbury and the Kerbela of Hussein, the son of Ali. In Europe, Rome was the foremost Holy City, the shrine of Peter and Paul, re-founders of the City of Romulus and Remus.

For the Catholic world, Rome is still 'eternal' among Holy Cities. The Holy Father, its first citizen, continues to exercise therefrom a charismatic influence, acknowledged regularly by thousands assembled in St. Peter's Square. To these appearances there is nowhere an equivalent: the clownish balcony appearances of Mussolini belong to an unlamented past. Since the death of Stalin – who in his lifetime was endowed with the attributes of a god – the leaders of the communist world have exercised decreasing psychical influence. Indeed, it would be difficult to imagine an ex-head of the KGB such as Yuri Andropov assuming such a role, and he never did. Nevertheless, the Third Rome, Moscow, has not become so totally secularized as the Second Rome, Constantinople (Istanbul). Lenin's tomb in the Kremlin is visited by devotees passing through it both day and night, glancing furtively at the livid figure in the glass case as at a recumbent deity.

In fact, the idea of the Holy City has never died. In literature, Bunyan's pilgrim was seeking the ultimate goal, the Celestial City. Many cities, or their near equivalent, have continued to qualify as

Holy, because the Idea of the Holy (as Rudolf Otto made plain in his book of that name) is an idea innate to the human psyche. There are pilgrimages to Lourdes, to Compostella, to Walsingham, to Benares, to Ise. The *pélérinage à la source* is above all a pilgrimage to a source of psychic and spiritual nutrition. Spokesmen at Lourdes acknowledge that most afflicted pilgrims, if they derive any benefit at all from their visit to the shrine of Bernadette Soubirous, obtain psychic enrichment.

The 'atmosphere' of which people are in search when they walk through the Holy City is not the composition of gases – nitrogen, oxygen, argon and carbon dioxide, etc. – which make air, but an evocative constellation of feelings: veneration and reverence, curiosity and nostalgia, surprise and wonder.

So today, we have the secularized Holy City and even the Holy Secular City. People need to go on pilgrimage, either alone or, like Chaucer's pilgrims, in groups, as thirsty animals will trek for miles to find a water hole. In the 1950s and 1960s, the road to Katmandu, littered with dropouts, symbolized this desperate need. There is some evidence that Liverpool, once a great industrial and mercantile centre, will be associated in years to come with the first pop group to obtain unparalleled international renown, the Beatles. Elvis Presley's home in Memphis, Tennessee, is already a flourishing shrine. As the media obtain a firmer grip on the communal psyche, so the pop hero – who in life enjoys a fame and notoriety superficially greater than that of all the leaders of the world's religions put together – will at death, and even before, cause a shrine to be erected, which will afford a continuous supply of nutrition to the inconsolable faithful. In fact, it is the purely *secularized* shrine and its influence which will demonstrate better than the sacred one the reality and potency of PN. In due course, such secular centres may come to fulfil the function of the old sacred ones so successfully as themselves to qualify as sacred.

Just as the Holy City will have its 'psalms and hymns and spiritual songs' (Ephesians 5: 19), so the secular sacred city will have ditties associated with it – 'Arrivederci Roma' (eulogizing Rome in its secular aspect, which is becoming more pronounced), 'Goodnight Vienna', 'Maybe it's because I'm a Londoner', 'I belong to Glasgow', and songs extolling San Francisco and even Chicago. All this testifies to the psychic enrichment provided by the city, even if it be no more than a City of Dreams. Perhaps of all the world's cities today, the one that, though almost wholly secularized, still preserves for most people the aspect of a Dream City, is Paris – still the Paris of Baudelaire:

> . . .cité pleine de rêves,
> Oú le spectre en plein jour raccroche le passant.

(o) Virtue

Although we have emphasized the degree to which the hero or the star, through achievement or glamour or both, feeds the communal psyche, it must not be forgotten that goodness as well as fame can also prove sustaining. In fact, the desire to lead a virtuous life, though seemingly rather out of fashion, is involved as much with the psychic as with the spiritual domain.

What is out of fashion is *moralizing* – possibly because morals have tended to be associated exclusively with sexual morals, and these are supposed to have undergone a revolution. Certainly the tiresome moralizing to be found in some Victorian fiction, from the *Christie's Old Organ* type of book (where the failings were usually taking a drop too much or poaching) up to the high-minded passages in George Eliot, is unlikely to return to the novel. People no longer read to be edified. One cannot imagine Anthony Burgess or Gore Vidal interrupting the text to indulge in ethical homilies, though one suspects that the former is a moralist *malgré lui*. And there is supposed to be a moral theme running through popular films such as *Star Wars* and *ET*. So morals, if not moralizings, are back.

When the psalmist spoke of 'the beauty of holiness', he was certainly referring to a reality which was PN-purveying. And judging from the hyperbolic sentiments expressed in announcements of decease, especially in some provincial papers, the world is more peopled with saints than one had been led to believe. Even so, these tear-jerking tributes to Dad and Mum and Nana do suggest that virtue and virtuous example are such as can supply a psychic need. It remains true that this need is chiefly met unobtrusively, because virtue, being its own reward, does not require trumpeting far and wide:

> Neither clerisy nor outward colour can reveal Charity to you,
> Nor words, nor deeds, but only the knowledge of men's hearts;
> And these are known to no clerk or other creature on Earth
> . . . .[17]

The Greek who advocated the ostracism of Aristides because he was tired of hearing him called The Just, certainly has our sympathy. Having said that, just men have our respect, and they may excite our awe.

The other type of man to radiate charisma was the sage – a figure revered in the Orient more than in the West. This was no doubt because the West has had no figure exactly comparable. We can boast neither an Imhotep nor a Confucius. As it is, the intellectual, or *savant*, a lesser figure, has received much greater respect in France and Germany than in Britain, unless we except Scotland. The Scottish diaspora has dispatched throughout the world men of intellect and men of practical reason, i.e. engineers; but they have, like the engineer in Kipling's poem, 'McAndrew's Hymn', tended to keep in the background.

It may be that the cultivation of ideologies has brought about the eclipse of virtue as something to be admired and revered. For the ideologist is one obsessed with '. . . dreaming of systems so perfect that no one will need to be good',[18] whereas no future age can be conceived – even with the elimination of poverty and disease, and with the development of powers at present undreamed of – in which man will not be concerned, in some manner, with goodness and the way to achieve it. And this will demonstrate what was obvious to our ancestors, that man needs for his sustenance the incentive not merely of success or of power, but of moral goodness. It is not an accident that a person of real virtue should be held up as a 'shining' example. Schiller pointed out (Letter XXVII) that whereas there is no moral transcendence of duty, an aesthetic transcendence makes for noble conduct. Nobility of character, as Plutarch was perhaps the first to demonstrate, is therefore the source of a particular kind of PN. Bunyan exemplified it in the character of Mr. Valiant-for-Truth: 'My sword I leave to him that shall succeed me in my pilgrimage, and my courage and strength to him that can get it'.

(p) Music

In dealing with the environment (pp. 44–50), we spoke about music and the part which it played in the lives of so many people. Of all the arts, music remains the most mysterious. It is that in which form and content, the saying and the said, are one. While possible to imagine how painting and the plastic arts originated – possibly at first as directional or warning signs – the discovery of melody, and in due course the underpinning of that melody by harmony and counterpoint, is an innovation for which it is more difficult to account. That music and speech developed together, and were for many millennia inseparable (not that they are completely separate now), is very likely. In that case, the development of sound for its own sake or as an *art* may have been due to the discovery that music, or concordant sound, exerted a composing effect on the emotions. This discovery – one of man's earliest perhaps – was exploited in due course in the musical therapy available at medical centres such as the great Aesculapion at both Pergamon and Cos. Apollonius of Tyana (4BC – AD97) advocated music as therapeutic, as had Aristotle at the end of his *Politics*, though he held that music had other uses too. For Boethius (*c*.480 – *c*.524), music was not merely a consolation but 'a clue to the interpretation of the hidden harmony of God and nature'.[19]

Even so, the idea has not been widely accepted even today. Despite his devotion to the art, Dr Burney (1726-1814) was content to call music 'an innocent Luxury, unnecessary indeed to our Existence, but a great Improvement and Gratification of the Sense of Hearing'. Yet the appetite for music, not as an innocent luxury but as a psychic need, has never been greater, especially among young people, judging by the avidity with which they seek and make music.

If the function, or indirect effect, of music is to compose the emotions – a gift attributed first to Orpheus, who employed it also to calm wild beasts – then music is a form of PN. Since all music is pure music in the sense that it is the abstract exploitation of sound, we may go further and say that music is pure and undiluted PN. For that reason, music is, and has been recognized to be, the highest of the arts. Indeed, musical order or melody may be the prototype – perhaps the mystical prototype – of an order at the heart of reality. Apart from its nutritive qualities, therefore, music is audile metaphysics. It is the art where opacity is most nearly broken through.

As well as the ancients, some of the great figures of the Renaissance realized the calming function of music. In his fifth Letter, Marsilio Ficino, the Platonist (1433-99), made clear that the body and soul were linked by the 'spirit', by which he meant the psyche. This, he held, was 'nourished' (his word, be it noted) by 'sounds and song'. He also held that sweet perfumes were nutritional. In his seventh Letter, he stated explicitly that 'the soul receives the sweetest harmonies and numbers through the ear', which thus remind it of, and render it pervious to, the divine music and universal harmony of the heavens. He also pointed out that the Egyptians, who practised what we should today call holistic medicine, regarded medicine itself, music, and the 'mysterious' (theology) as one and the same study.[20] In addition to being a philosopher, a doctor (our word medical is derived from his friends, the Medicis), and from 1473 an ordained priest, Ficino was a skilled musician, expert at playing the lyre.

Therefore it is true to say, with Walter Pater, that all art approximates to the condition of music, because all PN aspires to its purest state. The best condition of the psyche is a serene, reconciling repose; and music, from the lullaby upwards, is in its final effect both serene and reconciling.

If music is the highest of the arts and the purest form of PN, it does not follow that it should take precedence as a cultural force over all other aesthetic forms. Few people, even dedicated musicologists, could rely for cultural enjoyment on an exclusive diet of music. In any case, there are tone-deaf people, or people like Winston Churchill who cannot stand 'good' music, as the great man made clear when, during a wartime visit to the United States, he was obliged by President Truman to sit through a piano recital. Music is indeed the prototype of PN; and at its highest level its perfection and purity have always earned it, as Ficino pointed out, the reputation of being the art cultivated in heaven. In the ancient cosmogonies, beginning with that of Pythagoras, it was the medium generated by the turning celestial spheres and therefore inaudible to the human ear, though according to Porphyry, Pythagoras himself was able to hear it. But for us who are not in heaven but very much on earth, and who have speech and vision too, a diet of ambrosia, if available, would soon pall and cause us to long for a good succulent steak. So music is but one of the arts to be practised, if still that affording intimations of perfection which are all we can hope for in an imperfect world. Music remains the most compelling reminder of truths which are reflected, though more opaquely, in the other arts.

What is needed, and what has often been vaguely felt to be lacking, is a distinction within music equivalent to that obtaining in literature between poetry and verse. Verse has always been recognized as a legitimate literary form, and good verse possesses features which lend it an enduring quality. There are some genres – hymns for example – which can be written only in verse: the attempt to bring poetry into the hymn book has been markedly unsuccessful. Indeed, the writing of good verse requires considerable talent. Usually, it takes the form of *vers d'occasion*. The same applies to what may be called verse-music. Since such music is associated with a particular moment or event, it becomes identified with experiences that remain in our minds for years – as, for example, the dance-music and revues of our young days. Music critics tend to dismiss as of no consequence this large body of material; but precisely because it is, so to speak, a *cordial* for the ear, the effect is *heart*-warming. It follows that it is an important and perhaps indispensable form of PN.

If well-composed, such music deservedly captures the allegiance of thousands, if not millions. Some (not all) of the original American musicals fall within this category; the T. S. Eliot/Lloyd-Webber revue, *Cats*, certainly does. Even the severest of critics have given it praise, however grudging, though the principal song, 'Memory' – a significant title and a perfect example of verse-music – was predictably dismissed by the critic Sheridan Morley as 'dreaded'. We have given other examples of such songs of sentiment.[21] It is a pity that the word 'sentimental' – as for instance in 'Sentimental Gentleman for Georgia' – should in current English have a vaguely pejorative meaning. Sentiment is a legitimate and necessary nutritive ingredient of social life; the lack of a proper word has prompted the media to use the unsatisfactory 'emotional'. A goodbye, if heartfelt, ought to be conveyed as such, though with due restraint, and the same is true of the sincere welcome. If such occasions are allowed to pass without the appropriate expressions of feeling, we remain psychically unfed. Our psychic appetite is cut. Rhetorical speeches would be out of place: the need is precisely for the sentiment which acts as a PN cordial. And that which is needed repeatedly in daily life must come within the category of the nutritive.

Negative PN

We now append a list of examples of *negative* or neg-PN. This is naturally provisional, as PN can be acquired, just as it can be lost, and that which provides PN in one age may not do so in another.

Positive and negative nutrition

(a) Supermarkets

Compare a grocer's – in France, for example – with its stock of fresh and wholesome food, its pâtés, its cheeses, its cream, etc., laid out for inspection. The sight of such rich abundance not merely stimulates the gastric juices, but provides PN; for the food is, so to speak, living and expressive, like the flowers in the vase in the hospital ward. Consequently, it feeds us psychically. The packaged food in a super-market, on the other hand, is 'dead'. Although it is capable of physical nutrition, its provision of PN is neglible. It evokes no instinctive responses. Moreover, the premises themselves, being depersonalized, are deficient in PN; and the bored girl at the pay-desk, who is hardly more than an adjunct to the cash-register she operates, purveys the minimum amount of PN. In time, the girl herself will be replaced by a machine, and then the depersonalization will be complete. There will be a closed circle of neg-PN. Already the purchasers move round the place like somnambulists or ghosts, creatures in a low state of psychic vitality.

(b) Empty houses

Unless it be of great antiquity or otherwise associated with some striking event, an empty house has a devitalizing effect upon the psyche. Indeed, it used to be thought that a neglected building provided an open invitation for mischievous or evil powers to take up residence. As Richard Carew observed:

> If there be a house, great, dark, foul, putrified, melancholic, and void of dwellers to make abode therein, the devils soon take it up for their lodgings; but if the same be cleansed, the windows opened, and the sunbeams admitted to enter, by and by they get them packing, and specially if it be inhabited by much company, and that there be meetings and pastimes, and playing on musical instruments. [22]

If Carew's diagnosis be mistaken, his remedy is valid. A house that is 'lived in' and made into a *home* provides PN. The negative forces, Carew's 'devils', have 'got them packing'. A home is a power-house of PN, which is why the inhabitants resort to it for psychic recupera-tion. The same is true of a garden. Tended and ordered, a garden displays a beauty to which the psyche immediately responds, whereas a garden gone to weeds causes a sinking of the spirits. The

Ideal Home always has its garden, and *Homes and Gardens* is an appropriate title for a periodical devoted to elegant family living.

The truth is that *order* is psychically satisfying. When we open a cupboard and observe its contents to be neatly arranged, we know that *intelligence* has been at work. This 'passage of intelligence' is understood most fully at the intellectual or spiritual level, for it is to the intellect that the books in a library disclose their meanings. At the 'closed' psychic level, PN is afforded by order in the aesthetic sense. The footprint in the sand to Robinson Crusoe was initially the occasion of psychic excitement, as was (and is) the discovery of the first evidence of our earliest palaeolithic ancestors. This stage is followed by intellectual speculation upon the meaning of the forms or patterns presented. The footprint and the fossil are symbols or expressions of life, and as such are in different degrees nutritional: the footprint because of its promise, in cases like Robinson Crusoe, of imminent meeting and inter-subjectivity, and the fossil because of its evidence of others who, having inhabited our world, signal across to us, however feebly, from remotest time.

(c) Warehouses

It is for a similar reason that buildings containing furniture or goods no longer in use are examples of negative PN. In a warehouse or storeroom, the structures are massed not according to their use or value but according to the accident of contiguity. The objects are related externally. Not order but pseudo-order reigns. Their utility and purpose are suspended. Therefore there is no nutrition. The goods in a removal van are likewise reduced to the lowest level of PN; they regain such PN as they have by being put 'in place' in the home. Conversely, the exhibits in a museum, being carefully arranged and shown to advantage, are potential sources of PN. Quite apart from its contents, a picture-gallery provides PN because the exhibits are tastefully arranged, with suitable lighting, etc.

(d) Routine

Hitherto, the examples given of negative PN have been associated chiefly with spatial structures. But just as human culture is specifically a time-culture, so there can be times and seasons in which PN is at a low ebb. On returning from a holiday or from a special occasion, we may feel in 'low spirits'. This is understandable, since the supply of PN has been suddenly cut off. Similarly, the 'Monday morning feeling', which afflicts office workers in particular, is a feeling of negative PN. The psychically recuperative weekend is over: the working-routine must be resumed. The change is not physiological but psychic, which may of course have neuro-physiological consequences. At the outset of the new week, we need to adjust ourselves afresh to the presence of our fellows. This sets up a tension between the instinct of solitariness and the instinct of gregariousness, the instinct for co-operation and the instinct for competition, which the break has disrupted. At such times even our most congenial colleagues may slightly 'get on our nerves', because they too are engaged in the same process of partial adjustment. In normal times colleagues may 'quicken' one another: it is this which makes them congenial. In a factory, where contact, being mediated through the machines and their functioning, need not be so close, the 'Monday morning feeling' is usually less acute. But, as we shall see, factory workers have their own psychic problems to cope with.

In all cultures, there are special 'off' seasons, when the level of psychic energy is deliberately lowered. For reasons of spiritual health, an attempt is made to live on a psychically reduced level. In monasteries and nunneries, these periods are recurrent; their purpose is to cultivate greater spiritual energy. A season such as Lent and, in the Moslem world (though in varying degrees of observance), Ramadan, are intended to effect a kind of collective psychic spring-clean, preparatory for the great psychic and spiritual renewal to follow. Deprived of such rhythmic psychic exercises and training, the modern urban dweller may suffer more than he realizes. Hence the onset of mild accidie, neither psyche nor spirit being afforded the periodical renewal of energy which each urgently requires. Many people are bored with their work, and regard it merely as a means to gaining a livelihood; and their leisure more often than not is correspondingly sterile. For some, the 'Sunday morning feeling' is as acute as that of Monday; *tuer le dimanche* is a problem facing many a wage-earner, discontented with his work and unable to find a proper means of recreation. For there comes a time when distraction is not enough.

Boredom is therefore the condition in which the capacity for PN is reduced virtually to zero. It is the state in which routine becomes jejune and unendurable, and the interruptions to it no less abhorrent. Although routine is always a trifle boring, the psychically healthy person does not find it uniformly tedious. Better the dullness of routine than the strain of prolonged disorder and confusion. Just as a life of physiological routine is a condition of bodily health, so a measure of uniformity is a condition of psychic health. The trouble with much factory routine is that its sameness deprives it of interest; it lacks the 'creative dullness' of the life of the intellectual. Meanwhile, there are certain moments in the working day of most people, but particularly of brain-workers, when the need for PN is particularly acute. One of these, and perhaps the most universally felt, is mid-morning, which has given rise to the now hallowed custom of 'elevenses'. This provides an excuse not simply for the partaking of refreshment but for a brief moment of social contact and gossip. One suspects – but this could no doubt be verified – that the custom came in with the general employment of women in offices.

(e) Loneliness and the herd-life

Whereas solitude is a psychic need, loneliness involves psychic deprivation. Solitude is correlative with gregariousness, as concave to convex, whereas loneliness is enforced solitude. In the modern world, large numbers of people live alone. True, few individuals can long support this state of isolation; but never to be alone is also psychically damaging. To achieve psychic health is to effect, as usual, an equilibrium between the two states. One of the great problems of marriage is to work out a means of permitting both partners to enjoy this balanced, rhythmic life of society and privacy. No two people were ever intended to live in constant and unremitting association; and until recently the marriage-bond was 'complicated' by other factors, which prevented direct psychic collision. Such factors were often regarded by idealists as obstacles to a satisfactory partnership, little realizing that they were often the means of achieving harmony. A woman who is so close to her husband as to lose all 'mystery' may still be a satisfactory sexual partner, but she will fail to give him the PN he needs as much as he needs sex. Then it is a case of waiting to see how much longer her sexual attractions will continue to prove all-sufficient. In the wife's attitude to her husband, the distinction between sex and PN is not so clearly drawn; for it is doubtful whether a woman can sustain a purely sexual relation with a man with whom she has decided to live. (Prostitution is possible for a woman, precisely because there is no question of cohabitation.) But even given women's admitted adaptability, the husband can be too 'near' to her to afford her the PN she needs. In order to retain a hold on the other, each partner must remain something of a stranger. Unfortunately, the modern house or flat does not always provide that degree of privacy which is so essential for psychic compatability. For the rest, there is evidence, some of it rather repulsive, that men and women are tending increasingly to take their pleasures separately; and this may be due to an instinctive reaction.

For evidence of the beginning of this new development, an article in the *News of the World* (26 September 1971) was instructive. Entitled 'How the Stag Wives Hit Back', the first paragraph set the tone:

> The curtain is going up on Britain's hottest-ever season of stag shows. Pubs, clubs and halls all over the country will echo to the belly-laugh and ribald encouragement to the girls who bare their all – to entertain husbands and boy friends 'off the leash' for a night on the tiles.
>
> Men might think they've got it all their own way with stag shows, but the wives are hitting back.
>
> They're organizing Hen Parties – a naughty night out for the ladies. . . .

The whole article, which with its detailed account of male strip-tease is too sordid to reproduce, forms a disturbing comment on modern *moeurs*.

Substitutes for PN

The next category of phenomena we need to examine is that of substitutes for PN. We have already referred to *ersatz* PN, but we can isolate the substitutes into four kinds. It is noteworthy that two of these are closely linked with the physical or physiological sphere, and therefore with a form of nutrition cruder than that adapted to the psyche.

(a) Alcohol

The chief and most potent substitute for PN in the history of mankind has been some stupefiant or narcotic. For the modern world, and in particular since the industrial revolution, this has been alcohol ('the shortest way out of Manchester'). The dependence of modern man upon alcoholic stimulant is demonstrably great and would appear to be increasing. The advantages of alcohol, as a PN succedaneum, are its rapid effect, its efficacy as an indulgence both solitary and communal, and, though depending on the country, its relative cheapness. As its primary influence is to relax the higher cerebral centres, alcohol can in moderation open the individual to a measure of psychic enjoyment. This is its well-known function in ceremonies, from the informal 'cocktail hour' to the formal banquet. But for the large numbers of men and women for whom alcohol is a means of escape from emotional stress and anxiety, it can lead to the temporary suppression of 'intellectual' life altogether.

The increasing use of alcohol is paralleled by the increased indulgence in amusement. To some extent the first results from the second. The state of emotional inanition following upon the pursuit of amusement for its own sake is for most people so intolerable as to require a quick and effective anodyne. This means that the already heavy consumption of alcohol in the modern world is likely to become greater as the supply of genuine PN runs short. There is evidence that certain periods in the past have depended heavily on alcohol, but usually the partakers have been groups in society whose way of life has been threatened or disrupted. For instance, gin-drinking became especially prevalent among the displaced workers in the early days of industrialization ('drunk for a penny, dead drunk for twopence, straw free', as the advertisement put it). And there have been entire peoples who have resorted to alcohol upon the break-up of their traditional society. This applied to the Ainu of Japan, the aboriginal inhabitants, after they had been forbidden in 1887 to hunt and fish.[23] The reason is clear: a 'traditional way of life' is itself the chief source and purveyor of PN, and something without which society cannot live.

(b) Eroticism

The second major substitute for PN is eroticism. Whereas that form of sex-appeal called glamour is a potent and necessary form of PN, the commercialization of sex today is no more than the scraping of the barrel of a form of nutrition which has been over-exploited. The purveyors of such nutrition, far from being the champions of 'liberty of expression' or harbingers of a breakthrough into sexual freedom, are scavengers of the psyche. The continued public response to this material, which is not confined to the masses but includes a branch of the intelligentsia, suggests that some part of the immense expenditure upon education is not effecting that 'raising of standards' which was intended. The psyche is not merely being fed; it is being overfed and/or over-stimulated.

> We had fed the heart on fantasies,
> The heart's grown brutal from the fare.[24]

The 'branch of the intelligentsia' is not a figment of prudish fancy. During the debate in Britain in early 1983 on cable TV, there was a determined attempt by a pressure group to establish an 'adult', i.e. pornographic, channel. The Home Affairs Editor of *The Economist*, Brenda Maddox, writing in *The Times* (25 February 1983), observed. 'To my knowledge, Mr Chris Dunkley, television critic of the *Financial Times*, is the only one who has dared to admit during this "winter of debate" on cable that he would like to see more, not less, erotic subject matter on his television set. Me too.'

An attempt has been made by some to draw a distinction between the erotic and the pornographic. Nobody minds being accused of eroticism: there is still an aversion, though no doubt dwindling, to be called a pornographer. (We speak of serious writers, not those engaged in the industry itself, though even these sometimes pose as social benefactors.) In practice, the distinction can easily become blurred; and since the appetite for the erotic grows with what it feeds on, the partition is soon broken down, and the result is the open exploitation of sex for the purpose of titillation. Save in the Communist contries and in certain Islamic states, a stage has now been reached where this aim is openly acknowledged. Films, cassettes, magazines vie with one another in its systematic exploitation. There are always those who, averse to being called reactionary, declare that this trend – and to call something a trend today is held somehow to excuse it – will soon lose its momentum, forgetting, or failing to observe, that this has already happened, and that the sexually meretricious is speedily giving way to the scatological. A feast of so-called delights of the flesh, which the crusaders of pornography (including a batch of ecclesiastics) claim to be hymning, turns into a festival of *cochonneries*.

Increasing doses of the erotic and still more the scatological and the sadistic have the effect, as we are now beginning to see, of *cutting the psychic appetite*. To cut the psychic appetite, especially at an early age, is highly injurious; but our educationalists of a 'progressive' turn of mind seem not merely oblivious of this danger but are sometimes prepared to encourage it. There is such a thing as psychic anorexia, as we shall see.

(c) 'Education' or 'culture'

There is, however, another and third substitute for PN, and this is one to which we have already briefly alluded. We refer to 'education' or 'culture' itself, especially in the snobbish sense as that which qualifies a man to enter, or to hold his own, in certain elevated social milieux. In writing of Blake, Eliot spoke of 'the eternal struggle of art against education'. We can frame that expression in a different way by speaking of the eternal struggle of true education against false. Basic education is the provision of PN at the requisite stage, and therefore the promotion of psychic growth. Concerning this process there need be no mystery, apart from the mystery associated with all growth; the development of psychic response in his pupils or students is one of the few genuine satisfactions which a teacher can hope to experience. Apart from the capacity for psychic response, education is nothing but instruction; and the more methodical such instruction can be, the better. The attempt to liberate the pupils from necessary rote-learning is having the effect of bringing into existence successive generations of illiterates.

Of the petrification or disintegration of education, due partly to the information deluge, we shall speak more in the sequel. It is sufficient here to draw attention to a tendency much to be deplored. As education becomes a desperate means of keeping in school young people whose minds have already been trained – if they have been trained at all – 'beyond school' by the media, the aim is to provide 'packaged' education which they can take away with them and use as means of getting through life. Small wonder that so often this provision fails them, and that they find themselves either persisting in slavery to the media or surrendering to some irrational cult which stimulates, if only briefly, an impoverished psyche. Or there is the recent cult of so-called 'working-class culture', usually promulgated by those who have vacated that class or who have never belonged to it. For the few, there is 'culture'. This is a synthetic grasp of such literature and art as is in vogue. To the culture addict, the task is to 'keep up' with what a small group of pundits pronounce to be 'advanced'. For 'their word alone decides whether a pile of garbage poured on the floor is just a pile of garbage, or the most wonderful new art sensation, worth twenty thousand dollars.'[25] This is an activity involving great effort but productive of increasing dissatisfaction. One representative of the avant-garde gives place to another, often without any plausible reason, so that the aspirant is encumbered with a quantity of miscellaneous knowledge and judgement which represents neither a guide to life nor a psychic solace. Nor are the instructors in any better situation: a university teacher, who seemed not untypical, once confided to the author that he had been obliged to keep up with his subject in a fashion so intensive as no longer to enjoy any new book on it. Whereas our forefathers were raised on half a dozen books, of which the Bible would normally be one, we are choked with 'modern literature' which in its bulk is getting out of hand and its intellectual weight steadily lighter. And whereas the influence of the Bible was conveyed at more than one level, the most important perhaps being the subliminal and therefore most psychically satisfying, 'modern literature' is accompanied by a stream of 'criticism', comment and exegesis, whereby the best is turned into archaeology almost as soon as it has come on the market. At universities the vogue for 'analysis', which in the case of a critic of true sensibility like F. R. Leavis is a *means* but which in the hands of many a young practitioner has become an *end*, ensures that a piece of living literature is reduced almost at once to a cadaver. Anxious to satisfy the examiners, the student finds himself reading the criticism (usually assembled in a convenient handbook) instead of the work itself. Meanwhile, the glossy magazines, sometimes, concealing their true purpose under the guise of giving counsel, enjoy immense circulations, and, precisely because they represent a diversion, exert the greater subliminal influence. For what we turn to with relief achieves the maximum impact upon a sensibility relaxed and caught off its guard.

In such circumstances, it is hardly surprising that people should seek to rediscover the sources of PN by devious and often obscure paths. Hence the renewed interest – which has never been far below the surface, as our newspaper horoscopes testify – in magic and divination, as indicated by the sale of Tarot cards, copies of the *I Ching*, joss-sticks in shops in certain urban districts, and now by astrology on Breakfast TV.[26] As our education becomes more arid and seemingly removed from life, so the search for 'meaning' outside the classroom and the lecture-room is intensified. Similarly, as our religion becomes increasingly demythologized, so the search for a new mythology will be the more enthusiastically pursued. It is all part of the belief-explosion. For meaning at the psychic level is best transmitted or suggested by mystery, the elusive promise of meaning.

Of the resurgence of interest in witchcraft there is ample evidence. 'Witchcraft is not dead. For many intelligent and educated people, witchcraft is very much alive and flourishing. They see it as a modern and workable religion.'[27] The phrase 'for many intelligent and educated people' is worth noting.

(d) Abundance

The fourth substitute for PN is abundance, or excess of goods and possessions. We have spoken already of the psychically impoverished life of the wealthy. That the declared aim of almost all governments, whether democratic or totalitarian, right or left, is a raising of the standard of living remains a fact of significance. Equally significant is the fact that the criterion of such a standard is a material one. Implicit in this policy is the belief that, by granting the ordinary man increased prosperity, the organs of authority can fill the psychic void within him. It is somehow assumed that more goods and possessions will augment happiness and contentment. The ideal state seems to be that of the Marquis de la Mole in Stendhal's *Le Rouge et le Noir*, who was 'encamped amid his wealth'. During a visit to the Soviet Union, the writer chanced upon a periodical in which advice was given to youth leaders on how to deal with the persistent questions raised by young people concerning the meaning of life. The answer was blandly naive. Such restless persons were to be assured that when a true socialist society were built – whereby the standard of living of the Soviet fatherland would match or exceed that of the capitalist world – these disturbing thoughts would vanish, never to return. It was interesting to observe that a generation grown to maturity in Soviet society should have found the social climate so inclement as to leave them psychically exposed. More interesting still was that its mood should have been thought capable of cure by the application of standards derived directly from the bourgeois world. The supposed cure was responsible in large part for the disease itself.

The very 'progress' of Soviet society was no doubt the cause of that *taedium vitae* which many people were experiencing, as it had long overtaken a section of the youth of the advanced capitalist countries. Yet there is little sign as yet that the world's leaders have come to a realization of the bankruptcy of their cherished nostrums, and this includes the 'leaders of opinion' or taste. One has merely to observe the opulent decor of many a TV pop programme – the location of the network now being a matter of indifference – to realize how oppressively materialistic the standards of value of these performances have become. And there is some evidence that the new generation of affluent youth is demanding even more luxury on the model of their 'gods'. We have today psychic poverty in the midst of material plenty: that is perhaps the key-point of this book.

In the past, the above substitutes for PN operated often in isolation, or in temporary combination, or in one particular section of society to the exclusion of the others. Today, at least in the Western world, all four are found to be operating together over the majority of the population. Although in the Communist countries there is an absence of overt eroticism – so that to visit the Soviet Union or China is to experience a momentary feeling of returning to the world of one's childhood – these countries are unlikely to remain long unaffected, especially as the standard of living rises.

Addiction to alcohol is almost world-wide, with exceptions such as India and some Moslem countries, which serve merely to highlight the general tendency. As to the increase in drug-taking, from mild sedatives such as cannabis to killers such as heroin, so much has been written on this subject that its relevance to our theme need hardly be stressed.

Since material progress is the universal goal, we shall likewise not linger over this particular substitute, save to point out that, under Western influence, primitive societies have themselves been possessed by the mood of acquisitiveness. Apart from the potlatch ceremonies of N. American Indians, this is reflected in the strange 'Cargo Cults' of Melanesia, whereby the inhabitants daily expect the arrival of a ship or even an aeroplane filled with material goods (including sophisticated firearms) for free distribution. Such goods are regarded as the gift of the ancestors, believed to be the real inventors and manufacturers of machinery and consumer goods, which the white man, determined to hold down the natives, had hitherto managed to conceal.[28]

What of the substitute which we have called 'education' or 'culture'? This deserves more extended treatment. As minority phenomena, these appear not to exert an influence over society in general; but, as we shall see, this is only partly true. The élites of most countries today are conditioned by a form of education and culture based largely upon the Western model. To take the fine arts alone, almost any exhibition of 'modern art', wherever it is held, resembles any other, even to the point of including its selection of blank (or almost) canvases, and not omitting the familiar pin-head sculpture. A similar uniformity applies to music, and, if the Little Reviews are examined, to literature, especially poetry. 'Culture' is international in a way in which true culture can never be; but the ubiquity of such 'cultural' products, the encomiums they elicit from official spokesmen for the arts – for 'no degree of dullness can safeguard a work against the determination of critics to find it fascinating'[29] – and the fantastic prices which they sometimes command, afford the ordinary person the illusion of being in contact with the creative forces of society. Such products are for the most part clever exercises in pastiche, which, at a given signal, may undergo change into something different and even contrary, much as this year's fashions are deliberately made to differ from those of the last. It is the avant-garde, usually thought to be the enemy of convention, which is most conventionally enslaved.

One of the curious features of this by now familiar situation is that the avant-garde, despite its having acquired an international dominance, still encourages the idea that it is engaged in a life and death contest with Philistia. But as Hilton Kramer has pointed out in his *Age of the Avant-Garde* (1974), the myth of 'its struggle against impossible odds with little hope of just recognition, is an indispensable instrument in the consolidation of its influence'. Meanwhile, it has entered into a 'profitable alliance' with its traditional antagonists, the mass media, the universities and the market-place. Thus the 'struggle' is mere shadow-boxing; and as the world's various media enter into closer co-operation, so the avant-garde is able to reinforce its claim that no other form of art has any justification or right to exist. This ensures that any artist, even one from a region remote from Western civilization, will soon be turning out work in the authorized manner.

Despite the alliance in question, some members of the public view the products of the avant-garde with bewilderment and incomprehension. The response of the official critics is usually to suggest that such persons have failed to see the light, and that their condition deserves pity rather than sympathy. For what the mass media have agreed to sponsor, the masses are expected to approve. This situation has become so normal that the expression of genuine minority views may occasion surprise. When, for example, a schoolboy once referred to the Beatles as 'noisy extroverts', the pronouncement was considered so unusual and heterodox, especially coming from a young person, as to deserve extensive notice in the press. The matter was then given hurried but decent burial and the official adulation continued, as it has to this day.

The truth is, however, that all genuine art is *local*, as W. H. Auden said. There is no international style. The promotion of an international art is a matter of cultural politics, which, as we said earlier, has become an important weapon of government. In that case, it might seem all the more strange that nations, anxious to promote their cultural image, should tend increasingly to exchange material of similar nature; but in fact this is merely a way of demonstrating that each sponsor belongs to the same 'exclusive' club. In another medium, the film or the video, a similar desire to conform to current standards of taste prevails. Entries to film festivals will, in the prevailing mood of the avant-garde, consciously exploit the scabrous, with the most successful essays in this field carrying off prizes. Not for a moment does anybody seriously suppose that the majority of these films possess artistic merit, though they sometimes are held to carry a 'message'. In a recent cartoon, depicting a couple sitting before a TV set, the husband says: 'I don't believe this film can have a message. Where is the violence? Where is the explicit sex?' But the alliance between the avant-garde and the media is such that at one level the fare is acceptable and at another lucrative, and such combined success is supposed to rule out the legitimacy of contrary opinions.

In view of what we have already said on the subject of eroticism, we should perhaps warn against adopting too exclusively *moral* an attitude to these tendencies. The present trend is in many ways a form of Puritanism for which we twit the Victorians, only in reverse. (To take a minor instance: to speak, as Trollope does, of 'unmentionables' and 'inexpressibles' is merely another way of *thinking* about trousers and the sexual organs they conceal. It is the very opposite of an 'innocent' attitude. But this does not excuse the present obsession either.)

Such remarks might be taken to suggest that all cultural activities organized for prestige purposes between countries, or within the same country, are so much imposture. The aspersion applies above all to packaged culture, of which the plastic arts can so easily become examples. It does not apply to activities where there is genuine *re-creation*, as in skilled performances of drama, opera or ballet. In such activities, a great actor, singer or dancer, not simply by possessing 'charisma', can provide authentic PN; for such nutrition, like physical nutrition, must remain fresh, and the re-creation by a great artist in each performance is the guarantee that the emotions evoked are genuine. Moreover, the advantage of the arts involving personal interpretation is that they are a two-way activity. An actor is not speaking into the void, any more than a dancer is dancing in isolation. As every artiste knows, the performer is no less in receipt of nutrition than the audience. A great personal performance is a communal nutritional feast. Such are those 'memorable' aesthetic occasions which everybody may experience half-a-dozen times in life.

This is the reason perhaps why the distinguished actors and ballet dancers of the world have on the whole successfully avoided becoming slaves of the avant-garde. For one thing, they cannot be everywhere at once, as can the 'typical' work of art; and where their ubiquity can be simulated, as in the film, the nutritional capacity is manifestly reduced. In the film, it is the director rather than the actor who now tends to hit the headlines; and where, in a film which attains notoriety because of some affront to accepted taste, such as *The Last Tango in Paris*, an actor, Marlon Brando, is hailed for his performance, the critics have been hard put to it to elucidate in what his achievement consists.

4

The nature of PN

Culture, conscious and subconscious

In this chapter we shall be concerned with issues of a more general character. The sphere of the psyche has been described as characterized by a certain opacity. This means that in the psychic sphere values are not directly apprehended but only implied. A work of art avoids saying explicitly what it means – if it does so, the mystery vanishes, and we get didacticism. The apprehension of values, though never total, is found at the higher level of intellect or spirit: hence psychic 'values' partake more of the nature of valence than of value. Since the psychic level is an intermediate one, it is that at which the personality is partly 'possessed' by instinctive forces and feelings. Of the animal it can be said that he is wholly subject to such 'possession'. When an impulse of panic passes through a crowd, there is momentary total instinctual 'possession'; and it is therefore at such moments that human beings subsist almost wholly upon the animal level. The specifically human is a sphere of tension between the pull of instinctive valencies and the attraction of values. To be human is to be 'disintoxicated', a condition not easy to sustain and never complete.

Since instinctual 'possession' is largely an unconscious process, it follows, as well as from what we have said earlier, that culture is in large part an unconscious or subconscious process too. The human psyche is like an iceberg in that only the tip is visible. Being a realm of instinct and feeling, it emerges into the conscious realm only in so far as the pull of values exerts its dynamism, and this may undergo marked variation. There is a limit to the amount of psychic energy on which we may draw, and sleep is a psychic as well as a physiological necessity.

How is culture transmitted? Rarely, or perhaps least effectively, by exclusive or deliberate indoctrination. It is transmitted rather by unconscious or subconscious imitation, whereby ways of behaving, dress, habitual responses, style, are passed from one generation to another, beginning at a stage in infancy where such acquisitions take on the aspect of instinct. By contrast, the part played by *education* is 'superficial'; but even here the education most telling and permanent may be that which is absorbed outside the hours of formal instruction. There is an epigram to the effect that education is that which is left when everything learnt has been forgotten. In school or university, it is the rites, traditions, and *esprit de corps* which, being subliminally absorbed, implant themselves most indelibly. How superficial is much official teaching or indoctrination may be gauged from the example of totalitarian countries threatened with assault or annihilation. When the Soviet Union came under attack from the Nazis in 1941, the leaders, abandoning the appeal to communism and dialectical materialism, sought desperately to revive the traditions of Holy Russia. With the help of the Orthodox Church, this appeal was remarkably effective. And we can imagine a similar reaction if the People's Republic of China were placed under threat. Precious little would be heard of Marxism, which, as a Western doctrine derived from the Hegelian school of German philosophy, has no deep emotional appeal to the Chinese peasant anyway; but a great deal would be heard of the kingdom governed by the righteous ruler wielding the mandate of heaven, and divinely appointed its saviour and deliverer. The shrewd ruler knows his people; the dictator above all is aware of the limits of propaganda.

It may be that the convulsion within the sphere of education in our time, which is a world-wide phenomenon, is due precisely to a quarrel over PN. Progressive educationalists are nearly always political ideologists, anxious to alter or even to destroy the prevailing social order; but their campaign – in which many students have enthusiastically joined – to abolish discipline, examinations, and even final degrees, and to confine education, at the higher level, to a dialogue between students and their teachers (who are reduced to a level of equality with their charges), and presumably to change education at lower levels to free assignments or projects interspersed with mild political indoctrination, is designed to destroy the 'spirit' of traditional education. Ordinary educational reform, for which there is periodical need, would not require so drastic a propaedeutic. Many ideologists realize that nothing short of uprooting the system will suffice for their purpose, for their ultimate aim is to effect an emotional change in their contemporaries. In China, the communist take-over of 1949 was a matter chiefly of politics and economics; but when Mao Tse-tung wished to change the 'tone' of the Reform, he launched what was appropriately called a *cultural* revolution; and it was this movement, whether successful or not, which later inspired so many ideologues of the West. In other words, it was the would-be destroyers of the system, or what the French call the *casseurs*, who called themselves Maoists. And their textbook, or opusculum Bible, was not, as with the old-fashioned radicals, Marx's *Capital* or the works of Engels or Lenin – large, unread volumes – but a little red book of moral maxims, some pithy, some prissy, some fatuous, but all designed to provide a kind of capsuled PN, capable of being put to incantatory use, and regularly so put at times traditionally associated with communal worship or ceremony. It was even employed as a 'magical' charm in the event of illness, thus fulfilling the part which PN always plays in such cases.[1] In short, the enemies of the PN provided by our traditional system were only too ready to substitute another form, which, examined *au fond*, was not so very different in nature. For not merely can PN never be dispensed with, but its make-up is remarkably uniform. Indeed, the substitution of Maoism for Marxism was a shift back, so far as PN was concerned, to orthodoxy; for although Marx himself was a man of cultivated tastes, with a particular love of poetry, especially Dante, his economic writings, apart from an occasional flare-up of moral indignation, make arid reading, whereas it was not for nothing that Mao was a poet. The Soviet Union, possessing no equivalent figure, might have suffered a much greater psychic crisis if its leaders had not been men of bourgeois morals and outlook (as Svetlana has provided fascinating confirmation in the case of her father), and if the 'great patriotic war', as it was aptly called, had not drawn so heavily upon tradition. No doubt that is why the country, in some of its aspects, conveys to the visitor even today an almost poignant impression of Europe's traditional past, while the official Marxist publications in the show-windows steadily accumulate dust.

This was brought home to the author not long ago when, staying in Moscow at the beginning of the Christmas season, he looked across in the silence of the night from his hotel window to Red Square carpeted with snow, and suddenly realized that the star on the summit of the Kremlin, its 'red shift' dominating the scene, could easily have been taken for the Star of Bethlehem. Nevertheless, the policy of the Soviet government is still nominally to *changer tout cela*, to win over 'hearts and minds', as Yuri Andropov affirmed. Hence the bitter conflict between Marxist orthodoxy and 'rebel' writers, on whom the role of Opposition has largely devolved. Yet here again it is interesting to observe that the 'rebels', unlike the Western Maoists, display an attitude not unlike that of champions of Western Christendom. In works still banned in the Soviet Union, such as *Dr Zhivago* and the novels of Solzhenitsyn, there is a 'reactionary' atmosphere which may have been responsible for their ready and even enthusiastic acceptance by the general public in the West: for advanced or experimental literature is cultivated only by the practitioners of minority culture. Meanwhile, the Soviet public is still obliged to subsist upon 'socialist realist' literature and art which is nothing if not psychically sterile. This is varied occasionally by nostalgic glimpses into the 'pre-Revolutionary' European era provided by such imports as *The Forsyte Saga*, which the authorities permit because is it supposed to illustrate the evils and 'contradictions' of bourgeois capitalism. One suspects that the people lap it up because of its evocation of a colourful and hierarchical social order, a 'high life,' so remote from their own dreary egalitarianism.

PN and national cultures

A country in which the traditional sources of PN partly dried up, necessitating urgent supplies from other quarters, was Japan. With the 'unheard of' defeat of 1945, the traditional religions, Shinto and Buddhism, suffered a serious, if temporary, eclipse. This was inevitable, since Shinto especially had been identified with a regime largely discredited. But the enormous part played by Shinto and Buddhism in nourishing the Japanese psyche required to be compensated from some other quarter, and this gap was filled by a variety of 'new religions' (*shinkō-shukyō*). On the surface, many of these religions appeared to be thinly-disguised forms of materialism. In return for formal adherence and the payment of a subscription, they promised health and prosperity in this life; and the most successful and publicized of them, Soka Gakkai, sought to gain political power through its political wing, *Komeito*, the 'clean government' party. Yet what would seem to have attracted adherents to this as to some other new faiths, and to older ones such as Tenrikyo (a remarkable religion founded by a poor housewife in 1848), was the degree to which they purveyed a sense of 'togetherness'. This was induced by ritual, lustration, music and sometimes dance, culminating in mass ceremonies in which the individual was 'taken out of himself' and subjected to powerful pressures of a hypnotic kind. Many of the new religions will no doubt die, but others will take their place. They supply, if only by means of an *Interimsethik*, a permanent need. And their appeal is chiefly to the middle-classes, namely, that part of society which felt itself most betrayed or let down by the old order.

Meanwhile, the traditions associated with Shinto and Buddhism are by no means dead. Behind the 'new' faiths are recognizable Shintoist or Buddhist elements: Soka Gakkai is directly inspired by Nichiren Buddhism, a militant creed in its day. Nor is Christianity without influence. Amid all these changes, however, one focus of psychic feeling has remained in many ways unaltered, namely, the Emperor himself, the nominal high priest of Shinto. With timely wisdom, the Americans decided to keep him on the throne. Thereby the entire people were maintained in something like psychic security. This is a circumstance capable of almost sensory verification by the visitor, whereas a very different feeling is evinced by contact with another defeated power, (West) Germany. Nor need we pay much attention to statements in Japan to the effect that the Emperor enjoys no official position in Shinto. That is as it may be. To the ordinary Japanese, he is (though less explicitly no doubt) what he always was, a focus of loyalty and a powerful source of charismatic influence.

As an exercise, it would be tempting to go round the world for the purpose of assessing, in so far as one's competence permitted, the amount of PN prevailing in different countries. Such an investigation would provide some revealing results; for countries can vary in this regard to a marked and significant degree. In view of its great importance, the United States may perhaps be selected for special consideration, though generalization is here hazardous, because one region of that vast country differs so widely from another. The foundation of the United States was inspired by an idealism nourished by elements in the British tradition, and the struggle for independence was in one sense a British civil war. No one was more authentically an English gentleman than George Washington, whose estate, Mount Vernon, was named after the British admiral in whose service his younger brother had died. Combined with notions of 'manifest destiny' and the 'American dream', such idealism was the power whereby people of diverse origins were turned into American citizens in a single generation; and this steady process of Americanization worked well, and hardly without opposition, until the end of the Second World War. At that moment, and in the early days of the Marshall Plan, America was perhaps the most powerful and prestigious country ever to have existed, not merely by reason of her huge industrial potential but because of her capacity to disseminate Americanism — an ideology or gospel propagated as much by her missionaries as by her businessmen. Nor were the missionaries confined to persons wearing clerical collars: every part of the world was affected by America's great powerhouse of synthetic PN, namely Hollywood.

At what point American pre-eminence, both in the material and in the psychic sphere, began to show signs of waning, is difficult to say. The change was due partly to that very pre-eminence itself; for the recipients of 'aid', while gratefully and even greedily taking what they were offered, resented the ideology, and more subtly the PN, that were included as part of the 'package'. This inclusion was not always deliberate: American propaganda, while being put out officially by organs such as the USIA and the Voice of America, more frequently 'seeded itself'. Simultaneous with the growing reaction against Americanism were signs that America herself was beginning to undergo a psychic convulsion. The American dream, it seemed, had been dreamed through to the end. And when the United States became involved in the Vietnam war, the psychic deficiency became all the more evident — though the first signs of weakness had occurred at the end of the Korean war, with the evidence of successful brain-washing of American prisoners. A great deal has been written about the troubles at Berkeley, California, which sparked off student troubles elsewhere; but what was interesting was the degree to which they were involved, as were the troubles in Paris a year later (May 1968), with the 'sexual revolution'. Many of the *manifestations* marking the troubles at Berkeley and elsewhere — Nanterre, for instance — were definitely erotic in character[2]: the usual sign that PN is in short supply. What had happened, in general, was that Americanism had begun to lose faith in itself, at its psychic core, at the moment when the United States, as a world power and as the oldest of the new countries, was being put to its severest test.

The effects of secularization

A force making for the systematic erosion of PN is secularization. Every country must have its share of idealism; but the idealism must rest upon a firm cultural foundation, which means a reservoir of psychic energy. American idealism, however, was born of a reaction: a reaction against British traditions which, in other respects, were taken over wholesale by the Founding Fathers and their successors. American culture, in the majority and the minority sense, was English culture up to at least the time of Henry James. In the world's greatest pluralistic society, no one element was theoretically allowed predominance, at least among the competing idealisms. The result was an emerging secularism. 'Secularization threatens to become a sort of state religion established by court decree.'[3] Now secularization is the enemy not simply of religion but of PN in general; and countries which, like the United States, encourage the process of secularization are likely to generate strong reactions. These are seen in the proliferation of religious cults, like the Jesus Movements, or the varieties of Buddhism (considerably diluted), such as inspire the characters of novels like Kerouac's *Dharma Bums* (1958). A people cannot live without a proper supply of PN. Such movements appear to be providing it.

Granted, there are persons by no means hostile to religion who stoutly defend the secularization process. 'Secularization rolls on,' says Harvey Cox, author of that still influential work, *The Secular City* (1965), 'and if we are to understand and to communicate with our present age we must learn to love it in its unremitting secularity.' Cox makes a distinction at the outset between *secularization* and *secularism*. 'Secularization implies a historical process, almost certainly irreversible, in which society and culture are delivered from tutelage to religious control and closed metaphysical world-views. . . . Secularism, on the other hand, is the name for an ideology, a new closed world-view which functions very much like a new religion.' This distinction is certainly important; but if the process of secularization is 'irreversible', and if we must learn to love our present age in all its 'unremitting secularity', it is difficult to see how the process we are asked to encourage will not end up as something very like secularism. What Cox seems to be saying is that the journey itself is valuable only so long as we do not reach our goal. And, as he rightly adds, echoing the American archbishop, secularism 'must be watched carefully to prevent its becoming the ideology of a new establishment. It must be especially checked where it pretends not to be a world-view but nonetheless seeks to impose its ideology through the organs of the state.' That which needs to be 'watched', and still more to be 'checked', is not an abstraction but a powerful movement: and this movement can be none other than that of secularization itself, which Cox believes to be so salutary. Secularization is thus a form of creeping desacralization, and as such it is damaging to the psyche. In fact, no process of desacralization can proceed very far without producing the kind of reactions of which we have spoken. If desacralization were really irreversible, it would end by undermining the entire basis of culture; there would be cultural deprivation of an extreme kind, a condition of neg-PN.

Cox pursues his argument with rigour, employing paradox ('the Genesis account of Creation is really a form of "atheistic propaganda" '), and not fearing to use the arguments of the enemy ('religion is, in a sense, the neurosis of cultures: secularization corresponds to maturation'). And he destroys almost all the idols to which modern man has given veneration – all, that is to say, except sex. Here, curiously enough, his iconoclastic mood suddenly changes. Instead of supporting the efforts to desacralize sex, as some clerics have done, he reproves such organs as *Playboy* for seeking to do just that. 'This futile attempt to reduce the *mysterium tremendum* of the sexual fails to solve the problem of being a man.' *Mysterium tremendum*! In other contexts, this would represent the very epitome of the sacred which he has sought to 'defuse'.[4] But not at all. 'Sexuality,' he says, 'is the basic form of all human relationships, and therein lies its terror and its power.' (He even slips in a sentence which goes against his whole approach: 'Another antidote is simply to de-romanticize sex.') In short, Cox perceives implicitly that a desacralized sex would deprive it of its meaning and power. What he is seeking to justify is sex not merely as a sacred function but as a purveyor of PN.

It is interesting to compare Cox's views on this matter with those of John Robinson.[5] Arguing in *Honest to God* and other works that the Christian tradition has suffered from a failure to come to terms with the erotic, Robinson approves of sex-magazines such as *Playboy* in that, in his view, they relate sex to the rest of life. This is what Cox says they do not do. Robinson would seem to wish to make sex into an activity like any other; Cox, though going against his central argument, realizes that this cannot be.

In other words, Robinson is a thoroughgoing secularist, for whom there are no *mysteria tremenda*. Cox preserves at least *one* reserve of mystery; and perhaps his dread of secularism, as opposed to secularization, is due to his instinctive perception that a life deprived of all mystery, though rational and ordered, would not be worth living. 'This *futile* attempt. . . '

Secularization as a social process began, we may suppose, in Europe with the 'waning of the Middle Ages'. During the mediaeval period, an immense capital of PN had been built up, chiefly through the influence of the church and a group of charismatic monarchies ('Il y avait la Sainte Vierge, il y avait le roi'[6]); and even now this capital is far from exhausted. The Catholic Church has always possessed a quality which has distinguished it from almost any other, including Orthodoxy, and that is a kind of wordly wisdom. From the beginning it saw the necessity of coming to terms with certain features of paganism. In this it resembled Japanese Buddhism in its accommodation with Shinto. Moreover, it devised a liturgy which, though often above their literal understanding, enabled the majority of the congregation to know vaguely what was going on at the altar, and to give their own interpretation of it when they did not. Nevertheless, if the truth were known – which fortunately it is never likely to be – it might be found that in the sphere of faith and morals misapprehensions of the most ludicrous kind prevail. The American Catholic who, at an audience at the Vatican, exclaimed in a breezy way, 'Hullo Pope, I knew your father the late Pope,' was not necessarily so isolated a figure as might be thought. Moreover, the Church's 'year' corresponded to the agricultural year, conferring a religious relevance on rural life that the Church today cannot match in the case of the 'secular city'. This ecclesiastical influence survived revolutions, anti-clericalism, and movements for disestablishment. The 'hold' of non-Roman institutions such as the Anglican church was chiefly that they never completely shed their Catholic character, while the non-conformist churches retained a vague attraction to the Anglican establishment to which they have of recent years been negotiating their return. Even the most resolute of Protestants seems to feel, in his heart of hearts, that Rome possesses some special source of spiritual energy. Nor was it for nothing that Rome should have been called at times the Whore of Babylon; for this was to add another to the succession of female figures, beginning with the

Mother Goddess, who have been worshipped as the apex of so many religions. The Scarlet Woman *is*, in an oblique sense, an avatar of the Mother of God, immaculate; for, as Blake wrote, 'every harlot was a virgin once'.

More recent attempts by the Catholic Church to accommodate itself with 'the world' have been less successful than its former accommodation with the nature cults; for nature was not the World but rather the Earth, the womb of life in its primal innnocence. It was the 'innocence' of certain nature cults that the Church sought hurriedly to veil, since it seemed to condone licence. The motives of those who would make the Church an agent of social revolution, especially in the impoverished Latin American countries, are understandable; but the Church needs no revolutionary ideology but its own, which is far more extreme than that of any secular gospel. To surrender to a secular gospel would be to surrender parts of its 'spell': with the result that the faithful would finally be left cut off from their emotional sources, and therefore having to make do with the thin fare provided by a materialistic ideology. This would lead either to total disillusionment or to the embracing of secularism in the closed sense defined by Cox. Meanwhile, the Church, having abdicated its traditional position, would disintegrate from within; a process which may already have begun if we are to judge by the annual departure of several thousand priests. This was not the outcome envisaged by those advocating *aggiornamento* or 'renewal'.

Within the next few years, a growing number of persons outside both church and political party (for the number adhering to the purely secular gospels will, unless under political pressure, be small) are likely to be psychically disorientated. Living in the Secular City, they will be prone to seek ever-increasing distraction. Curiously enough, Cox takes the view that urbanization, in addition to conferring a welcome anonymity, must necessarily 'enhance' our manhood. 'Residents of a city of 10,000 may be limited to one or two theatres, while people who live in a city of a million can choose perhaps between fifty films on a given night.' It is interesting to observe that Cox takes an example from the field of PN. But in what respect is our manhood (as *homo symbolicus* or man the communicator) 'enhanced' by the fact that our range of choice, in this sphere, is apparently so much greater than it was in the past? Of the fifty films available for viewing in a large city, the majority are likely to be so inferior that the choice of really good films is bound to remain small. Will all the people who want to see a film on a particular night be sure to see something of quality? On the contrary, many people, anxious for an evening's light amusement, will wish to avoid precisely the 'good films' and to stay at home and watch videos, nice or nasty. This tendency was concealed in the past because, in many towns and in all villages, people drew their PN largely from the folk-festivals distributed throughout the year, not least those hallowed by the Church: and because of the rarity and relevance of these festivals, the resultant psychic satisfaction was much greater than anything derived from modern *ersatz* PN. Today, people may 'go to a show' to celebrate some crucial events in their lives, but the show is rarely of immediate relevance. A couple with whom the writer was acquainted went to see *Oh! Calcutta!* to celebrate their golden wedding – it is difficult to believe that this experience induced nostalgia for past love or a feeling of renewed affection.

The almost universal presence of the TV set testifies to the fact that PN, or rather *ersatz* PN, is now laid on like light and heat. But a psyche which is in perpetual need of stimulation is not in a healthy condition. During most of history, disasters apart, the psyche was subject to gentle and regular nutriment in accordance with periodic natural rhythms. These rhythms have now been broken or interrupted, and the result has been a haphazard overfeeding and intoxication of the psyche.

Moreover, the Secular City has deprived the psyche of one of its most imperative needs, and that is silence. The healing power of silence is in some parts of the world almost totally forgotten. It is forgotten often in hospitals, where its therapeutic power is most needed. It is certainly forgotten in our large towns. There comes a point when people come to *want* noise, because silence has become insupportable. Like the painful oral sensation of first taking food after long abstention, silence after long habituation to noise can hurt. But the psyche through many thousands of years has been nourished periodically on silence – that silence which is the sleep of the psyche; and it is difficult not to believe that the racket deliberately maintained in our discotheques, with electronic amplification which in the past would have been found unendurable, is a kind of determined invasion of the psychic sphere, a deaf-wish, aimed at leaving the devotee psychically as well as physically exhausted. The reasons for this calculated assault are for the psychologist to explain. At any rate, two University of Michigan audiologists discovered not long ago that the sound level in rehearsal rooms of beat groups rose to 130 decibels, which was above the noise-level of a Saturn Moon Rocket, namely 120 decibels. (The present EEC recommendation is for a limit of 85 decibels for industrial noise. As the decibel scale is logarithmic, 90 decibels is 10 times as loud as 80 decibels.)[7] It seems possible that the cult of pop music itself is an anti-cultural force, in the wide sense: a force no doubt harmless in moderation but damaging when taken in regular draughts. 'Ultimately, alas, music can be a way of saying: to hell with mind.'[8] It is likewise possible that the interest taken in oriental cults of 'transcendental meditation', which have significantly been patronized by pop musicians, are an instinctive reaction against the tyranny of sound. For ultimately, 'only the silent hear'.[9]

The Secular City or Metropolis, which in Cox's view provides opportunities for a new kind of freedom – no longer the pre-urban ethos of spatial proximity in neighbourliness but a means to acquiring the friends we really wish to cultivate – suffers the defect of failing to provide a satisfactory psychic environment. Cox virtually admits this by citing the case of Christian ministers who, conducting a survey of a new urban high-rise apartment area, found to their surprise that the recently-arrived apartment dwellers 'did not want to meet their neighbours socially'. The pastors later realized that 'what they had encountered was a sheer survival technique. Resistance against efforts to subject them to neighbourliness and socialization is a skill apartment dwellers must develop if they are to maintain any human relations at all. It is an essential element in the shape of the secular city.' In that case the secular city has a shape not altogether desirable. To say that people need to practise 'survival techniques' is hardly a good advertisement for the secular style of life. Not the art of living but the art of surviving becomes the goal. This means that a whole tradition of living must forcibly be abandoned; cities *qua* cities, ceasing to be unified, organic wholes, must become huge dormitories; and the only hope of organizing a satisfactory life is by throwing out lengthening antennae, life-lines, in various directions if the beleaguered inhabitants 'are to maintain any human relations at all'.

If this desperate stratagem is the pattern of the future, the task of organizing a satisfactory life will prove beyond the capacity of all but the grimly resolute. The rest will suffer psychic inanition to a degree never before experienced.

A human being in the 'wrong' environment is ultimately reduced to a condition as lamentable as a displaced animal. True, the trend towards anonymity in living has been going on for some while; the fact remains that for many millennia mankind lived (urbanly) in much the same way. 'Goethe's Weimar was the same kind of city as Abraham's Ur, or, indeed, as the lowest stratum of the *tel* at Jericho.'[10] And Goethe, in his Autobiography, *Poetry and Truth*, has described with realism, but also with nostalgia, what life was like for the inhabitants of a city-state (Frankfurt). How can we deny that the cathedral towns of England, or the university towns of Europe, or Venice, Florence, Toledo, or Avila, or Ch'ang-an or Kyoto, in their heyday, provided an environment not merely physically but psychically rich, even allowing for much squalor and the prevalence of disease? A people that could go to such trouble to beautify their environment must, we feel, have lived life to a fuller degree than others. These places therefore remain monuments which, when threatened by exploitation, arouse a world conscience. The task today is not to acquiesce in conditions which permit *bare survival*, but to plan, or rather replan, cities in which the person will be able to live a satisfactory psychic and spiritual life. The great Japanese architect Tange Kenzo would appear to realize this. What Cox ignores is that such life involves not simply establishing 'personal relations' – and reaching out for most of them beyond the city's confines – but cultivating a measure of enriching solitude. The defect of the Secular City is that it is a place both difficult to be neighbourly in and difficult to be alone in. In the traditional city, a balance was struck between the claims of solitude and the claims of society. The flat-dwellers of the survey mentioned by Cox not merely showed reluctance to meet their neighbours, but 'had no interest whatever in church or community groups'. Admittedly, such groups can sometimes be a pretty dull lot. Whether this lack of interest applied simply to groups in the area he does not say; but the presumption is that it applied to all such groups, no matter where they might be. Such antipathy to corporate or community life is unnatural and inhuman; for the personality cannot retain its health without a certain group-life, some of which must be provided by the immediate neighbourhood. What the champions of the Secular City forget is that man is not merely a creature capable of living off selected 'personal relations', most of which are enjoyed at a distance, but an animal, with animal instincts, albeit overlaid with human emotions. He therefore

113

needs an *Umwelt*. His 'shared zoology' is a fact which no amount of secularization can obliterate. Indeed, secularization can do as much harm to his *animal* nature as to his *human* nature; for, as we have seen, part of the psyche is the sphere of instinctive valencies, and if these are not activated by appropriate evocative signals in the environment, there will be psychic impoverishment for which no amount of material welfare, still less 'spiritual' activity, can compensate. While spiritual life can be led 'at a distance', the same is not true, beyond a certain point, of psychic life. That is the reason why prolonged residence abroad, or at least in an alien environment, can present serious problems for many people, and why the expression '*culture* shock' is appropriate in cases where initial contacts with foreigners or aliens prove bewildering. As for the city-dwellers of whom Cox speaks, they were, it would seem, already suffering from a kind of psychic deficiency disease, and it would have been interesting to know how many of them had managed to cultivate 'personal relations' at long-range. Very few, one suspects. Throughout his book Cox tends to treat people solely as *intellectuals,* for it is only such persons who can survive in an alien or alienated environment; but no community possesses more than a minority of such people – people who can create their own inner solitude and who can communicate across a gulf with other like-minded persons – and it is the bulk of decent, instinctively-orientated citizens whose needs require to be taken into account.

By contrast, F.R. Cowell, in his book *Culture in Private and Public Life* (1959), took the line that cultural activity is the pursuit of truth, beauty and moral worth; and because he realizes that only a few people pursue these values consciously, he tends to give the impression that the rest of the community must blindly follow. 'The mass of humanity, impotent itself to create or to devise great traditions of truth, beauty or goodness. everywhere tends to follow cultural standards devised or elaborated by the *élite*.'[11] Do they? What about today? In the strict sense, the point may be conceded; but a community which lives a rich psychic life can be regarded as cultured in another sense, and this is the culture which will matter as long as the human race lasts. Citing the fact that the per capita spending on books in Britain in 1957 was about 3p per week, Cowell concludes that 'for the vast majority of the great British public, cultural interests are at present no more than a marginal interest in their lives'.[12] But this is explicit, intellectual culture again; and if Cowell thinks that such culture will one day diffuse itself throughout society, he is surely mistaken.

Equally mistaken is the view that the Secular City is anything but a transitional phenomenon. In fact, it always imposes a threat. If it actually came into existence, its inhabitants would soon be afflicted by the most oppressive *taedium vitae*. Those 'scientific humanists' who hold that all metaphysical beliefs should be expelled as so much mumbo jumbo would be the first, one suspects, to find life in the Secular City insupportable.

Countryside and the church

Although Cox is no doubt right to associate secularization with urbanization, the countryside, or what is left of it, can be secularized too. This is a dangerous development, because the beauty of nature remains a most potent source of PN. It is here that the maximum of intersubjectivity is possible; which is why it is not inaccurate to speak of 'communing' with living things. Environmental influences which have prevailed for the greater part of history cannot be renounced in a few years. Cox's 'personal relations' are exclusively human ones. Too much stress on 'the personal' can be harmful: we need relations with the infra-human too.

How ill-advised is much of our policy towards the countryside, scarcely needs stressing. In order to make money, but sometimes in the innocent belief that the public weal is being served, stretches of country, especially near the coast, are 'developed' with the connivance of the very planning authorities whose duty should be preservation. The idea is to encourage people to patronize beauty spots, oblivious of the fact that such development, if pushed too far (as it nearly always is), will destroy that which is valued, leaving the countryside desecrated and the countryfolk worse instead of better off, since the visitors will stop coming. The only way to 'develop' the countryside is to conserve it. At long last there seems to be a public conscience on this issue, but it is still necessary to fight short-sighted policies. What is at stake is not mere antiquarian or aesthetic interests, but a reservoir of psychic health.

From at least Neolithic times, the village has been the unit in which most of the human race grew up. Today, even though the countryman is in a minority, the sight of a well-kept village arouses more than sentimental emotions. What we behold is a kind of norm of human habitation which may well resume its importance with the achievement of megalopolis. For the latter will 'liberate' much of the countryside and there may be a revival of rural life, preparatory for the day when the planet earth, evacuated of its surplus inhabitants, will return to its pre-industrial beauty. Meanwhile, an attempt must be made to keep the rhythm of country life going; and this can be done only by people unbitten by the amusement bug and willing to live a life of quiet labour.

The position of the village institutions, above all the church but not forgetting the school and even the post office, is paramount; for it is in the country that the sense of the sacredness of life is most forcibly brought before us, and the church was until recently the 'focus' of the emotions aroused by life and death. Hence the harmony of the church building with its surroundings, the irreplaceable music of church bells, and the solemn peace of the churchyard. Curiously enough, it is often the unbeliever who realizes most keenly the social importance of the church (we refer here chiefly to the English church, for this is for us the Catholic institution most integrated with the countryside, though the Methodist chapels of the West Country are very much part of the land, and the 'marooned' aspect of so many of them today is a sad sight). Thomas Hardy, a thorough-going agnostic, was greatly exercised about the condition of the Anglican church in his time. His plea for its support was as much that of the moralist, anxious to hold 'the shreds of morality together', as that of the poet who realized that the church supplied man's psychic as well as spiritual needs.[13] This is in many ways a more responsible attitude than that held by Bernard Shaw, who believed that churches should be turned into museums.[14] Museums they are in danger of becoming, and this will spell the end of most of them. The issue is vital, because unless the church continues its mission, the countryside will lose one of its last bulwarks against secularization.

On the other hand, we have to recognize that the church's message has come to be for many people frankly unacceptable. To them, the artificial maintenance of that institution is no more than a sentimental exercise, using sentimental to mean that which is continued for the sake of the residual emotion it is capable of arousing, while its *raison d'être* has vanished. And such sentimentalism could give rise to some ludicrous results and practices, comparable to the playing at druids at Stonehenge, or the antics of fire-worshippers, or, for that matter, of witches.[15] Yet although a large part – perhaps the greater part – of the public may not care two hoots for either church or clergy, Bible or Prayer Book, the once-familiar liturgy has only to be threatened with modification or revision, and a cry of alarm and anguish goes up not least from the agnostic and atheist establishment – quite apart from a number of the faithful – with passionate appeals to desist from such sacrilege. Indeed, one of the most doughty champions of orthodoxy in this respect was an author who had in the past pleaded for the retention of the broadcast of Choral Evensong, and yet who in the same breath, or perhaps a few breaths later, had protested her 'vehement unbelief'. Marghanita Laski was not of course advocating the retention of the creeds or the formularies, which she must regard as so much nonsense. She was fighting for the maintenance of a rapidly-diminishing source of PN, as her pleas for more ritual in a well-known discussion with Archbishop Anthony Bloom made clear. Similarly, it was a group of secularists for the most part who endeavoured, though without success, to prevent the burial by the Department of the Environment of one of the oldest Celtic chapels in the country. As for the church, she lined up with the bureaucrats.[16] The agnostics and atheists – who would be unlikely to declare themselves as such unless they had reflected deeply on what Paul Tillich called 'ultimate concern' – are surely in some manner right. That same concern included the instinctive feeling that the churches, with all their pomposity of ritual, their moral flaccidity, and their eagerness to compromise with the world, remain, as no other institutions, guardians of both past and present. They represent, even if they occasionally travesty, a dimension of experience to which human beings need access. A clerisy, to use an old word, is indispensable to a community. So is a shaman, by whatever name he or she is known. Just as the Nigerian tribe, the Abuan, chose an Ake-Abuan, 'so that he might be holy on our behalf, keeping all the laws that ordinary people have no time to remember because of their regular work',[17] so every community needs a select group – a profession set apart – to supervise the 'rites and ceremonies', and to guard the institutions dedicated to their performance. You are going to have such people anyhow. A host of officials, from social workers to psychiatrists, and a growing number of un-officials, have sprung up around the administration of the democratic welfare state. As for the totalitarian world, it has its own often sinister sodality of overseers and guardians. Among this largely secular army of helpers or hinderers, the authentic guardians of the sacred are not the least important, and need at all costs to be retained. Even secular, anti-clerical France contrives, in however indirect a manner, to aid select confessional institutions, and now undertakes to keep in repair ecclesiastical buildings associated with the *infâme* which her great rationalist, Voltaire, sought to *écraser*. Tough-minded men are sometimes better 'guardians of the faith' than mitred *fainéants*.

We cannot relegate the conduct of the liturgy to amateurs of folklore, though even that might be preferable to its performance by certain followers of avant-garde theology. We need to supplement a diminishing band of dedicated clergy by volunteers from the laity, in order to keep the liturgy relevant and alive; for if the Orthodox Church under communism can survive, the Western churches under the threat of secularization ought not to perish. What seems clear is that the Church will not be saved by compromising with the world, or by holding services to commemorate the anniversaries of commercial sex-revues. Such attempts to show that the church is up-to-date are rarely the work of the laity, and it is the laity whose views are sometimes less tinged with idiosyncrasy than their spiritual overseers. A return to the full liturgy, without frills, would be far more effective: the experience of countries where the church is under persecution suggests that men will endure much for the sake of authenticity.[18]

Nevertheless, the authority – we need not talk of prestige in such a connection – of the church has reached, in western Europe at least (it is different in some more distant countries), a point so low as to suggest that any further decline will spell dissolution. In *De Profundis*, Oscar Wilde spoke of the need for a Church of Unbelievers. He need not have worried, for that is virtually what we have already. Perhaps such a brotherhood has always formed an integral part of the universal church. Just as among all the verse produced in the world – and today alone there are more poets than in the whole of past history – there is very little real poetry, so the amount of genuine conviction among persons nominally religious is probably very small. What the intellect cannot explicitly subscribe to, however, the psyche can grasp. And in any case, if we look back, we find that the situation of the church or churches has repeatedly been a source of alarm and despondency, often verging on despair. But she endures.

This is a sign that, at heart, even those who fail to give her active support are not altogether indifferent to her fate. What, however, of religion itself? This raises more fundamental questions, especially in relation to culture. To this subject we now turn.

5
Religion, culture and counter-culture

What religion is

Lucretius observed that 'tantum religio potuit suadere malorum' ('so much evil could religion prompt'). People have taken this to mean that religion can do nothing but harm. Yet this is much like saying that Dr Johnson's statement that 'patriotism is the last refuge of a scoundrel' is a condemnation out of hand of patriotism, instead of meaning (as it surely does) that scoundrels, anxious to excuse their basest actions, may lay claim to patriotic motives. What is now generally realized, even by the indifferent, is that religion is one of the 'forms of the spirit': that it can no more be 'abolished' than can art; and that those who try to abolish religion are often animated by a passion which is religious in quality and in its way proselytizing. And no one can deny that religion and culture are closely associated – so closely, in fact, that there is doubt whether one can exist without the other. Culture without religion is empty; religion without culture is blind.

One of the proofs that religion cannot be dismissed out of hand is that humanism, which some hold to be an attitude more mature than that of religion, is in fact parasitic upon it. By a paradox, humanism is the one point of view which leaves man ultimately in doubt of his humanity. Hence, if the works of humanists are examined, it is usually found that they leave a 'place' for religion. This 'place' comes to assume more and more importance. The purely humanist aspects one by one fall away, and 'religion', sometimes tricked out in rather fantastic guise, re-emerges as dominant. This happened most strikingly in the work of Auguste Comte. For Comte, religion is outgrown only to grow into the religion of humanity.

Even so, these post-humanist religions themselves begin soon to wilt. The reason is that they are too explicit and conscious. In the worlds of Dilthey, they tend 'to achieve the sovereignty of the mind, the tendency to that intellectual quality which aims to make all activity conscious and to leave nothing behind in the darkness of mere behaviour, ignorant of itself'[1]. Dilthey, like Cowell, would seem to have regarded this movement towards intellectual explicitness as both inevitable and to be desired; but the truth is that such wholesale transcendence of the psychic realm is impossible. It would involve, as we shall see, a transcendence of the *human*, the conduct of life at the level of pure spirit or intellect: an impossible angelism. In academic circles of extreme refinement such intellectual culture has sometimes been considered an ideal, just as a life of pure spirituality has been aimed at in certain monastic communities. To the chagrin of the more ardent, the ideal is never so much as approached. The mistake is in failing to see that religion is an activity, a movement, whereby the opacity of the psychic sphere is penetrated, not permanently but as a constant process. The religious phase *is* this passage from psychic to spiritual, neither the total supersession of one nor the permanent attainment of the other.

In youth, when everything seems to be within reach, the impression is sometimes received that by some feat of spiritual athleticism, moral perfection can be attained at a single bound. But in life there is only effort, and falling away, and renewed effort, just as there needs to be eating and sleeping as well as thought and action. The mundane activities are not so much interruptions of spiritual activity; they are elements within that activity, which is an expression of the human. In a fruitful life, eating and sleeping are a part of culture, since they are means to psychic and spiritual renewal.

Collingwood observed:

> To fancy that religion lives either below or above the limits of reflective thought is fatally to misconceive either the nature of religion or the nature of reflective thought. It would be nearer the truth to say that in religion the life of reflection is concentrated in its intensest form, and that the special problems of theoretical and practical life all take their special forms by segregation out of the body of the religious consciousness, and retain their vitality only so far as they preserve their connection with it and with each other in it.[2]

That in religion the life of reflective thought is concentrated in its intensest form is surely not the case. The life of reflective thought is

121

concentrated in its *intensest* form at the intellectual or philosophical level. At its most intellectual level, religion does attain the level of reflective thought; but its springs are below this level, that is to say at the level of the psyche. Religion provides a cure for what at the psychic level has become a burden, an incubus. All religious experience is represented as a kind of awakening: the awakening precisely from a psychic sleep. Or, to preserve the metaphor of psychic closure, religion is the throwing open of the personality to a world of explicit values. Thus religion has always work to do; the accumulating psychic burden must continually be lightened, there must be a perpetual bringing to birth. It is because of this movement towards explicitness, towards the discovery of a world of values, that, as Collingwood was right to say, the various activities of theoretical and practical life take their origin from the religious consciousness. They 'retain their vitality only so far as they preserve their connection with it and with each other in it.' This is true above all of the scientific impulse, as all great scientific intelligences have realized, and lesser ones denied. The 'rationalist scientist' is a figure belonging to the brief phase of secularization through which we have been passing, a hero of the popular scientific press. The great men, from Newton to Heisenberg, have been men of deep spiritual insight.

Because religion is the act of conversion of the psychic into the spiritual, it lives in a psychic ambience, just as the psyche itself partly lives in the ambience of the organic. There are supposed to be religions totally devoid of ritual; but it will be found on inspection that such religions, even those which entail sitting in a meeting-house and remaining silent until 'the spirit moves' one to speak, are dependent upon a psychic atmosphere; for silence, as we have seen, is a prepotent source of PN. In the case of many devotees, *all* that is gained by attendance at a service of this kind is PN, and this is not a matter for ridicule: the psyche is gently brought to a state conducive to spiritual perception, which may or may not attain expression in another phase of life. Love can be experienced at moments other than those of 'making love': indeed, love-making, a physico-psychic experience, may be symbolic of a mutual devotion expressed in quite different fashion, or in the natural course of living together. On the other hand, the hieratic gestures, incantation, and singing associated with most religious observances are psychic expressions which, like all art, fortify the feelings and thus serve to further spiritual insight. No doubt shelling peas, or sweeping a room,[3] can do the same. But in ritualized religion the technique of psychic opening has been worked out methodically. It is remarkable how closely the various Christian 'cults' resemble one another, and how the Moslem manner of praying has remained uniform since the seventh century. Granted, there are moments when the traditional liturgy loses its efficacy, and we have suggested that this has been happening of recent years to Christian observance; but there is also reason to think that, after a period of experimentation, the old forms will in part be resumed, because they are compatible with the human norm, just as the drama, after a period of experiment, tends to move back to its traditional forms.

If that is so, a world without religion and culture is inconceivable. Even though the human race may transfer itself bodily elsewhere, perhaps to some of the comets believed to be behind the solar system, the pursuit of *values* will still be the *human* activity; the particular place in which that activity is pursued is immaterial. Although Eliot says that we may 'anticipate a period, of some duration, of which it is possible to say that it will have *no* culture',[4] he is presumably meaning culture in the sense of minority culture. A situation in which the psyche itself were deprived of nourishment would, if prolonged, mean extinction.

The relation between religion and culture

The point still to be clarified, however, is the exact relation between religion and culture; for while it is agreed, if not always for the right reasons, that culture is desirable and its continuance a social necessity, no such consensus of opinion exists regarding religion, even though we have contended that the religious impulse is an enduring activity, a necessary 'moment' in human development.

While it may be hazardous to make prophecies about future developments, we still return to the notion of the *human* and its implications. A purely rational being, actuated by what the philosophical radicals called the 'felicific calculus' and governed by logic, would not be human in the true sense. A race of such rational creatures might conceivably come into existence, perhaps as a result of genetic experiment or behavioural engineering like that envisaged in B. F. Skinner's *Beyond Freedom and Dignity* or the novels of Asimov; but they would be logical machines rather than human beings. Nor would they have anything resembling a culture. And if culture is that which makes life worth living, such rational automata would have nothing to 'live' for.

It is sometimes argued that the perfectly rational society would be Utopia. The originators of Utopias seek usually to demonstrate that the rational life is the truly natural life, as if man, placed in a suitable environment, would spontaneously act in conformity with reason. On the other hand, when ordinary people have time to spare, or are afforded the least excuse, they *tend* to frolic like little animals, to play, to dance, to make music, to throw a party, to get out into the open, to rush down to the sea: in short to 'have fun'. And while such activities may be largely a reaction against the routine of daily life ('Que la vie est quotidienne!'), there is reason to suppose that behaviour of this lighthearted kind is nearer to the human norm than action according to reason and calculation. At least it remains a periodical social necessity. As Huizinger said, 'Real civilization cannot exist in the absence of a certain play element'[5]; and Schiller spoke not merely of *ein ernsts Spiel* (earnest play) but of the fact that man is only a fully human being when he plays.[6] Indeed, before the Industrial Revolution, the drudgery of daily life was considerably alleviated in two respects: first, by exposure to the natural rhythm of nature which gave men time to breathe, and secondly by the introduction of festivities into work itself. Rice-planting in Japan was accompanied by special music and dancing. Traditional folk-songs like those of the Hebrides contained 'labour lilts and croons' – songs of walking, reaping, quern-grinding, milking, spreading the seawrack, etc. Such pleasurable accompaniments would seem to have been customary in the case of every fundamental activity, in both Orient and Occident. The *solemnity* associated with modern culture is due largely to the influence of minority culture.

Man is therefore a cultural animal as well as a religious animal; and the answer to the question how religion is related to culture is that religion 'secretes' culture in the course of its activity. That is why it is doubtful if culture can long continue to flourish in the absence of religious practice or at least a religious background, though it may be preserved for a while in an artificial state, along with certain weakening standards of 'good behaviour'.

Needless to say, such an association has given rise to much controversy. Even Eliot, who argued strongly in favour of the close link between religion and culture, admitted that he was able to perceive this association 'only in flashes'.[7] And a man of similar outlook such as the historian Christopher Dawson was prepared to argue that 'the rise of humanism and the modern sciences has created an *autonomous* sphere of culture which lies entirely outside the ecclesiastical domain and in which any direct intervention on the part of the Church would be resented as an intrusion'.[8] Whilst the second part of this statement may be accepted, the first is open to doubt, above all if the word 'religious' is substituted for 'ecclesiastical'. Dawson thereafter spoke of culture as being *national*, though not *political*. 'What is necessary is some organization which is neither political nor economic, and which will devote itself to the service of national life and the organization of national culture.'[9] And again:

> We need something in the nature of a non-political party to cover the ground that is left unoccupied – the issues outside party politics which are nevertheless essential to the national life. Such an organization would have to be completely free and non-official, since its supreme end must be to preserve the freedom of our national culture. It must find room for everyone who is not committed to a totalitarian ideology, and who is loyal to the national tradition and to national institutions and ideals.[10]

Written just before the last war, these passages have today a somewhat old-fashioned ring. What is the national culture of Great Britain? One is aware that an organization such as the British Council is supposed to be disseminating it, but that does not necessarily mean that it exists. Moreover, in what could a non-political party, devoted to the propagation and support of a national culture, consist? It would be either a folklore society, or a national – and therefore political, and hence nationalistic – party in disguise, rather like the Japanese Soka Gakkai.[11] Himself a Catholic, Dawson either did not see, or chose not to stress, that the national institutions of the United Kingdom, as at present constituted, include an Established Church, so that it is not true to say that national culture, such as it is, 'lies entirely outside the ecclesiastical domain'. In speaking of the former power of the Catholic faith, Dawson observes that 'today this universal background of popular culture has disappeared, and even among practising Christians religion no longer occupies the same psychic territory as it did in the past.'[12]

The second part of this statement, which is couched in terms congenial to our argument ('psychic territory'), may be accepted; but the first part is still not quite true – or rather it is so nearly true as to reveal its inadequacy. For what is left of popular culture, and what has meanwhile arisen as pop culture, is by no means devoid of religious content, taking religion in its widest sense, and this is true even more of European countries, above all France, to which in some respects the United Kingdom is drawing closer. To find oneself constrained to pronounce our culture more religious than it was before the war is distinctly odd, given the fact that secularization has gained such ascendancy, and that certain ministers of religion have exuberantly paraded their agnosticism. But the truth is that the 'national' culture of which Dawson speaks has all but disappeared (if it ever existed), while 'popular' culture, however diffuse, has moved in to occupy some of the 'psychic territory' left vacant.

Religious revivalism and outbursts of 'enthusiasm' sometimes attaining frenzy are periodical features of social life; but the new religious movements, especially among the young, exhibit a spontaneity which distinguishes them from more conventional 'returns to religion'. Organizations such as Moral Rearmament tended to fit in with conventional upper-middle-class cultural traditions, despite the Group's work in the industrial field and in race-relations: whereas the new movements seem to be upsurges of genuine, or at least thwarted, religious feeling. Moreover, they are revolutionary in a more fundamental sense than those ideological movements which call for the destruction of the established order. That some of the movements have grown out of hippy cults, such as that of flower-power, is significant; for we may see in them an impulse towards universal 'brotherhood' struggling for expression. By contrast, in Maoism, or in more recent Marxist movements, there is little evidence of love-of-one's-neighbour, though the original anarchists were passionate idealists. Hence the ugliness with which these creeds surround themselves.

It will be immediately apparent that we are speaking of religion and culture as primarily affording PN; and what we may deduce of 'primitive' religion and culture suggests that they were fundamentally joyous activities, bringing exultation to the worshippers. The artists who depicted the animals in the Lascaux caves, and those who represented the Great Mother in Anatolia, not to speak of the builders of Angkor Wat and Borobudur, were surely expressing fervour and adoration; and what we know of the beginnings of Christianity lends substance to the view that the converts were filled often with 'the spirit'. The early Christians were known for their 'love feasts'. Indeed, the original form of the Mass involved a gathering of friends. The stern, forbidding, elements in religion – or what passes for it – grew up with an organized priesthood and above all with the establishment of churches wielding social power. Even so, those peoples who have retained traditions of communal acts of worship, such as certain African communities and the negro element in the United States, practise Christianity (and other religions) in a manner more vital than most Christians of the Western tradition. True, the Easter services of the Orthodox Church retain something of the old ardour; and there is a growing tendency in Protestant churches to follow the service with a gathering in the Church Hall, where an atmosphere of fellowship is created often more in keeping with the spirit of Christianity than the sometimes dreary ceremony preceding it. Here, as elsewhere, we take examples chiefly from Christianity. Of the mood of fellowship engendered by certain Buddhist and Shinto rites we have already spoken.

Religious institutions

It is because emotions cannot be generated at will, but are always by-products of directed activity, that institutions are necessary, even though such institutions can sometimes inhibit the consumption of PN. Hence the recurrent need, already alluded to, for reform and renewal. Religions can no more survive without some elementary organization than education can survive without schools. True, every so often there will be movements for abolishing the church or for 'deschooling society',[13] but these are merely preludes to the foundation of different institutions. Moreover, for the purpose of launching their attacks upon institutionalism, the reformers themselves make use of institutions, such as the publishing houses which issue their books. So far as culture and its transmission are concerned, the need for institutions is imperative. Hence the importance of libraries, museums, and above all universities, which 'cultural revolutionaries' wish to abolish in favour of 'freer' institutions (such as anti-universities), of which the least one can say is that they will not remain free for very long.

If cultures are 'secreted' or precipitated by religions, it is hardly surprising that we should find in every age a certain measure of cultural petrification and stagnation; for the rites and cults of a culture are no less compulsive and enduring for being less obvious and marked, than the stereotyped cults of religion. To define the 'style' of a culture is extremely difficult, just as it is difficult to isolate the subtle differences in behaviour of peoples geographically contiguous, such as the French and the British. A culture is therefore like an *Umwelt*; it is an *Umwelt* in which the human animal, or a particular group of human animals, finds itself psychically and spiritually 'at home'. For our culture is our psychic and spiritual home which we must collaborated to maintain, just as animals collaborate in maintaining their 'ecological niches'. A whole science, that of cultural anthropology, has recently arisen in order to study such human *Umwelts*, and to compare them with those of the animal kingdom. What this science may fail to grasp is the part played by PN in maintaining the *Umwelt* and in providing its *raison d'être*. People cling to their homes, or establish others of similar 'style', for reasons we have given; but the home can prove oppressive to its inmates if its stimulus-signals and sign-symbols become too limited in scope. This oppression is experienced by many an adolescent, whose biological mutation brings on a corresponding mental crisis, as psychic religious emotions are partly transformed into spiritual ones (the transformation is never complete). The resulting outburst of 'religious' zeal may sometimes take political form. The adolescent becomes a dedicated crusader, seeking to realize in practice the new values of which he has become aware. At this point, there is usually an awakening of love, which, often in contradiction to the new sexual urge, reaches out to someone who can 'respond' on the idealistic plane. This is the moment, too, when the heroes are no longer (if they ever were) the parents or guardians of the home; they are men bent on the reform of society, ostensibly in the name of human brotherhood or 'universal love', and preferably those lent enchantment by distance (both geographical and psychic), such as in the 1960s a Mao or a Che Guevara. These become the more heroic and exalted if they have combined their mission with an element of romance, which the Bolivian revolutionary so successfully managed to do, lending his reputation to movements of sexual liberation which the conventional revolutionary, almost always a puritan, might otherwise have repudiated.

In such circumstances, violence exercises its attractions. 'It is the violence of Che Guevara, his life, his rapacious good looks, his fabulous death, which constitute his appeal. Nobody decorates their bed-sitter with posters of Bolivian miners.'[14] This is of course a signal demonstration of the inadequacy of the 'materialist view of history'. The youth who should strictly be impelled by purely material motives is carried on the wings of an exalted idealism. This lasts until such time as the ardour, which seemed at first so pure and disinterested, encounters its first disillusionment, usually because the movement has become a prey to petty jealousies. Then it is that the conventions of one's culture may come to seem not so superannuated after all; that the institutions to be ruthlessly swept away show themselves to possess a certain merit, if not quite the same as before; and that the home, now perhaps deserted, evokes a wistful nostalgia. Those countries which have undergone a genuine revolution tend, as soon as the dust of turmoil has settled, to establish a regime of almost humdrum conformity. The leading ideologists, if not the instigators, of the revolt, are usually removed, and police vigilance ensures that no one shall venture to repeat the revolutionary experiment. Meanwhile, it is surprising how much of the old religio-cultural tradition still remains. Visitors to Russia or even to China may, as we have pointed out, find traces of the former regime more clearly in evidence than in countries which have undergone revolutions much less violent. This is no doubt because the Marxist-Leninist gospel possesses scant appeal for the bulk of the Russian and Chinese people, for there is precious little psychic nourishment to be found in Dialectical Materialism – a doctrine which most of them probably regard in private as a load of rubbish. It needs an intelligentsia to take rubbish, especially theoretical rubbish, seriously. Indeed, if the official regimes were to be abolished tomorrow, it would probably be found that the psychic loss had proved negligible, and that the old religious tradition would speedily reassert itself, if in the case of Russia it has not already done so.

The alternative society

Notwithstanding the tendency to cultural petrification, and the short-lived character of so much youthful revolt, the idea of the 'alternative society', which really means the irrational society, must apparently be taken seriously: for it would seem at first sight to offer a complete break with the values of the culture, both Christian and post-Christian, which for centuries has sustained Europe and, in some respects, the whole world. Yet is this really so? Is not the alternative society rather another case of an ideal remaining parasitic upon the religious traditions of the West, though reflecting those traditions in a distorted and often crude fashion? Let us examine some of its credentials. According to Jeff Nuttall, who is our best guide to the *Sturm und Drang* epoch, the dropping of the atom bomb was the first signal for the movement towards an alternative society. 'The people who had not reached puberty at the time of the bomb were incapable of conceiving life with a future.' Young people found that

> Dad was a liar. He lied about the war and he lied about sex. He lied about the bomb and he lied about the future. He lived his life on an elaborate system of pretence that had been going on for hundreds of years. The so called 'generation gap' started then and has been increasing ever since.[15]

The discovery that there was no future was coeval, it will be observed, with the beginning of the 'sexual revolution'. This was also mixed up with the jazz-cult. 'Charlie Parker's records began to be distributed', and we have already been told that 'in truth, if Charlie Parker was not possessed by supernatural forces, then there's nothing supernatural about genius'. Jazz, we are told, is an American slang expression meaning 'copulate'; and 'in the underworld jazz produced an ethos and a pattern of behaviour that the world's young were ready to grasp like drowning creatures, rushing towards hip as their parents were rushing towards the merciful oblivion of death'. Moreover, 'the hipster, or hep-cat, was the first exemplary citizen of the alternative society', to which is added the rather bewildering information that the hipster was 'the big-city twentieth century descendant of the post-emancipation big-talkin' gambler'. Finally, we are told that ' "one is hip or one is square . . . one is a rebel or one conforms" ' (this illuminating statement is from Norman Mailer's *White Negro*).

Now for some history. The 'first public showing, in England at any rate, of radical divergence on the part of young people' was the teddy-boys, though

> no teddy boy, at that time, was sufficiently clear in his own mind to know, or sufficiently articulate to say, what his deepest responses knew, that the established world was the emanation of

a gigantic falsehood and he wanted out. He also wanted to stop using the shield of the official poker-faced popular culture.

The next group to wear a new style of clothes were

the motor-cycle cowboys, the 'Wild Ones'. Their uniform, the second to emerge in England, possibly the first in America, consisted, still consists, of skin-tight jeans and black leather jacket. Accessories could include peaked cap (further shades of the SS), calf-length boots, neck bandanas, Nazi war relics, big brash transfers and later, in England, where the 'ton-up boys' became the 'rockers' (indicating a defensive adherence to the simple early forms of rock 'n roll) ornate patterns of brass studs, tiger-tails, fringes, chains and bells.

With its 'shades of the SS' and 'Nazi war relics', this uniform is then described in lyrical terms:

Very little has come out of the whole teenage development that has more beauty than decorated rocker-jackets. They showed the creative impulse at its purest and most inventive. Without any sentimentality it's possible to say that they constitute tribal art of a high degree, symmetrical, ritualistic, with a bizarre metallic brilliance and a high fetishistic power.[16]

In other words, we have here a definite religio-*culture*, but, surprisingly enough, in view of the opposition to the Bomb, it is a culture not infused with compassion but with something like its opposite. Very soon there were 'the huge pitched battles (between mods and rockers) of 1964'; and 'everywhere there were zippers, leather boots, PVC, see-through plastics, male make-up, a thousand overtones of sexual deviation, particularly sadism. . . . ' Indeed, the author licks his lips at the 'satisfying' way in which 'a traffic stream on a hot Saturday, stalled, crammed with sweaty pink families trapped with one another as the Mini-Minor was trapped in the queue, could be utterly negated, cancelled, by a column of gleaming rockers hurtling past them to the round-about'. The author further explains that this was 'the only way the growing mind could deal with the constant probability of unprecedented pain and horror which the squares took such trouble to preserve.'

The squares were not the only ones, it appears. 'Eulogized by poets Ginsberg, Kesey and McClure, the Angels, under their president Sonny Barger, terrorized Californian society by their arrogant mindless brutality, the extravagant splendour of their filthy array, and their custom of multiple rape.'[17]

Yet, writing in 1966, Nuttall maintains that 'the Beatles were and are the biggest single catalyst in this whole acceleration in the development of the sub-culture' – a rather strange diagnosis to be made in the case of young men who, whatever they may later have said, accepted decorations from the Queen[18], accumulated vast fortunes, and lived what were essentially Establishment lives. Moreover, their generally decent behaviour, despite the occasional antics of one of their number who was tragically murdered, contrasted markedly with the preoccupation of the Underground with the aberrant and the scabrous. 'Both Brady and Hindley (the Moors murderers) were working-class libertines in a world where the working-class libertine, from Sillitoe's Arthur Seton to Genet's Claire and Solange, had been eulogized by the rebel culture.' The author admits not only that 'a good many of us were trying, like Mailer, to move out of deadlock by breaking all taboos', but also that 'we had all applauded and romanticized the American leather-jackets, particularly Hell's Angels, with their swastikas and cheese cutters'. Moreover, 'there were numerous Nazi overtones in literary life, like the distinguished writer who sent his mistress iron crosses and photos of Hitler signed by himself'. Nuttall recounts that 'Keith Musgrave and I were discussing publicly disembowelling a human corpse and hurling the guts at the audience. Nitsch lamented the fact that corpses were available to medical students but not to artists. So did we.' And he adds, with a show of honesty, that 'moral shame, moral absurdity, moral abuse, moral paradox and moral outrage had frozen us at a point of almost total negativity'.

Reading this book, one is driven to the view that Nuttall's so-called Underground movement and its obsession with aberrant sexuality, and with jazz as a sexual expression, was nothing but an ungainly product of Puritanism. This is a point which he all but acknowledges in one place. When he states that 'Boroughs currently attempts control of people's living by playing tapes of obscene or pleasant sound in their vicinity', he does not appear to realize that the obscenity only works, if it does work, because of the presence of still powerful taboos. You can shock only what is there to be outraged. Sick humour is humorous, and not just sick, because of a prevailing state of moderate health. He argues *ad nauseam* that the hip is aware of 'the fact of imminent nuclear destruction which the square persistently ignores', and that 'the significant division is no longer between east and west but between square and hip all over the globe'; but his case reaches a level of bathetic absurdity when he declares, upon what evidence we do not know, that the squares 'are so largely suicidal because they never get a good fuck'. Moreover, the book abounds with approving references to 'distinguished people', to writers' conferences, to Albert Hall meetings, and to the fact that this or that jazz-number got into the Top Twenty. His pages are bespattered with name-droppings. About such surface glitter there is not much that is 'underground'; and indeed towards the end of the book he admits that about 1965 'the Underground was suddenly there on the surface, in open ground with a following of thousands'. And so, after the *Oz* Trial, Richard Neville's writing for the capitalist press, and Jerry Rubin's working for the system itself, it has remained.

In the light of such developments, it is difficult to see in what the alternative society is supposed to consist. True, Nuttall talks about 'a new culture, based on total freedom, extended sensibility, and spirituality of some kind re-established in place of politics', and a concern 'for the business of being human'; but the actual attitude – 'a maturing of the hip point of view' –

> was, and is, one in which despair, neurosis, mental unbalance are all part of the day-to-day norm, everybody's starting-point, at which all former reference-points – society, morality, religion – are eradicated, where the individual may move to establish his own values and relationships according to his own experience.

Now this, if examined closely, is found to be either total anarchy or simply 'morals in reverse'. Speaking of Genet's *Our Lady of the Flowers*, Philip Toynbee wrote:

> This book subscribes, morally speaking, to the tired old myth of 'the Bourgeois and the Outlaw'. It was a myth when Goethe evolved it in *Werther*, when Byron expanded it, when Baudelaire and a dozen other great nineteenth century writers subtly transformed it. But if it had not exhausted itself with Jarry, it had certainly done so with Dada and the Surrealists. . . . Genet is enslaved by the conventional – and therefore inadequate – morals of his time. He accepts them unquestioningly, and believes that when he has reversed them he has achieved a new morality.[19]

That is a pertinent observation, not least because it deals with writers and movements with which Nuttall is also concerned. He and his fellow-advocates of the alternative society are quite simply 'enslaved to the conventional'. Their alternative society is in fact the correlative society; one battens upon the other. It is interesting to find Nuttall casually throwing away the remark that, in the mid-1950s when 'the rich odour of marijuana became, for the first time, a familiar part of the London atmosphere', youthful affluence was playing its part. 'Teenage wages were going up *and so were student grants* [my italic]'. In short, a good deal of protest was financed by the very authorities against whom the young were supposed to be in rebellion.

Although 'the route to God is insanity, the dissolution of identity through the dissolution of rational relationships', and although 'the future is a void' and 'the only way to deal with void is by a game of chance, some absurd pattern of behaviour', Nuttall does from time to time issue remarks which have the ring of truth and a direct bearing on our theme. 'Art', he says (and by art he would appear to include culture in general), 'is knit to society by religion. If religion becomes non-religion, corrupt, then art, in order to remain art, must divide itself off from society.' This is surely true; but it does not follow that art, divorced from society, must take on the aspect of absurdity, any more than it follows that the 'route to God is insanity' even when religion is not corrupt. Here again Nuttall is taking the traditional point of view of existence as rational, and reversing it. In the Preface to his book, he states that what is irrational in its nature can only be irrationally understood; but an understanding which is irrational is not understanding in any accepted sense; it is a mental state which, having failed to trace back the irrational to the point at which it deviates from the norm, has not yet reached understanding. Like everything else, religion is always in *some* degree corrupt, and culture will necessarily reflect that corruption. Far from being the true enemies of corruption, the Underground movements are in secret agreement with that which they oppose; and that is why they exude the sado-masochistic influences of which Nuttall seems lingeringly to approve. Hence the violence which he so deplores in Vietnam as to rank it higher in the scale of evil than that of the Moors murders (but only the violence committed by the Americans, needless to say, not that of the Viet Cong), calls up a counter-violence in which he exults. Jacques Maritain had something to say about that:

Man is so formed that the worst scenes of violence, far from causing him to react in accordance with reason and endeavour to prevent the infection from spreading, finds within him a secret ally, a kind of wicked resignation, a temptation to his fatalistic inclinations.[20]

That is precisely the impression with which Nuttall's book leaves us. The real Underground, such as that which opposed the Nazis or resists the present repressive regime in the Soviet Union, is never tainted in this way, because these men knew, and know, that they have in the people a silent ally. Consequently, they seek by every means 'to prevent the infection from spreading'. The false Underground, while claiming to condemn the violence of the Bomb, etc., openly proliferates its own violence, and, while condemning the bourgeois 'hypocrisy' about sex, cultivates 'a thousand overtones of sexual deviation'.[21]

Rejection of the scientific world view

Many theories of culture, and perhaps most conceptions of the counter-culture, do not recognize the province or relevance of religion at all. One work on the counter-culture, written at about the same time as Nuttall's, ignores traditional religion altogether, though stressing the importance of eastern religious influence. This is Theodore Roszak's book *The Making of a Counter-Culture: Reflections on the Technocratic Society and its Youthful Opposition* (1970). It is on the whole a balanced and temperate book, much better written than *Bomb Culture*; for the latter is often hysterical, as well as being interspersed with passages of what is called 'experimental writing', some of it barely intelligible and often, like much writing of the kind, exceedingly dull. And Roszak is a useful authority to look back to.

The assumption with which he starts is that the orthodox culture opposed by youth is 'fatally and contagiously diseased'. This culture Roszak defines as a technocratic totalitarianism: that is to say, it is the result of rule by experts who have a 'relentless quest for efficiency, for order, and for ever more rational control'. And he maintains that 'nothing less is required than the subversion of the scientific world-view, with its entrenched commitment to an egocentric and cerebral mode of consciousness, and its replacement by 'a new

135

culture in which the non-intellective capacities of the personality – those capacities which take fire from visionary splendour and the experience of human communion – become the arbiters of the good, the true, and the beautiful'. Furthermore, he believes that only among youth can 'the radical discontent and innovation be found that might transform this disoriented civilization of ours into something a human being can identify as home'; and he believes that 'what a mere handful of beatniks pioneered in Allen Ginsberg's youth will have become the life-style of millions of college-age youth'. He adds: 'Is there any other ideal toward which the young can grow that looks half so appealing?'

When we examine Roszak's statements closely, we find a number of important but stealthily induced qualifications. After his eulogy of the young, he admits that the creation by youth of a new society 'is too big a job for them to do successfully'; that while the youthful appetite 'is healthily and daringly omnivorous . . . it urgently requires mature minds to feed it'; that 'once a cultural disjunction opens up in society, nothing can be guaranteed'; and that the new youthful counter-culture is 'a culture so radically disaffiliated from the mainstream assumptions of our society that it scarcely looks to many like a culture at all, but takes on the alarming experience of a barbaric intrusion'.

Although he argues with great skill that the counter-culture is entirely different from anything that has appeared since the birth of Christianity, he acknowledges that Christianity in its time was upheld by 'the very scum of the earth', people 'whose own counter-culture was, at this stage, little more than a scattering of suggestive ideas, a few crude symbols and a desperate longing'. This is very much as the counter-culture appears to us today. But, despite the disorganized condition of youth, its confused aspirations, and the 'outlandish' nature of the comparison with what he calls the Christian *scandalum*, 'all revolutionary changes are unthinkable until they happen. . . and then they are understood to be inevitable'.

It is when we inspect the *content* of the new counter-culture that we begin to have our misgivings. Certainly, the prescriptions for our salvation issued by Allen Ginsberg, and quoted at length in *Bomb Culture*, bear a remarkable resemblance, not least in his insistent recommendation of 'moral codes and standards which include drugs, orgy, music and primitive magic as worship rituals', to the way of life of ancient Rome *against which* Christianity resolutely set its face.[22] Indeed, when Roszak speaks of 'the need of the young for unrestricted joy', we begin to feel that he is recommending that bleak permissiveness which, in referring to the 'executive morality' of *Playboy,* he appears to condemn. For of one thing we may be certain: in this life 'unrestricted joy' is not within the reach of anybody, young or old, and to suggest otherwise is seriously to mislead. In 1973 Father Kenneth Leech, in *Keep the Faith, Baby,* told us that today there is a 'rediscovery of the body and a search for physical ecstasy'. Well, the body is always being rediscovered. Brigitte Bardot rediscovered it some years before. The *Sun* newspaper is daily rediscovering it. Young people, as Roszak says, 'bring with them almost nothing but healthy instincts'; and that is to bring with them appetites which, if allowed unrestricted exercise, will most certainly invite that 'barbaric intrusion' which he describes as constituting an 'alarming experience'. In fact, however, we understood – did we not? – the young to bring a great deal more than simply their instincts. We understood them to bring, along with those instincts, new values and ideals which are to act as 'arbiters of the good, the true, and the beautiful': such a culture being a living and nourishing one because of its repudiation of 'the scientific world-view'. If all that youth can contribute is sheer appetite, however healthy, no wonder that mature minds are needed to impose some control over that 'omnivorous' and clamorous hunger.

Next, it is impossible to subvert a view of the world like that of science unless that view can be shown to be false. Such a *Weltanschauung* cannot be overthrown merely because it is antipathetic to a particular generation. Admittedly, most people, if given the choice, would prefer a magical to a scientific view of the world. It would save a good deal of trouble and drudgery. It would be most convenient if we could control the weather, or destroy our enemies, by the performance of simple rites. The point is that we know, or we have found out from experience, that the magical view of the world is false. What Roszak is repudiating is not so much the scientific view as the materialistic philosophy – due to an 'egocentric and cerebral mode of consciousness' – which has become associated with it. He is not the first to have done so. Blake, whom he quotes, did so. Rousseau did so. The Romantic poets did so. Scientists and philosophers such as Whitehead did so. So have all the higher religions. In any case, the espousal of 'the non-intellective capacities of the personality' is nothing new. And if, as Roszak says, the scientific community no longer regards Jung and Bergson as major thinkers, that is because the work of these men has been assimilated into a point of view which, already adumbrated by Nietzsche, Schopenhauer and Kierkegaard, has gained enormous influence, so that it has assumed for many the status of orthodoxy. Apostles of *reason* are hard to find these days, while every gospel of irrationalism has its enthusiastic band of followers.

We have dwelt at length on the testimony of Nuttall and Roszak because, looking back twenty years, they mirror with reasonable accuracy the mood of the time. Since then, the 'alternative' mentality has gone somewhat into recess: but we have the birth of a new irrationalism with the advent of *kitsch* – a movement of deliberate 'bad taste'. This again battened on the 'good' taste of the previous epoch. There followed a *dégringolade* into another and more extreme uprush of bad taste, Punk Rock. The death in 1979 from a heroin overdose of Sid Vicious, the Punk idol, while on bail in New York for murdering his American girlfriend, marked the horrendous end of the first stage of the movement; but the Punk hairstyle – semi-shaven and almost rainbow dyed 'Mohican' style, sticking up in spikes – continued to be observed in urban streets as these lines were written. It is possible that Punk was a desperate effort to extract PN from the commission of sheer outrage; but the outrage is now largely a theoretical one, and the revolutionary fervour seems to have subsided. The movement bears some resemblance to a heretical religious sect. The members act with a degree of solemnity; they are prepared to suffer discomfort – safety-pins through the flesh, etc; they have distinctive costume, usually black, with various accoutrements (studded dog-collars, etc.) purchased at special boutiques. Finally, they still depend to some extent upon drugs – LSD and 'speed'. In order to counter the bleakness of their lives – the majority would seem to be unemployed but obviously not destitute – they insert between themselves and their environment an environment of their own, which is precisely their 'outrageous' costume. In the section on environmental matters, we referred to this not uncommon habit. It is a way of asserting identity. Such is their way of subsisting within the bosom of what, compared with the 1930s, is an affluent society though, for them, a psychically famished one.

This is very different from Roszak's 'visionary splendours', etc. Punks seem to have no philosophy and, so far as one can see, no social idealism. What Roszak is seeking, especially in his references to the non-intellective capacities of the personality, is precisely the source of PN which 'the scentific view of the world' has so often stifled. He says as much. 'Building the good society is not primarily a social, but a *psychic* task' (my italics); and by 'society' he presumably means 'culture'. This is true. But, as we have argued, the springs of PN cannot deliberately be made to flow; they are a by-product primarily of genuine artistic and religious activity. All action which generates emotion capable of fertilizing practical life is psychically nutritive: but the action must be directed to an end, there must be a *work* of art, a moral or charitable act. An aesthetic or a moral experience is psychically nourishing as a foundation for spiritual nourishment derived from the apprehension of values. Culture is at once the residue of such activity, awaiting activation in books, works of art, etc., and the style or way of life maintained by communal action. That is why we have called culture the secretion of religious activity.

Not only is culture the secretion of religion, but this secretion helps in turn to sustain religious insight. As Hardy said, 'poetry and religion touch each other, or rather modulate into each other'.[23] Pictures, sculpture, and music inspired by religion are used to furnish and grace churches and temples. What religion gives to art, art may give back to religion; and what is not fitted for such restitution is lacking in genuine aesthetic inspiration. The secular art of our time is not, in the true sense, *dedicated,* but too often merely a sterile pattern-making; but where a Matisse or a Chagall or even a Cocteau reach the highest point of their genius, is in a religious context, as recent years have shown. Just as 'tout le reste est littérature', so all that is not at root living religious art (not that its overt *content* need be religious) is art for the collector, the dealer, the connoisseur, the gallery – that is to say, art as investment or as status symbol, devoid of all but *ersatz* PN. The most sensitive in any generation shovel this form of art out of their minds, and start creating afresh; but this does not prevent the 'artistic world' from purchasing the junk and selling it off to the public at considerable profit. Then there are the purveyors of culture *per se*, aesthetic antiquaries who produce anthologies of past artistic achievements. Such catalogues are of dead or fossilized artefacts, which, divorced from their contexts, cannot enrich the psyche.

There is one final point which requires clarification. If art, or the aesthetic mode of activity, is not directly open to values, does the religious apprehension imply the transcendence of the psyche? No, because spiritual and intellectual activity, deprived of psychic breath, cannot exist in such a transcendent state. The religious insight results from the achievement of a new transparency. The visionary who sees a *vision* is still seeing through the medium of art; and Shelley was right to say that 'poetry is the breath and finer spirit of *all* knowledge'.[24] We may compare the psychic realm to a lighted room of which the curtains are drawn. Life has a comfortable but self-enclosed aspect, and the occupants of the room feel reasonably at home. But when the curtains begin to let through a vague light, the impulse is to open them, upon which the real light of day streams in. The world outside is still observed through the windows, but the vision is now greatly extended and it is real. We do not ever leave the chamber of the psyche, but we are aware, if we choose to be, of a new world outside it, into which we have an urge — for ever denied us in the human state — to venture.

> A man that looks on glass,
> On it may stay his eye;
> Or if he pleaseth, through it pass,
> And then the heaven espy.[25]

6

Psychical distance, the fine arts, amusement and 'magic'

Bullough's essay

In 1912, Edward Bullough, Professor of Italian at the University of Cambridge, wrote an essay entitled ' "Psychical Distance" as a Factor in Art and as an Aesthetic Principle'. This essay came to exert considerable influence, even outside the sphere of pure aesthetics, and it is still the subject of controversy.[1] Bullough's argument may be summarized as follows. There are moments in life when our 'affections' – that is to say, anything which affects our being, bodily or spiritually, i.e. as sensation, perception, emotional state or idea – are somehow switched off, or put out of gear, and as a result we contemplate objects or phenomena 'objectively', as if a certain measure of 'distance' separated us from them. This distance, which is different in kind from physical distance, is called by Bullough 'psychical'; and he argues, with some telling illustrations, that distance in this sense is an aesthetic principle, the sign that we are entering the realm of art or the province of the beautiful as opposed to the merely agreeable or pleasant. It is also peculiar to man. Only man can keep his distance.

In this context, the relation of the self to the object is by no means an *impersonal* one. On the contrary, it is highly personal; but the relation has been 'cleared of the practical concrete nature of its appeal', and involves the contemplative attitude. In this sense, Bullough's theory resembles that which S. Alexander put forward in his *Beauty and Other Forms of Value* (1933), whereby art was said to be the result of the constructive impulse become contemplative.

To assert that aesthetic appreciation results merely from the existence of psychical distance, however, would be too simple. There is what Bullough calls the 'antinomy of distance'. Aesthetic apprecia-

141

tion, and indeed aesthetic production, is genuine in so far as distance, though present, is reduced to a minimum: in other words, 'the antinomy of distance' entails that distance should decrease to the point just short of disappearance. Everyone must find his distance-limit, but the artist has a special gift (not of course always a conscious one) for judging what, in any particular work of art, this limit shall be.

The bearing of such a theory upon the concept of PN and its relation to culture will be obvious, as will be the divergences between the two approaches. Bullough is striving to uphold the view that there is such a thing as pure art, an activity completely removed from 'the realm of practical systems and ends'. Moreover, it is an activity which, as we gather, increases in aesthetic purity in so far as it depends upon the specifically aesthetic senses, such as sight and hearing ('the ground for the rejection of the lower senses has always been that they mediate only agreeable sensations'). We have pronounced this type of art 'fine art'; but we have not yet enquired whether such fine art can exist *in itself,* as an independent faculty, though the conclusion of the previous chapter would suggest that this is a heresy peculiar to the modern era. On this subject, Bullough ventures an interesting remark, but one of which he seems hardly to appreciate the implications. Speaking of the art and literature of the past, he observes that

> provided the Distance is not too wide, the result of its intervention
> has everywhere been to enhance the *art*-character of such works
> and to lower their original ethical force and appeal. Thus in the
> central dome of the Church (Sta Maria dei Miracoli) at Saranno
> are depicted the heavenly hosts in ascending tiers, crowned by the
> benevolent figure of the Divine Father, bending from the windows
> of heaven to bestow his blessing upon the assembled community.
> The mere realism of foreshortening and of the boldest vertical
> perspective may well have made the naive Christian of the six-
> teenth century conscious of the Divine Presence – *but for us it has
> become a work of Art* [my italics].

Perhaps the chief key to the meaning of this passage is the suggestion, or indeed the assumption, that, in comparison with Christians of the sixteenth century, *we* are mature, of age, grown-up. Our predecessors were so naive as to interpret the painting as meaning or symbolizing that which the artist intended it to mean and symbolize. To us, sophisticated twentieth century observers, Distance has, so to speak, lent disenchantment, or the capacity to demythologize, so that a religious painting, far from making us 'conscious of the Divine Presence' or aware of any 'original ethical or social force of appeal at all', has left us merely with an aesthetic impression; or, to be more exact, it has made us aware that, having been stripped of all its original significance, it has *become* a work of art – whatever a work so thoroughly *dépouillé* may be said to have turned into.

Distance in this sense clearly means Distance in time rather than Distance in the psychical realm: or rather psychical Distance pushed to such a degree that the work is no longer contemplated in Bullough's intended sense, even though he has entered the qualification 'provided the distance is not too wide' and has spoken of the 'intervention' of Distance as having everywhere enhanced the '*art*-character of such works'. The truth is that if a work of art is wholly emptied of its intended meaning, and cannot move us as the artist intended, nothing is *enhanced* about it but rather diminished; and this reduction of content, instead of presenting us with 'pure form', leaves us precisely with a pattern, dependent to a large extent on 'mere realism of foreshortening and of the boldest perspective', which, if it has thereby *become* a work of art, has turned into something other than a work of art as normally conceived.

The implications for PN

In the light of this criticism, Bullough's thesis, stimulating and provocative as it is, seems at root unsatisfactory; but for our present purpose what matters is its implications for PN. If we recall Cowper's remarks about nature and the psychic nourishment with which it provided him, we realize that he was referring to a concrete, living experience, though rendered in metaphorical terms. He 'drank' the streams, etc.; he was not contemplating 'pure form'. Similarly, the art of the past appeals to us, and nourishes the psyche, only in so far as it is alive or relevant: that is to say, the 'consciousness of the Divine Presence', as in the example given, must still in some fashion be experienced. And if we, modern grown-ups as opposed to naifs of the past, are unable to attain such consciousness at all, the work of art ceases to be nutritional. Bullough speaks of 'the twofold character of the aesthetic state in which we *know* a thing *not* to exist, but *accept* its existence' (his italics); but, *pace* all those who have subscribed to Coleridge's 'willing suspension of disbelief', how can we *accept* the existence or reality of anything if we know it not to exist (e.g., if, while unable to believe in the Christian faith, we repudiate the sacred in general)? The 'willing suspension of disbelief for the moment' (Coleridge's actual words) is a disbelief in inessentials, in order that our attention may be released to probe a deeper core of meaning. For that reason it is a *suspension*; it is not an imposition; and it is only for the moment. Bullough's variation on Coleridge errs in being a good deal too rigid.

On the other hand, there is a measure of truth in Bullough's concept of psychical Distance, and he is not to be impugned because he is stating something evident. All PN must undergo some kind of initial preparation, or be transmitted through a refining medium, or submit to interpretation, before it can be efficacious. The development of a culture is precisely the building up and codifying of this refining process, which, because it is a process, is continuous. For this reason, we should prefer in general the expression 'psychic refinement' rather than psychic distance, because the latter can only with difficulty be distinguished from *physical* distance, as at least one passage of Bullough's essay testifies. The development of more and more delicate instruments for transmitting information, or for recording music, the increasing attention paid to acoustics, the measures taken to improve lighting and temperature in the display of pictures, are means to the more effective absorption of PN; so that the attempts recently made to render orchestral music in conditions resembling those which originally prevailed are not necessarily more 'faithful to the original'. We may suppose that Palestrina or Bach would have welcomed, had the opportunity presented itself, the technical advances of our time. We cannot pretend to know what the original may have been in their minds.

Again, Bullough's essay makes it abundantly clear that art for him consists solely of the 'fine arts'. This is the reason why he promotes seeing and hearing above the other senses, and perhaps why he remarks that 'the more intense the aesthetic absorption, the less one "likes", consciously, the experience'. For it is recognized that the fine arts involve, both in their creation and in their appreciation, a form of discipline. Small wonder, therefore, that he declares that 'attempts to raise "culinary art" to the level of a Fine Art have failed in spite of all propaganda, as completely as the creation of scent or liqueur "symphonies" '; whereas what is clearly wrong is not the arts themselves but the 'attempts to raise' them to an unnatural level. There is a hierarchy in the arts as in everything else. We have already said that the culinary art, cooking, belongs not to culture but to civilization; it is a technical phenomenon; whereas gastronomy is a psychophysical science which, because it is bound up with particular social instincts and customs, belongs rightfully to culture and has a legitimate, if neglected, place in it.

A man who fails to appreciate gastronomy but who remains devoted to the fine arts is a cultured man in the sense understood by the apostles of minority culture, but he is not cultured in that broad sense. Culture need not necessarily impose undue strain on the participant. Rather PN should promote that relish of which Thomas More spoke, or that worthwhileness of living referred to by Eliot. A poet such as Dylan Thomas, who seems deliberately to have gone over his poems in order to make them obscure, is engaging in minority culture snobbery;[2] for, as we said earlier, whenever culture is regarded as a social minority affair, there is a tendency for the cult of snobbery to flourish. Membership of a set or clique assumes an importance greater than the need for genuine appreciation. Anyone who has had occasion repeatedly to attend *vernissages* will have remarked on the scant attention paid to the exhibits, even by the critics whose job it is to write about them, and the importance attached to being seen 'to be there', to be greeting the 'right' people, to be making the 'correct' remarks.

Similarly, many an exhibition programme contains an introduction, usually by a well-known name, which is evidently not meant to be understood in the accepted sense but consists of a message to the initiates composed largely of 'in' jargon. A decade later or even sooner this will be scrapped in favour of one equally obscure but no less designed to suggest that you and I belong to the same set and that all the rest are philistines. This is very different from making genuine war on Philistia, as a Matthew Arnold or an F. R. Leavis did, because the minority culture snobs depend upon a large community of illiterates to offset their exclusiveness. The minority culture snob derives his PN not from art, which he often does not understand (Lord Clark, who should have known, spoke of the 'contemporary attitude of pretending to understand works of art in order not to appear philistines'[3]), but from the sense of prestige or status, due often to the presence of a charismatic leader; and, being snobbish first and cultured second, he is willing to switch allegiances if circumstances dictate. The leader, too, can swiftly change his role, as in the case of the member of the intelligentsia who is in the habit of putting himself at the head of successive artistic or politico-artistic movements. This happens more often in France than in Britain. In Britain art is not merely less involved with politics but less inclined to excite partisan passions.

Thus it soon becomes clear that although the minority intelligentsia *appears* to be cultivating art, the art in question is merely the symbol of a way of life, sedulously cultivated and often expounded in manifestos. Both the Futurist Manifesto and the Surrealist Manifesto were about *life*; and when the Marxians criticize an artist or writer who appears to be producing work in conflict with the party-line, they accuse him of 'bourgeois aestheticism', whereas what he is doing is to reflect a new way of life. This is often an implicit protest against those bourgeois tendencies to which Marxism itself is subject.

Often the 'new' art which the genuine artist creates is recognized and seized on by women in advance of men, because in the modern world the female psyche tends to be undernourished. That women are 'nearer to life' than men is a commonplace; and genuinely new art – as opposed to much 'experimental' art – satisfies her, because it provides or stimulates a renewal of the emotions, a reiteration of 'the true voice of feeling', which is both liberating and nutritive. Since feminism and Women's Liberation have meant on the whole the investment of the feminine domain by masculine ideals, and since self-appointed champions of women such as Simone de Beauvoir are in fact advocating the incorporation of women in the masculine order, some of the rebellion of women is directed, though subconsciously, against her 'liberators'. These liberators are often partisans and advocates of the pornography which dehumanizes her. The release of new emotional resources was the achievement of D. H. Lawrence and the reason why he has become a major cultural influence, though not always one to be safely followed. In the same way, the cult of frankness, though superficially in harmony with the female instinct to be 'down to earth', fails to be nutritive, because it is incompatible with the true feminine *mystique*. Recent research has confirmed that, despite the sex-and-violence cult, the romantic novel still retains its popularity, and some authors specializing in this *genre* have reported markedly increased sales. Meanwhile, enormous success is achieved by TV serials written by Victorian or Edwardian authors, both British and foreign, in which the men are masculine and the women on the whole feminine, though the script-writers feel the occasional necessity of adjusting the moral behaviour in order to lend certain characters greater verisimilitude. One suspects that the most ardent admirers of these national entertainments are women, who are no doubt helped thereby to feel whole again. For in wholeness there is calm, the *Yin* principle.

Minority culture, true and false

That the minority culture referred to is culture of a false kind will have been obvious. Nor is it an accident that such minorities, now generally in league with one another throughout the world, believe themselves to be cultivating pure art, pure music, and even pure literature. The last is the purer, apparently, for approximating to the 'absurd', whereas the art is of an evident representational type, though deliberately distorted, and the music is discordant only in presupposing the basic melodic system. In other words, the meaninglessness or absurdity of the literature battens upon sense, even of a quite conventional kind, just as its 'immorality' or claim to 'transcend values' is merely a direct reversal of established principles, which are all along presupposed. As a general rule, when words such as 'beyond' or 'outside' are employed, we may be fairly sure that we are dealing with persons anxious to join an Establishment.

What then, is the sign of *genuine* minority culture? In the modern world, it is very rarely associated with the political Establishment; and when, as in the case of the BBC Third Programme, it is sponsored by the media, the experiment is short-lived. Moreover, whatever the merits of the Third Programme – and it had great merits – it provided a certain amount of pabulum for the culture-snob; and there were certain aspects of contemporary culture with which it was reluctant to have anything to do (intelligent criticism of linguistic philosophy, for example). Genuine minority culture is the by-product of small communities engaged upon dedicated work, as with the old monastic orders; and the first sign that they are cultural is that they do not consider themselves to be such. There is no more pure culture than there is pure art; there is only the elaboration of religious myth, for 'when man loses the capacity for myth-making, he loses touch with the creative forces of his being'.[4] When universities (for instance) devote themselves purely to intellectual research – using the adjective intellectual in its modern, etiolated sense – they tend to operate in a spiritual void. This issues either in the production of erudite compilations, or, because the intellect abhors a vacuum, work infused with secular gospels, such as Marxism or anarchism; or, since much of this is now threadbare, doctrines which go 'beyond' these teachings, providing such doses of myth, mystery, miracle and authority as are sufficient to nourish a famished psyche. During the student turmoil of the 1960s, the phenomenon most interesting, or disturbing, to note was the similarity of the actions and reactions of the young people, their earnestness, their credulity, their impulse to proselytize. There was the case of the LSE students who set out to instruct groups of apprentices in the new revolutionary doctrine (which their pupils ungratefully dismissed as 'a load of rubbish'), or that of the students occupying the Odéon in the Paris Latin Quarter, who held prolonged sessions at which they answered questions or invited guest speakers. (Characteristically anxious to put himself forward as a spokesman for youth, Sartre received a welcome somewhat less warm than he expected.) Even those students who later realized that they had acted foolishly, admitted to a feeling of exhilaration, of solidarity, almost of religious millenarianism, compared with which the return to work proved an anticlimax. There followed a period of calm; but since that time, the interest in ideas of a new life, of being spiritually reborn, far from having ceased, has merely assumed less strident forms. After the initial youthful turmoil, the popular press was fond of using phrases such as 'it will never be the same again'; but in reality the protest movement, despite its extravagances, marked a partial return to the human norm, since youth without an outlet for fervour inevitably vents its frustration in anger. The destruction was largely the work of professional agitators. On the whole, punk is pacific.

A new religion?

Do we therefore want a new religion? This is a question often asked. In fact, the market, as we pointed out at the start, is already overstocked. If some of the spiritual wares on show are carefully examined, they will be found to be either disguised heresies of the traditional faiths, ingenious syncretisms, or scarcely-veiled political creeds. Most of them possess escape-hatches which enable the devotee to pass from one to the other. Thus we find men of considerable ability and intelligence, such as the late J. G. Bennett, moving from adherence to Gurdjieff, to Subud, and to the Roman Church with an ease occasioning surprise even to themselves. Some of us who have investigated the situation are familiar with a circumstance alluded to by G. K. Chesterton in his *Autobiography*, namely, that in moving from one meeting-house to another, the same faces are encountered. This is not merely a case of taking out a succession of spiritual insurance policies; it is a case of wishing to experience pleasurable religious emotions for their own sake. It results from an imbalance between the conscious and the subconscious inevitable in a world imbued with secularism. No longer subject to the 'pull' of value, the psyche in its subliminal aspect drinks deeply at the vast irrational well of the collective unconscious.

The new faiths are in most cases those which in the United States would be called non-liturgical. By contrast, the liturgical religions were precisely those which successfully devised forms and ceremonies which put a degree of psychical distance between the worshipper and the object. He was thereby subjected to a measure of emotional control. Since the values of art-religion-culture at a certain level are opaque, the emotions they evoke must not be exposed naked, must not even be named, or, failing to discharge themselves effectively in practical life, they will be dissipated in what Collingwood called amusement.[5] That indeed is what happens in the case of the religious dilettante. He samples religious emotions as a means of diversion. His ordinary life remains unfructified, because he is assimilating *ersatz* PN. This leaves him in a state of staleness or, what comes to the same thing, perpetual psychic hunger. 'Hungering and thirsting after righteousness', or what C. D. Broad used to call 'spiritual diabetes', is an ailment afflicting many a religious devotee, whereas the authentically religious souls are those who seek to follow Jacopone da Todi, the thirteenth century Italian Franciscan poet, who defined the end of all genuine spiritual experience as 'an ordered life in every state'.

That the emotions discharged in everyday life are best not named or identified as such (or they will lose their dynamism) may seem at first strange, especially as their identification in amusement is seen as perfectly normal. The reason is that to identify an emotion is to squander instead of to conserve it; and such dissipation is precisely that which characterizes amusement, rendering repeated doses of it at once necessary and psychologically debilitating. It is notorious that amusement, in order to be tolerable, demands more of itself. The amusement-addict reads not one detective story but a series, views not one chosen TV programme but turns on the set as regularly as he turns on the tap; for it is a thirst that is in need of continuous slaking. Except for the purpose of making a study of technique or of social behaviour, no one would willingly submit himself to such a continuous dose of *genuine* PN. A really satisfying drama, like a well-performed liturgy, is sufficient to fortify the psyche and to enrich our psychic life as a whole. There has to be time for psychic digestion. Similarly, a relationship of profound affection or love is lived most satisfactorily in the absence of repeated verbal assurances of devotion – indeed, the 'naming' of the emotion may cause real, if temporary, rupture; which is why, as Collingwood pointed out elsewhere,[6] the suitor is wise not to press the question 'Do you love me?' unless he is so sure of an affirmative answer as not to put his case in peril. When we feel strongly, the best mode of communication is action, however trivial, for here words fail us; or, to quote the old saw, 'when lovers lack matter, the soonest remedy's to kiss'.

In view of our identification of PN with the emotions canalized into practical life, we are faced with the problem of Collingwood's terminology. It will be recalled that he identifies such fructifying emotions with those originally associated with magic.[7] His theory is extremely ingenious. Magical emotions, he argues, are those which are concerned 'to develop or conserve morale'. That of course is the function of PN. What, then, is the reason why, though morale-building is still a human necessity, magic as the primitive savage conceived it has no place in the modern world? Collingwood answers this question by affirming that magical actions were not conceived by the savage in the way generally supposed; that is to say, he never believed 'that the enemy is defeated or the tree felled by the power of the magic as distinct from the labour of the "savage" '. But surely he did, and this is why we (and no doubt he) considered the process magical. For 'such a person thinks, for example, that a war undertaken without the proper dances would end in defeat; and that if he took an axe to the forest without doing the proper magic first, he would not succeed in cutting down the tree'. Some, though perhaps not all, savages were firmly convinced that the *dances* ensured the enemy's defeat, just as they believed that sticking pins in an effigy might of itself bring about an opponent's death. If victory did not ensue, or the opponent remained alive, then obviously the magical rite had been inadequately performed: the practitioner, if he also engaged in subsequent action such as fighting, did not deserve to win. Magic is now regarded as primitive because this attitude is no longer considered valid.

Nevertheless, the arousing of emotion for discharge in practical life is still a normal and indispensable activity, in which, so far as we know, only man engages; and the means whereby emotion is so raised are those religio-artistic activities which, though in the past associated with magic, may well have antedated the magical phase and can be considered independently of it. (This does not mean that a war-dance observed by the enemy, or the latter's knowledge that effigies were being stuck with pins, might not seriously affect morale – a point to which Collingwood alludes – but this proves not that war-dances and effigies cause death but that low morale can be injurious to health and sometimes fatal.)

Nevertheless, Collingwood clings to the term magical art. When he enumerates contemporary or recently extinct examples of such art, he includes all folk-art, the 'traditional low-brow arts of the upper classes', much religious art, as well as ritual activities such as sport, ceremonial meals, pageantry, etc. But these are what we have included within the sphere of PN. If such activities are removed or dissociated from art properly so-called – that is to say, what Collingwood defines as the expression rather than the arousal of emotion – there is precious little left. Art, in other words, returns to the narrow aesthetic sphere to which Bullough, for one, had sought to confine it.

Furthermore, at the end of his book, Collingwood places upon art an important social responsibility. Art, he says, is 'the community's medicine for the worst disease of the mind, the corruption of consciousness'. This would seem to be a responsibility somewhat heavy for it to bear. For those engaged in 'expressing' emotion are a minority compared with those concerned with arousing it. If the community's corruption of consciousness is a disease as grave as he implies, there would seem to be insufficient medicine to go round, given the few genuine artists available. By expressing an emotion, Collingwood says, an artist becomes aware of what it is; and 'a consciousness which . . . fails to grasp its own emotions is a corrupt

151

or untruthful consciousness'. This 'malperformance' takes place 'on the threshold that divides the psychical level of experience from the conscious level'. Now, if our theory is valid, this conversion of the psychic to the conscious level of experience is not simply an aesthetic activity but a religious one. In its aesthetic *aspect* the emotions involved are not, for the reason given, those of which the devotee becomes aware, since to 'name' them would be to destroy that efficacy or dynamism which is needed in their discharge in practical life.

It would be more accurate to define the 'corruption of consciousness' as that which occurs when emotion is discharged for its own sake, thereby blowing a psychic fuse. Now this we have seen to happen in amusement. Does this suggest that amusement is necessarily a form of corruption? Surely not. To answer in the affirmative would imply a wholesale condemnation of much of the leisure-time activity of the contemporary world. On the other hand, the *cult* of amusement can, as we know, reach dangerous proportions. There have been societies, that of ancient Rome for instance, where much of the populace has been enslaved to amusement. After the reign of Marcus Aurelius (AD 140-80), the Roman people enjoyed 175 holidays per year, when they habitually attended the circus. And because of the need to discharge emotions in *vacuo*, the amusements became increasingly brutal. A bored community needs increasing doses of violence for its psychic sustenance; and the greater the need, the more 'mindless' the violence becomes.

The organizers of the entertainment industry today know their audience rather better than some critics, who, though anxious to praise the 'brilliance' of films depicting acts of sadism, protest feebly at the 'lengths' to which such violence goes, as if the amusement-purveyors were not perfectly aware of what they were doing. The latter even protest, when gently upbraided, that they have the reputation of their directors to consider. 'The British Board of Film Censors has refused to issue even an X certificate for the film (about Billy the Kid) without the removal of the more violent scenes and gushing blood. The Distributors, MGM-EMI, fear that this will destroy what is considered the distinctive style of its director, Sam Peckinpah.'[8]

On the other hand, a certain amount of amusement is a necessity in a community, especially one that is subject to tension or boredom in its daily work; for the emotions thus pent up are in excess of social needs. The psyche must therefore be voided of such excess emotions,

152

must shed its burden, before it can proceed to its reconditioning – that is to say, to genuine recreation. The football match, once and still partially surrounded by a religious aura, performs a necessary social function. That such matches are so often associated with unruliness proves that the emotions due for discharge are in excess of the means available. The remedy is not more football matches but less psychically debilitating work. For in the modern era, work has been thoroughly secularized.

Collingwood's definition of the corruption of consciousness is outlined with less than his customary clarity. That is perhaps the reason why there exists a disparity between the ailment, which he describes as 'the worst disease of the mind', and the cure. It is also the reason no doubt why, when we have put down his brilliant book, we experience a feeling of vague dissatisfaction. 'The remedy,' he says in the last paragraph, 'is the poem itself.' The poet has told his audience 'the secret of their own hearts'. But has he? What is the secret divulged by *Hamlet*, or, to take the example of which Collingwood makes great play, *The Waste Land*? The secret, such as it is, is *locked in these poems*, which are distinguished by what we have called their opacity. In other words, the emotions they arouse are not named. Collingwood came nearer to the truth when, in an early work, he wrote that 'art is pregnant with a message which it cannot deliver'.[9] Precisely: in the last chapter, we spoke of something similar – of a psychic burden or incubus, of which the deliverance or lifting was the task of religion. Observe, it is not a case of art giving place to religion as negative to positive. The notion of the dialectical movement of the spirit, which Collingwood took over from Hegel, and for which he was criticized by Croce, entails some curious ideas as to the 'death of art', etc. Our argument, by contrast, is that 'the movement of the spirit' – to use for a moment the old and dated idealist terminology – is simply the development of the self from its implicit or subconscious phase to its explicit or conscious one. That is the reason why we have spoken of an activity called art-religion. The latter is a spiritual activity capable of being viewed from two aspects: as art at the psychic level and as religion at the level at which the psyche is, though momentarily, rendered pervious. To present the process in another way, it is the transformation of the individual into the personal. In this transformation, the psyche does not disappear, since we remain individuals or psychic beings. Nor is personality ever fully attained. We live on the spiritual level – that is to say, at the level at which values are apprehended – only at moments. The religious consciousness reflects the perpetual struggle towards individual transcendence, and therefore towards personal integration; it is not the end of the struggle but a greater awareness of its nature. (All this is reflected in the Christian liturgy. The General Confession finds us each week back where we were, with 'no health in us'; but at least it can be said that we are a little more aware of our condition, and this awareness is part of the movement towards spiritual health.)

Thus there is no such thing as the Hegelian 'death of art'. Art needs to stay alive because, as individuals, we need constant psychic sustenance; but as persons art is not enough for us. Religion as art must move towards completion by religion as spirituality, even though the movement is never complete. Religion *is* that movement, and that which moves is necessarily unfinished. Each of us, in St Jean Perse's phrase, is 'homme infesté de songe, homme gagné par l'infection divine'. Although we are aware that we cannot live without art (understood in the broad sense that we have given to PN), we know also that we cannot, in our present existence, live permanently 'in the spirit'. The author of *Revelations* declared that he was in the spirit 'on the Lord's Day': that is, there was a particular moment of elevation. We can be neither pure aesthetes nor pure gnostics. No condition of *Samadhi* is so complete as to render the guru's body invisible. Those who pronounce matter to be an illusion, such as the apostles of Christ Scientist, are careful to act *as if* the spatio-temporal dimension were real.

What, then is the nature of the burden or incubus of which we have spoken? *It is the burden of individuality itself*. Whilst to explain it would be to solve the mystery of life and suffering, the fact remains that we are locked in our individuality; we 'hear the key turn each in his prison'. Spiritual growth is both the awareness of this limitation and the development of the impulse to overcome it. That which is felt to be insufficient is already a burden, and the temporary surpassing of that condition makes its resumption scarcely more tolerable:

> Once more in man's frail world: which I had left
> So long that 'twas forgotten: and I feel
> The weight of clay again.[10]

As individuals we are all subject to gravity, as Simone Weil maintained; and a great scientist, speaking of the greatest dramatist and wit of his day, declared that he was able 'to liberate us and take from us something of the heaviness of living'.[11] This indeed is the function of art or the aesthetic mode; but it is also the reason why in the end art fails us. For the burden is merely shifted. We shut our eyes and imagine. In the end the world of imagination, the sphere of opaque values, palls, and we want truly to see, even if to see is only to glimpse or to descry.

We thus bring our thought into line with the conclusions reached in the previous chapter. If 'what religion gives to art, art may give back to religion', this is because there is only one activity or process, given various descriptions. With the theologians we may call it 'the progress of the soul', with the idealist philosophers the self-knowledge of mind, with the apostles of Vedanta (and by a profound scientist-philosopher such as Schrödinger) the identification of Atman and Brahman, with the psychologists such as Jung the process of individuation, or, as we prefer to call it, the transition between individuality and personality, psyche and spirit. Of this process, culture is the by-product. The transition is always taking place, like Hegel's coming to be and passing away which itself never comes to be nor passes away. In other words, there is a reciprocal movement from art to religion and from religion to art. The psyche reaches towards the spiritual: the spiritual re-immerses itself in the psychic. The movement itself may generate that moment of illumination which is spiritual insight; for unless the opacity were not from time to time rendered pervious, the psyche would remain self-enclosed, with consequent immersion in fantasy. But the transition to the spiritual – it will bear repeating – is never complete. We can apprehend, but not attain, perfection. The scene through the window is real; it is not painted on the glass. Paradoxically, the process is difficult to envisage because it is our everyday experience, as a generation fascinated by meditation should be the first to realize. Fix your mind upon ultimate matters and usually the effort rebounds into imagery. The opacity of this imagery you then endeavour to penetrate afresh, and so forth. No one understood this better than the psychologist whose ideas form the subject of the next chapter.

7
Jung on psyche and religion

Jung and Freud

In 1913, Carl Gustav Jung, who had worked for years with Sigmund Freud, his senior by ten years, decided as a result of disagreements to branch out on his own. Since that time, the Freudians and the Jungians have tended to keep apart; in some cases they have not been on speaking terms. With the controversy on this level of academic rivalry we are not here concerned, save to warn the unalerted reader that an uncritical enthusiasm for the theories of Jung may put him beyond the pale in certain psychiatric circles. The following appeared in *The Daily Telegraph* in October 1954:

> Dr. Carl Gustav Jung, the Swiss psychologist, celebrates his 80th birthday at his home at Kusnacht. . . Cables of congratulation arrived from all over the world, but none from 560 psycho-analysts meeting at Geneva. 'We belong to the other camp,' the secretary of the Congress said.

The dismissal of Jung as a serious scientific investigator is not uncommon. Peter Hays, Professor of Psychiatry at the University of Alberta, observed that 'one psychiatrist, Carl Jung, departed from Freud's ideas in a rather grand way, but his work soon became more redolent of philosophical discourse than of scientific writing, and today a psychiatrist reads his books more for background education than for technical assistance.'[1] Such a statement, with its underlying assumption that Freud is the acknowledged Pope of psychiatry, and its far from true remark about the approach of the average psychiatrist, is, alas, all too common.

The late J. A. C. Brown adopted a similar attitude. Having remarked that 'many critics have commented that the Jungian theory is more like a metaphysical system than a school of scientific psychology', he observed that

> the present writer may well admit that he comes into the Freudian category, and gets much the same impression from reading Jung as might be obtained from reading the scriptures of the Hindus, Taoists, or Confucians; although well aware that many wise and true things are being said, he feels that they could have been said just as well without involving us in the psychological theories upon which they are supposedly based.[2]

What is chiefly interesting about these remarks is their reluctance to acknowledge, or perhaps even to recognize, that Freud himself engaged in metaphysical enquiry and speculation, and that his ideas about the nature and direction of human life and death are closely involved with his scientific methods. Moreover, Freud's puritanical and pessimistic temperament may have had something to do with his postulation of primal malevolent forces, and his tenebrous notion of matter as having been 'disturbed by the appearance of life'.[3] And if Freud is allowed to write a book such as *Beyond the Pleasure Principle* (1920), which he described as 'speculation, often far-fetched speculation', why is Jung not permitted a similar measure of speculative freedom? The more we study Jung, the less far-fetched many of his theories may appear. This is especially the case if we bring to them some knowledge of the oriental thought which, as Brown admits, contains a large measure of wisdom. (For a study of the contribution which Buddhism, especially Zen, can make to psychotherapy, the reader is referred to Alan Watts's *Psychotherapy East and West* (1963), an acute analysis undertaken by a man sometimes considered to have been the champion of the counter-culture.)

Even if we welcome the speculations pursued by both Freud and Jung, we ought to bear in mind that neither claimed to have reached final conclusions. Both were men of disarming modesty. Jung laid no claim to have produced a system. His method was to proceed step by step. 'I have often made mistakes and had many times to forget what I had learned. But I know and I am content to know that as surely as light comes out of darkness, so truth is born of error.'[4] Again, 'our psychological experience is still too recent and limited in scope to permit of general theories'.[5] Finally, 'as I cannot claim to have reached any definite theory explaining all or even the main part of the psychical complexities, my work consists of a series of different approaches, or one might call it, a circumambulation of unknown factors'.[6] As so often, the dogmatic and often *ex-cathedra* remarks associated with the master are seen to be the work of over-enthusiastic disciples.

The primary reason why Jung is of interest to us, in our framing of a definition of culture, is that he has much of interest to say about the nature of the psyche. He assumed a psychic reality, convinced as he was that 'the materialistic hypothesis is too daring altogether: it goes beyond the available data and slips over into "metaphysical" arrogance'.[7] Naturally, psychic reality belongs to an order different from that of material objects; in Jung's view, the psychological is not 'only psychological'. But he insists that, as an empirical investigator, he does not *need* to presuppose any metaphysical or ontological view of the psyche's existence. He does not ask, where is the psyche? He merely states that there are psychic phenomena. And since the idea of God is psychically so important to man, Jung contends that it is psychologically real, whether or not the philosophical problem of the existence of God is a legitimate one.

Secondly, Jung differed from Freud in refusing to identify the libido exclusively with sexuality: for him, the libido was another name for psychic energy in general, and only one aspect of this energy, the earliest, was exclusively sexual.

Thirdly, that which belongs to both the unconscious and the conscious, linking the two together, is the symbol. A symbol is based not merely on something known but on something unknown, something that never becomes known save through the symbolizing process itself. This characteristic of the symbol makes it opaque. As the conscious mind cannot analyse it thoroughly, it remains to fascinate, as in dreams, myth and art. Through the symbol, some of the repressed material in the unconscious may come to the surface, and to that extent is 'known'.

Symbols can be of two kinds. First, there are representative symbols, such as myths. Secondly, there are behaviour symbols, such as religious rites. A symbol forms a kind of psychic cover. When, to use an expression from popular conceptions of espionage, a symbol's cover is 'blown', it loses its dynamic efficacy and survives merely as a sign. This means that a symbol, unlike a sign, cannot be deliberately made or fabricated; it cannot be reduced to some basic meaning, e.g., what for Freud is so often infant sexuality.

Nevertheless, the psychic life of a man is not merely derived from his own individuality and personality, which is necessarily unique, but from his membership of the human race. In Freud's view, the entire content of the unconscious was material which the individual had repressed; Jung came to the conclusion, as a result of work with patients, that beneath and apart from such personally repressed material, there were psychic layers derived from the common experience of humanity. (It is as well to remember that, while Jung's theories met and still meet with opposition and even ridicule, a psychiatrist as acceptable to the new generation as Dr R. D. Laing has suggested that the 'journey' towards the discovery of true selfhood involves 'going back through one's personal life in and back and through and beyond into the experience of all mankind, of the primal man, of Adam and perhaps even further into the being of animals, vegetables and minerals.'⁸) This was Jung's reason for studying ancient mythology, leading to his discovery, which is certainly exciting, that patients wholly ignorant of certain primordial myths nevertheless experienced, in their own versions, dream or fantasy-images of which such myths were evidently the basis. This bore fruit in remarkable works of collaboration, such as *The Secret of the Golden Flower* (1929), written with Richard Wilhelm, and the *Introduction to a Science of Mythology*, written with C. Kerényi (1951).

To this layer of psychic experience common to all mankind, including peoples having no known contact with one another, Jung gave the name of the collective unconscious. Although he retained Freud's view of the personal unconscious as that which resulted from suppression, he coined a word 'cryptomnesia' to signify the psychic condition whereby a memory, once present to consciousness but forgotten, arrived once more at the surface of consciousness and was taken to be a new datum of experience.

The archetypes

The collective unconscious is, so to speak, streaked with archetypes. Although Jung insists that the theory of archetypes remains a hypothesis, it forms the basis, and one of the most original components, of his psychology. Naturally, the archetypes cannot be apprehended directly, because they *are* unconscious; but we can catch them at the point at which they partially emerge from time to time into consciousness, that is to say, in the form of the 'archaic image' or symbol. If such images are associated with primordial myths, then, according to Jung, we may be sure that we are in the presence of the archetypes.

Although Jung's concept of the archetypes underwent modification, he never ceased to believe that the ambience in which they lived was a *timeless* dimension. This did not prevent them from exercising a dynamic influence. 'The archetype is the energic centre of the collective unconscious.'[9] Nor is it necessary to enquire of what they are themselves composed: only in respect of the conscious world can such a question be asked. Nevertheless, Jung employs a telling analogy with the axial system of crystals. Whilst it is true to say that the axial system determines the formation of crystals, it enjoys no material existence. An archetype is by definition a type, a form; only its ingression (to use Whitehead's term) into consciousness produces a perturbation in the spatio-temporal dimension.

Jung's explanation of the origin of the archetypes as the result of repeated human experiences leading to the stamping of the brain with 'engrams' (a word he borrowed from Semon and which has been used to explain the physiological basis of memory) is among the least convincing of his attempts to illuminate the contents of the collective unconscious. His efforts were in any case wasted. Few scientists now accept the engram theory even as applied to memory, though, as with preformation in biology, they often reject the concept only to resurrect it in another guise. The origin of the archetypes remains as mysterious as the origin of life; and as Jung tended in his later work to say that the two originated together, the question remains in suspense. But just as biology as a science continued to progress in the absence of an explanation of life's beginnings, so psychology may continue to develop in the absence of an explanation of the origin of the archetypes. What may confidently be said is that in the young child, and no doubt during the childhood of the race – an expression which we have to use carefully, because it is doubtful whether the hominid necessarily lived like a child – psychic life at the subconscious level is basically the mental norm. Consciousness, which for Jung always means reflective consciousness, was a later acquisition, and is even now only an intermittent activity, never to be dissociated or detached from its psychic substratum.

Since both Freud and Jung regarded the content of the personal unconscious as repressed material, it might be supposed that they entertained similar views of the opposition of the conscious and the unconscious. This is not so. The relationship between the two, according to Jung, is not exclusively one of opposition, save in the superficial sense that the unconscious opposes the conscious by exercising a compensatory function. The ideal is for the psyche to work in harmony with the reflective consciousness; then it is that we get true individuation, leading to a balanced personality. Such a balance is usually, and most desirably, the result of a process of auto-regulation; but in cases where a psychic trauma has occurred, the intervention of the psychotherapist may prove necessary. In such a trauma, or at the origin of it, the unconscious has been called upon to exercise so great a degree of compensation as to erupt into the conscious in the form of a neurosis. A neurosis is therefore a cure which has lost control of itself.

The task of religion

This provides us with a useful transition to Jung's views on religion. As Freud reduced the explanation of almost everything to infantile sexuality, it is not surprising that he should have pronounced this to be at the root of religion, which he held to be merely a sublimation of that primal phase. Although Jung began by following Freud, he slowly came to adopt the view that religion is 'psychologically true', because it is the bridge to 'all the greatest achievements of humanity'.[10] While Freud regarded religion as sheer illusion – although Jung claimed to have observed in Freud the irruption of unconscious religious factors –[11] Jung, though holding at first that it was not necessarily objectively true, maintained that it was of value, even supreme value, until such time as man arrived at moral autonomy. And just as Jung believed, at least to begin with, that the idea of God was psychologically true but ontologically meaningless, so he believed the self to be a psychic reality but essentially unknowable.

According to Jung, dogmatic religions arise not so much in order to explain or clarify religious ideas as in order to protect the believer from their psychic violence. If, Jung seems to say, the believer concentrates too much on the dogmas themselves, he may easily lose his faith when, as so often happens, some of these dogmas begin to seem 'incredible'. As faith is a necessity for man – who is always 'in search of a soul' – Jung takes the view that, except in the few cases where moral autonomy is attained, religious experience, whether or not it is a projection of the psychic need for a Father or a Saviour, remains the basis of human living. 'The gods cannot and must not die.'[12] In one celebrated passage, he goes almost as far as the orthodox believer:

> Among all my patients in the second half of life – that is to say, over thirty-five – there has not been one whose problem in the last resort was not that of finding a religious outlook on life. It is safe to say that everyone of them fell ill because he had lost that which the living religions of every age have given to their followers, and none of them has been really healed who did not regain his religious outlook.[13]

Moreover, despite recurrent outbursts of fanaticism, religion has on the whole succeeded in keeping dangerous instincts under control. It has also – and this is a point of particular importance for us – created recognizable *cultures*. Individuation as a process is never complete, because its completion might destroy that psychic link, that communication with the depths of the unconsciousness, which a purely intellectual existence necessarily precludes. We must strive towards a moral autonomy the complete attainment of which would be psychically detrimental.

This vital link with the unconscious depths is the means whereby we experience what Jung, borrowing the word made famous by Rudolf Otto in *The Idea of the Holy* (1932), calls the 'numinous', or the irrational *mysterium tremendum*. And in his book *Psychology and Religion* (1937), based on lectures given in the United States, Jung stresses the psychological validity of religion so emphatically as almost to suggest that it takes precedence over its ontological truth. 'Religious experience,' he affirms, 'is absolute. It is indisputable.'[14] Being the most profound experience which can happen to us, the *mysterium tremendum* takes precedence over all others, even, so he appears to hint, that of truth itself. For, as an effective expression of the archetypes, the *mysterium* communicates with the depths of our being, the foundation of our true self. Indeed, in the *mysterium* we are confronted with our own self at this level:

which is why an experience so overwhelming is at the same time a kind of *recognition*. In some contexts, indeed, Jung seems to identify the self, in its totality, with God: an identification similar to that between Atman and Brahman in Vedanta.

Curiously enough, Jung's most mature attitude to religion crystallized out during the studies he pursued in alchemy. His interest in this subject was due in part to his fascination with symbolism; but it was also his view that whereas the religious consciousness was concerned with faith, the goal of the alchemists was knowledge. The twin preoccupation of the later Jung may have been the result of an attempt to reach, by two paths, a goal which is at the terminus of both. For is it true to say that religion is simply faith? The mystics, surely, have sought something more than faith, something more than an 'overwhelming experience'. They have sought vision. What begins at the psychic level may end at a level at which opacity is at least partially overcome.

This brings us to a possible criticism of Jung, especially in the light of our argument at the end of Chapter 5. For Jung, the highest religious experience is still a *psychic* experience, and therefore one which is self-contained; and in this respect there is no essential difference between a religious experience and an aesthetic one. In that case, what can be achieved by the technique of psychotherapy? As Josef Goldbrunner remarks: 'Jung teaches his patients how to feel at home in the house of the soul, but he locks them up in it: the door to transcendence is barred.'[15] Or, as Victor E. Frankl, whom Goldbrunner cites,[16] contends: 'If psychotherapy is to be of any further help, it must be supplemented by a therapy based on spiritual values.' Although for Jung the psyche unites the unconscious and the conscious, religion at the threshold of reflective consciousness is still not a breakthrough into a higher sphere, that of value; it is a mere substitution of sign for symbol. The symbol is 'exhausted' and the sign points nowhere. Our argument, by contrast, has been that the *act* whereby the psychic becomes the conscious is the transition from the aesthetic mode to religion proper whereby, as if in an operation for cataract, a membrane is removed and values are apprehended.

This act of transition is therefore the passage from psychic culture, where values are incarnate and therefore opaque, to spiritual culture. But spiritual culture must continue to live in a psychic ambience, just as the *person* is still attached to the *individual*. The self that surveys 'all times and places' is still identifiable with a particular organism.

On the other hand, the human being composed of organism and psyche is possessed by a *nisus* to break out of its psychic chrysalis. The psyche needs to be fed and maintained in health so that the individual may move towards self-transcendence. 'Life is not possible without an opening towards the transcendent: in other words, human beings cannot live in chaos.'[17] That which begins as organic morphogenesis continues as spiritual 'growth'; and the human being is on the way to completion only if such growth is maintained. To develop in this manner is not to transcend humanity but to *penetrate further into the human*. And this is to acquire greater capacity for what is discoverable only on the human plane, namely disinterested love. Just as the maternal instinct is completed by maternal love, so maternal love becomes in turn a 'spiritual instinct' which seeks its own supersession (but not repudiation) in those acts of selflessness in which human nature discloses itself to itself. Acts of sheer benevolence are rare; so are selfless human beings. The task of the higher religions, and that in which their superiority consists, is to hold up to humanity an 'impossible' ideal so that man shall be reminded of his permanently unfinished state.

A second criticism of Jung is as follows. Even given the fact that he did not pretend to have elaborated a system, he clung to his archetypes as to the most stable part of his thought. But why, we may ask, are the archetypes confined to the unconscious? The word archetype or *to archetypon eidos* appeared first in the *Corpus Hermeticum* of the Neo-Platonists (third-century BC), and here the archetypes were naturally located in the heavenly sphere. Archetypes, indeed, belong to the spiritual as well as to the psychic world, and the latter are the shadows of the former. Jung's values, then, are wrongly or inadequately located. All action, in the true sense, involves final causality, which envelops 'push-and-pull' causality,[18] just as conscious-intelligence is the 'centre' of all mechanical process. The attempt to reduce final causality to mechanical causality *a tergo* is self-defeating. Now final causality is meaningless without an axiological dimension, a 'world of values', an archetypal realm, depending on a transcendent Logos.

It is said that at the end of his life Jung underwent a genuine religious experience or conversion, and that he liberated himself from the psychologism which, despite his efforts to shake free of it, had persistently dogged his thought. In other words, he realized that the opacity of the psyche could partially be overcome. But information on this point is scant, confused, and unreliable. If it is true, however, then his psychological work can be seen to have reached something like completion. 'Analytical psychology', as he called it, is sterile without *psycho-synthesis*; and this is the conclusion which he may have reached, and to which the more original psychologists of our time would seem to be moving.

8
The cultural prospect

Life as it is lived

It is obvious that no science can discuss normality unless it has some idea or apprehension of the normal. This is especially true of psychology, which is supposed to concern itself with mental health. Admittedly, there are those who seek to elude this obligation.

> The moralist and the psycho-analyst begin to part company. . . at the point of value-judgments. Many moralists feel that there is a virtue in conforming to a certain code of behaviour which should be acceptable to all. The psycho-analyst, by contrast, is not directly concerned with 'good' or 'bad' actions: his business is the growth of the personality, and the struggle towards emotional health.[1]

How can there be growth of personality or a struggle towards emotional health without *criteria* of some kind? In many cases, it would seem that 'personality' and 'emotional health' have a private meaning for the psycho-analyst. He has already made up his mind in what these things consist. Yet the very terms involve value-judgments.

Meanwhile, a psychologist can be so obsessed with the deviant, and at the same time so subtly influenced by the metaphysics popular in his day – or more probably surviving from his youth – that his view of normality becomes seriously warped. This happened to Freud himself. 'The professional bias of the psychopathologist often leads Freud to look upon *normal* phenomena as *deviations from the abnormal*.'[2]

Despite the criticisms of his work in the last chapter, Jung did implicitly realize that a conscious pursuit of values was essential to the fully satisfactory life. Even the eruptions from the unconscious needed to be interpreted according to ethical criteria. 'The images of the unconscious place a great responsibility upon man. Failure to understand them, or a shirking of ethical responsibility, deprives him of his wholeness and imposes a painful fragmentariness on his life.'[3] Or, as one of his disciples wrote with a clarity sometimes lacking in the master:

> The development of individual consciousness and the integration by the individual of unconscious contents are the only real safeguards against possession by the archetypes, and therefore against dangerous mass-movements. An archetype, like everything unconscious, is two-faced: it can produce completely opposite effects, be either good or evil, destructive or constructive. The aspect it presents depends largely on the conscious attitude, and its effects on the individual's capacity for understanding and moral elevation.[4]

But, as Jung himself admits, such 'integration of unconscious contents' is, if complete, an achievement of which only few persons are capable. These are the true moral leaders of mankind.

Although only a minority are capable of sustained moral elevation,[5] acts of benevolence, heroism, and devotion are within the reach of all, even the humblest; for, to quote Solovyev, 'each man is capable of recognizing and realizing truth, each may become a living reflection of the absolute whole, a conscious and independent organ of the universal life'.[6] And so when we refer to a consciousness open to the world of values, we refer not necessarily to the 'great moments' but to all deliberate action – indeed, to all action of our working life, as distinct from those apparently automatic activities which we perform from instinct or habit, though even here we act indirectly according to values: values that are opaque or 'crystallized'.

For this reason, all fruitful action is action which, because it seeks the *incarnation* of a value or values, lends the world by its performance greater sense or meaning. A great scientist – *pace* Lord Rutherford, who said 'let no one talk about the universe in *my* laboratory' – is one who renders the world more intelligible to us. He does not create or project this sense; he finds it, for it is there to be found. But why confine ourselves to a master mind? A housewife who successfully 'runs' the home is making sense of her environment, and at the same time maintaining it. Values can be incarnate only by a conscious centre, that is to say, a self; for only a self, a centre of value-realization, can communicate explicitly with the axiological (value) dimension.

This is the reason why life is movement. The human being 'gets up in the morning' and starts working at the business of living. The same is true of all the beings of nature, except the sub-atomic being-activities, which are perpetually *montés*. A conscious or a psychic being is impelled by a kind of inner dynamism or *nisus* constantly to reaffirm the sense of its environment by keeping it in order or repair. All these activities are mediated, at the stage of civilization, through institutions, civil, commercial, financial, etc., which themselves need to be maintained, periodically reformed, and sometimes disbanded. Just as the regime of the monastery, though apparently monotonous, is designed to 'free the spirit', so at a humbler level the automated kitchen is intended to liberate the family from drudgery, in order to enable its members to engage in supposedly more fruitful activities. Sometimes, as we know, the new activities entail another form of slavery, and at that point the psyche will have its own way of registering protest.

Nevertheless, much of life is a jumble of unfinished tasks, interspersed with automatic physical activities: the idea, possibly conveyed above, of a waking existence dedicated to purposive behaviour may seem a highly idealized picture of the life of the typical man or woman. Living is at all times approximate, botched, repetitive; tasks are begun, continued, postponed; speech is intermittent, halting, imprecise, productive of recurrent misunderstanding; relationships, even the most intimate, are often casual. And the natural succession of the hours obliges us regularly to fall into unconsciousness, when the self's link with the world of values is severed, and it lapses into a purely psycho-biological existence. In fact, we are so constituted as to render this abandonment of the task of conscious living highly salutary. Just as we can concentrate upon a lecture for hardly more than an hour, and often less, so a working-day exceeding sixteen hours imposes a severe strain on the nervous system, quite apart from the need of the organism periodically to close down its higher centres. We are children of nature, and nature exercises due care of humankind, not least in conferring periods of oblivion. For this reason we need institutions in which, during man's periods of repose, his culture may be 'frozen'. And the very nature of experience as fragmentary, yet somehow preserving continuity, testifies to its *thematic* character, and therefore to its unintelligibility save in the light of finality. A play purporting to demonstrate the *absurdity* of life is acted in an intelligible manner, and published in a volume with ordered pagination, designed title page, and fixed price. The potential readers are not sent a bag of assorted lead types to make what they can of.

There is a temptation to speak of cultures, or of a particular culture, as something fully formed; but this is due to the habit of historians – though a habit frowned on by many – of tracing the birth, maturity and death of cultures as if they were consistent and integrated wholes. No one has ever lived through a culture, as he might live through a war; and only a very few persons – a St Augustine or a Bede – have ever grasped the nature and significance of the point in time at which they were living. Yet it is all the stranger that these same epochs which *nobody* experienced should have become the subject-matter of historical speculation, or appraisal, as when Eliot speaks of a particular culture as having been 'worth while'.[7] In fact, the culture itself was probably a series of approximations and imperfections, with here and there a moment of 'crystallization' of which few at the time – very few – may have been conscious. Although today most people acquiesce in the way of life in which they have been brought up, they are full of grumbles about it; and there are those who, considering it 'rotten to the core', desire its overthrow. Meanwhile, everybody has to live; and since most people cannot live on a diet of fine literature and 'good' music, they seek nutrition where they can find it – usually in doses of amusement or distraction (today heavily spiced with eroticism) or at worst, in some narcotic: anything, in short, which, to cite Eliot again, may insulate them from boredom and despair.

Intellect and psyche

Even these few who attain intellectual vision do so only at intervals, and never without a measure of opacity. Dealing in remote abstractions, a higher mathematician may seem to be moving among essences; but, as H. H. Joachim used to point out, the mathematician brings to his work emotions appropriate to it, and these, as another great mathematician, Bertrand Russell, made clear, can be very powerful. Indeed, Russell's most lofty sentiments were expressed at a time when he was most preoccupied with mathematics and logic.

> I cannot bear the littleness and enclosing walls of purely *personal* beings. . . . In some way I cannot put into words, I feel that some of our thoughts and feelings are just of the moment, but others are part of the eternal world – even if their actual existence is passing, something – some spirit or essence seems to last on, to be part of the real history of the universe, not only of the separate person. Somehow that is how I want to live, so that as much of life as possible may have that quality of eternity.[8]

Furthermore, if we may judge from the passion that lurks behind Spinoza's *Ethics* (despite their being composed *de ordine geometrico*), the *amor intellectualis dei* which he believed to be the end of life was far from being an insipid sentiment. This was because the word intellectual up to his day, but decreasingly thereafter, implied an attitude charged with intense spirituality.

In other words, the highest moral and intellectual efforts of man are always *psycho*-spiritual. When we aim at the realization or actualization of values, our idea of value is always one that is already 'embodied'. In order to be faithful, devoted, or loving, we invoke not some abstract Fidelity, Devotion or Love, but an example or incarnation of these values made familiar to us often by the cultural ambience of our childhood or formative years. To most people, the embodiment is associated with the mother. In the same way, the artist does not aim at, or think steadfastly upon, Beauty, but rather upon some beautiful (i.e. PN-producing) scene, person, or design, which he tries to embody or incarnate afresh. The moral agent, like the artist, always has his model.

No doubt that is the reason why religious denominations which manifest the most loftily intellectual approach are often those whose churches are most heavily bedecked with statuary and images; where ritual (or what Jung called behavioural images) is most in evidence; and where a heavily charged atmosphere of olfactory imagery is engendered. Nor are the religions which forbid images, especially of the deity, devoid of 'visual aids': the illusion of emptiness, or the void, is itself an image and successfully incarnates one aspect of 'the beauty of holiness'. Perhaps the best example of this compromise is the Moslem mosque. Apart from the exquisite calligraphy, the suspended lights, the glowing colours of the carpets, and the silence, especially of tread, this is so constructed as to create an image of the sacred cosmos, making an absent or transcendent deity everywhere present.

The word 'aids' must be stressed, because the visual, olfactory, and tactile images are not the be-all-and-end-all of devotion, even though some people claim to worship images, such as an ikon or a statue of the Virgin. But to say that these images are not the food of the spirit is simply to say that they are the food of the psyche. Apart from the fact that it accompanies the spirit throughout its journey, the psyche demands nourishment all the more urgently once the higher values are sought; hence the higher the religion, the 'higher' the liturgical practices.

What Aldous Huxley was talking about in his two little works, *The Doors of Perception (1953) and Heaven and Hell* (1956), was not so much the nature of spiritual apprehension as the nature and function of PN. The 'vision-inducing' materials to which he refers, especially in *Heaven and Hell* – 'polished metals and precious stones', 'noble forms and colours artfully blended', etc. – are primarily sources of psychic nutriment, evocative signals, whatever the 'vision' may finally promote. As he wrote:

> Religious art has always and everywhere made use of these vision-inducing materials. The shrine of gold, the chryselephantine statue, the jewelled symbol or image, the glittering furniture of the altar – we find these things in contemporary Europe as in ancient Egypt, in India and China as among the Greeks, the Incas, the Aztecs.[9]

It is not for nothing that Huxley distinguishes between 'the visionary world' and the world of mystical experience. It has always been the function of 'art' to mediate between the two. The cult of relics, so widespread during the Middle Ages in Europe but also found in Buddhism, had also something to do with PN. The fact that these objects were so often adorned with precious stones, and preserved in reliquaries of sometimes extraordinary magnificence, tends to confirm this supposition. According to Lord Clark, the devotee 'really believed that by contemplating a reliquary containing the head or even the fingers of a saint he would persuade that particular saint to intercede on his behalf with God'[10]; but it is perhaps equally if not more true to say that the contemplation of the relics – often specially exhibited at certain times and places – afforded, because of this supposed efficacy, a powerful supply of PN. The collecting of relics is still common, as when a pop star's fans contest for a scrap of his hair or clothing which they later treat as a sacred object, not in the hope that by contemplating it they will gain favour with its owner but as a direct source of psychic nourshment.

Like the organism, however, the psyche needs its periods of fasting and abstinence: PN in perpetual supply or in too rich a form would produce an equivalent of surfeit. We may derive some of the most potent PN from looking at a favourite view, and we may build or acquire a house of which this view is one of the permanent attractions. But, as with a favourite painting or a favourite person for that matter, we do not wish to look at it unremittingly. To know that the potential source of PN is there is sufficient.

Much the most effective manner in which PN is absorbed, however, must always remain subconscious or subliminal. Urbanized intellectuals who look upon the country as a place devoid of true culture – or who consider the 'underdeveloped countries' as in need of 'the benefits of civilization' – fail to realize that such regions are often culturally far richer than their own, despite the absences of libraries, concert halls, art-galleries, and so forth.[11] Conversely, some of the countries most economically developed are those suffering from serious cultural undevelopment. Life in a small land-locked American town can be so psychically depriving as to cause distress which manifests itself in sensory or behavioural (neurotic) ways. T. S. Eliot described the Boston of his day as 'quite uncivilized, but refined beyond the point of civilization'. Even countries where the subconscious assimilation of PN is satisfactory to the indigenous inhabitants may prove psychically debilitating to the visitor – for example, the foreign student. Although Great Britain is a country skilled in student welfare, some of the breakdowns that occur among foreign nationals are due probably to the onset of psychic inanition, for which no amount of material care can compensate. Certain cases may be cured by habituation: in others, the only remedy is to return home where the right kind of PN is in supply. That is why there are 'homes from home', and why – to take an example already given – a young girl, removed from the bosom of her family, can rapidly organize a new psychic environment with a mate, part of whose supposed sex-appeal is a source of PN which she can amply reciprocate: for what is more satisfactory than to feed each other? As women tend to live a richer psychic life than men, deriving satisfaction from flowers, clothes, jewels, and above all 'human relationships', they provide more than their share of PN in the course of friendship and marriage. Anyone who has undertaken personnel or recruitment work knows how often women, as opposed to men, put on their application forms 'more interested in people than things'. When in his poem *Sensations* (1870) Rimbaud wrote of being 'heureux comme avec une femme', he was referring not to sex-appeal in the modern sense, but to the ambiance provided by female PN, as other lines suggest:

> Je ne parlerai pas, je ne penserai rien
> Mais l'amour infini me montera dans l'âme. . . .

Allusion to the young girl leads to the case of that same girl, inexperienced as she may seem, turned into a wife and mother. Looking back, many a son or daughter may reflect with gentle amusement upon the mother's superficial shortcomings; but in the majority of cases these reflections will be accompanied by a profound resepct, and even awe, for the way in which that woman, often harassed, overworked, and financially pinched, performed her maternal duties, coming straight to the job without training. In other words, the mother at the psychic level, guided by instinct, is rarely the failure that she might have supposed herself to be at the conscious level, where she was so often apparently outstripped in knowledge and wit by her partner and offspring. So universal has this veneration for the mother proved, that the Mother Goddess was one of the earliest of cults, preceding by thousands of years the rise of the Higher Religions, and so far penetrating those religions that Kannon or the Goddess of Mercy became one of the most venerated of Buddhist deities, and the place of the Virgin Mother in Christianity was sometimes elevated above that of her Son.

The promotion of culture

We therefore turn to our final problem, namely, what kind of culture is the most satisfactory, and how can we be said to instil a culture that is in part – and perhaps for the greater part – subconsciously expressed and absorbed?

First of all, we must refer to a faculty of the human mind to which perhaps insufficient attention has been paid. This is, as Bergson (who did give it attention) said, a capacity for forgetting, which he defined as one of the functions of the brain. This capacity, which is not of course voluntary, is one of the conditions of our living at all; for if everything were present to our memory, action would be paralysed. Progress in civilization likewise involves 'shedding the load' of a great quantity of information, and of certain capacities such as calculation, on to the computer. Thus much of our material life has 'gone unconscious' in the most desirable way, though with the result that calculations which could be performed by most people even before universal education are now proving tiresome even to the nimble-minded. If the original capacities were lost, a breakdown of the machinery would cause the breakdown of civilization. But the rusty iron staircase is there if the lifts fail, and both are finally supplementary to the human stride. Technics can progress only so long as man can still move of himself.

This would seem to suggest that *conscious culture,* if it is to thrive, ought to be reduced, if not to a minimum, then to a circumscribed area. There has been a tendency for this to happen by a kind of self-regulation, which is the reason why conscious culture is more or less conterminous with minority culture. Jung held the view that 'man's metaphysical task' was to raise 'the general level of consciousness'[12], but the metaphor might more appropriately be derived from the operation of the laser beam, conveying the idea of a powerful *concentration* of consciousness. The impression sometimes given is that, owing to the spread of education, there has been a great cultural diffusion at all levels of society. True, the huge sums voted by governments for education, and the implementation of vast school and university building-programmes, might suggest a rise in the general cultural level; but such expenditure – sometimes undertaken for prestige purposes – has produced, in the sphere of the humanities at least, a new kind of illiteracy, disguised by the use of an increasingly meaningless jargon. One has only to listen to certain public and broadcast lectures to realize that the 'new education' has called into being a language almost as far removed from common speech as the euphuism of the latter part of the sixteenth century. This is usually a disguise for extreme poverty of content.[13] It is unlikely that the numerous courses in creative writing in the United States have promoted more 'creators' of ability than would otherwise have arisen, and the same is true of the proliferation of art schools: we may remember that Henry Moore was expelled from the Slade, and Wyndham Lewis left because, as he said, he was found to be a genius.

And when the curricula of some of these institutions are examined, we experience no little surprise, until we grasp the evident fact that 'art', having been treated as an autonomous self-perpetuating activity, has in places degenerated into a diversion, no longer taken seriously even by those officially engaged in 'teaching' it, save as purveying a vaguely radical ideology. The following is of interest:

> Mrs Jean Nutter wanted to learn how to teach art to children. But after completing a year-long training course at an art college [the notorious Hornsey School of Art] she has complained to education officials that it was a 'training ground for anarchy'. She says she was taught about subjects like drug-taking and witchcraft and was constantly fed with anti-establishment ideas. And during the course, she claims, she was never told how to cope with day-to-day problems in the class-room nor given any practical advice. Instead she had to answer questions like: 'You are a tube of toothpaste. How does this help you to be a teacher?'. . . etc., etc.[14]

Although to belittle the work of societies for the promotion of the arts would be churlish, such organizations, however well administered, can undertake at best only holding operations. We must bear in mind that, while an enthusiastic audience may from time to time pack the one or two concert halls of our cities for music or perhaps for poetry-recitals, the mass media are discharging a torrent of *ersatz* PN for hours at a stretch; that governments plan to open up additional channels for the issue of more such mediocrity; and that every square yard of vacant or available wall-space is covered with crude imagery designed to promote the sale of wares claiming merits of often patent and recognized falsehood. It is the environment that men create for themselves, or allow to form around them, which reflects their true interests and tastes. It is the quality of their diversions which sheds light on their true (psychic) character. Finally, it is perfectly conceivable, given an adjustment in the law, that if the more brutal gladiatorial games of ancient Rome or their equivalent were to be staged in our great cities, the demand to witness the butchery would be overwhelming. As it is, the public enjoys the next best thing by patronizing pictorial or modelled versions of similar enormities; and the threshold of violence and scabrousness is constantly being lowered, often with the approval, and sometimes the acclaim, of intellectuals who, in another role, profess to be the upholders of minority culture.

What, then, is the task of the genuine apostles of minority culture? It, too, is a holding operation. The task of these men and women is, in E. H. Gombrich's words, 'that of recovering, preserving, and interpreting the cultural heritage of mankind'.[15] Here arises a paradox. Such a task would appear to be formidable, and we have said that conscious culture should be kept to a minimum.

Anyone who has visited or worked in some of the great universities in the United States – to take a country which, with Japan, has quantitatively the most impressive institutions of higher learning – soon comes to realize a disquieting fact: that the number of really eminent men in these sometimes gigantic institutions is constantly diminishing. On the other hand, the army of lesser scholars, epigoni, 'perpetual students' and administrators, etc., is on the increase. If we compare, without naming, some such institution with, say, one or perhaps two colleges at Cambridge before the First World War – Trinity and King's naturally spring to mind, with Keynes, Russell, Broad, Moore, McTaggart, Strachey, Duncan Grant, Rupert Brooke, Mallory, etc., in residence – we begin to suspect that the great expansion of higher education in our day has in many respects frustrated the most effective method of promoting fruitful learning. This is the regular contact of a small group of like-minded *savants*; such contacts are now virtually non-existent. If the group is too large, the degree of like-mindedness or compatibility will decrease. What will happen will be the development of a new academic *proletariat* devoted largely to 'research'. The individuals will sometimes enter into combination to pursue a special project, but usually they will tunnel away on their own among the book-stacks, planning works which, like an expensive psycho-analysis, will never reach completion. For academic respectability and the holding down of a job, however, a book will somehow be thrown together, perhaps with the aid of a special grant and leave of absence – for now we have to interrupt our everyday work in order to be able to justify it. This is, as already indicated, easier to achieve in the humanities than in the sciences. There is always something more to discover about a period of history, always something extra that can be said about a novel or a poem, always a philosophical problem, such as the theory of knowledge, which is sufficiently ambiguous to occupy the attention of generation after generation of excogitators.

Having cast aspersions on the humanities, we may find more encouraging prospects in the field of technical education. But is technical education really a form of education or culture at all? Granted, the bogus or phoney is less likely to gain a place in the field of techniques than in that of the humanities, because a man cannot claim to have 'his own science' or 'his own mathematics'. A bridge must be constructed properly or it will collapse. But, as we said earlier, scientific or technical education is *instruction,* and theoretically a man could successfully follow all the classes or courses in a certain technical field without acquiring any culture at all, and certainly without needing to bring to his task any cultural endowment of his own. That the engineers and higher artisans have always tended to form a caste or élite was shown by the first Industrial Revolution; and as our society becomes more automated, the engineers will probably form an increasingly closely-knit group. Nuclear engineers already do so, which is why governments at the beginning of the nuclear age were so nervous about their scientists, and why the security services of East and West were engaged in a tug-of-war over the loyalty of certain key-figures.

There are some disciplines today which, poised half-way between the humanities and the sciences, tend to lean for their vocabulary and terminology towards the latter, because of the continuing prestige of science. These are the social sciences. A great deal has recently been written about the nature of these sciences, and the radical ideology which they tend to breed. We need not linger over them,[16] save to say that, stripped of their jargon, they appear very naked indeed.

Unless there should be a nuclear war, and until the planet is largely evacuated, leaving the earth as a kind of international park commemorating the birth of humanity, the present tendency towards megalopolis is bound to continue. (The man who seems first to have envisaged the wholesale abandonment of the earth, a century before the technical deveopments that led to space travel, was Wynwood Reade, author of the once-famous *Martyrdom of Man* (1872).) We also have to reconcile ourselves to the fact that the media, especially television, are here to stay. In that case, conscious culture will continue to be minority culture, as it has never really been anything else; the problem will be to preserve the conditions for keeping even this minority culture alive. We have spoken of the link that exists, in Britain at least, between certain representatives of minority culture and manifestations of cultural decline; there can be few parallels to the case of a man holding anti-establishment views (though pretty conventional ones) yet for long filling an establishment job in the

National Theatre, and at the same time fathering a work so squalid as *Oh! Calcutta!*. Equally surprising is the tolerance shown by some members of the 'intelligentsia' to this and other productions (cheerfully labelled 'decadent'): we need not concern ourselves with the intellectual 'leaders' who have written rapturously about these pieces, for there are zanies at every social level. What needs to be stressed is that minority culture is not always to be found where we might expect it; it is only later that the true centres of intellectual and spiritual growth can be detected, and then it is too late – even if it would have been desirable – to dole out generous subsidies. The sixth century community on Iona under St Columba, or the group of devotees on Holy Island in the days of St Aidan and St Cuthbert in the century following, or Bede and his associates at Jarrow in the eighth century, did not realize that they were among the few genuine centres of spiritual creativity of their time, any more than did the seventeenth century members of Port-Royal or the family group at Little Gidding. The signs of genuine cultural preoccupation are an atmosphere of dedication, a rejection of the fetish of a high standard of living, and above all an indifference to publicity.

An amusing aspect of some movements concerned with promoting the values of the alternative society, or the Underground, was their readiness to avail themselves of the publicity organs of the social system they were committed to overthrowing. A publication such as *Do It!* by Jerry Rubin (introduction by Eldridge Cleaver), written by a man who 'for three years lived near the University of California as an Outside Agitator to destroy the University', was not only issued by a highly respectable publishing house, Simon and Schuster, but also used all the standard capitalist publicity methods, having been designed by Quentin Fiore ('the media magician'), as well as printing the word 'fuck' in upper case, lower case, and in line after line repetition, with the monotony of the Puritanism with which the author was so obviously infected, and recording with pride how much of this 'underground' activity was enacted before the cameras. Genuine cultural continuity will not be promoted by people who, as Rubin so revealingly claimed, 'want everything' (and apparently want it free[17]); for this is the very ethic or anti-ethic that has been eating at the heart of our present culture. The true cultural tradition will be handed on by those whose wants are few. Perhaps the most diverting development of all is that both Jerry Rubin and Eldridge Cleaver have now joined what they used to call 'the establishment.'

The prospect for culture

To venture to prophesy what centres of cultural growth are likely to survive both our media-ridden system and the revolutionary media that so effortlessly blends with it, is therefore not part of our task. In a previous chapter, we have dwelt much on the role of the churches, for they are the institutions which, depending upon continuity, re-enact the drama of the Fall and Redemption, which is the drama of all religion because it reflects the most profound needs of humanity. Every culture must have its myths, as part of its psychic equipment; and such myths have a habit of enduring, though with modifications, through centuries. Such was the myth of Oedipus, the myth of Faust,[18] the myth of Don Juan. Moreover, every great work of art or craft derives its nature from myth. 'Artists, even a whole nation of artists, city-builders and world-builders, are true creators, founders, and "fundamentalists" only to the extent that they draw their strength from and build on that source whence the mythologies have their ultimate ground and origin.'[19] Without myth, the emotional life of man would be seriously impoverished and even rendered incapable of proper expression. The myth of courtly love, for instance, was a means whereby the male-female relationship was 'regulated' at a certain social level (and not necessarily the highest level, for the troubadours and *trouvères* and some of the *jongleurs* moved among the people as well as among the courtiers). Nor is this myth wholly extinct. It began to show signs of wear towards the middle of the nineteenth century, as may be observed in Tennyson's *Princess* (1847), when artificiality had set in, and a good deal later still in such a curious novel as Ouida's *Othmar* (1905), where a court of love takes place. We are at a stage where this myth is in systematic liquidation; but it is more than doubtful whether the myth due to replace it, whereby woman is totally demythologized, will survive. Such a myth cannot engage the emotions, and it is based upon the elimination of taboos. In any case, a myth must have 'an ultimate ground and origin'; and this ultimate ground and origin, if it is really ultimate and properly grounded, must be reality itself. Man lives by myths, and myths live by truth.

If the various alternatives to the religious point of view are examined – with the exception of agnosticism, which is not so much a point of view as a mood: agnosticism as a permanent attitude tends to lean towards materialism – they will be found one and all to

179

constitute *ersatz* religions. Marxism is one. This is true of even such a farrago as that served up by Jerry Rubin. For when, at the end of his book, he recommended that 'the world will become one big commune with free food and housing, everything shared', and declared that 'there will be no such crime as "stealing" because everything will be free', and finally that the United States will become 'a tiny yippy island in a vast sea of Yippieland love',[20] he is repeating in modern form the old messianic dreams of the German Anabaptists, the adepts of the Free Spirit, the Taborites, or the Adamites, and even the early Christians who, according to Acts, IV, 'had all things common'. It was not for nothing that the word 'apocalypse' was given a two-page spread at the end of his book. He was a millenarian, dreaming dreams of which the realization was impossible; and like that less exuberant apostle of the Underground, Jeff Nuttall, his ideas were taken up and exploited by the cynics of the New Left, whose temporary alliance with the hippies to produce the yippies was not made without the most careful calculation. Indeed, we know well that, if revolution had come to America, Jerry Rubin, still dressed no doubt in his uniform of the 'American Revolutionary War soldier', would have been one of the first to be clapped behind bars, and that 'the vast sea of Yippieland love' lapping round the United States coast would have been swiftly mined, so that revolutionary zeal of a different order could be stimulated by the familiar bogey of a 'threat from without'.

Even so, the impulse towards a new social hygiene, the drive against the brute materialistic ethos of so much American and European life, is not to be despised; for it, too, is the sign of a religious conversion, the very language of which was employed in parts of Rubin's book, with its emphasis on 'change' reminiscent almost of Moral Rearmament, and on such ideas as 'politics is how you live your life'. Through much of the literature of protest ran the idea of redemption through love, and it was therefore not altogether surprising that a periodical devoted to the overthrow of the system such as *Ramparts* (Berkeley, California), while containing (July 1973) advertisements for such things as 'the new erotic jigsaw puzzle', and including illuminating remarks such as that 'the Stones, and certainly Jagger, are, if not always right, never wrong', carried on its back-cover a series of 'love posters', published by a firm called Celestial Arts, San Francisco, which called to mind, in their extreme sentimentality, the romantic postcards to which we referred. There were titles such as 'love deeply', 'love comes', and 'with each other', accompanied by scraps of uplifting verse, some in Gothic fount: all of which has a touch of amusing nostalgia for anyone over middle age.

The question is whether the traditional churches will ever revert to being the vehicle for cultural renewal, if we are right to suggest that they have largely ceased to fulfil that mission incidental to their true calling. Here again we must be careful how to frame our conjecture; there is evidence that the role of the churches, while diminishing in Europe, is increasing outside, particularly in Africa.

> Christianity is on the move southward to be predominantly a religion of non-whites. By AD 2000 the number of African Christians will have grown from four million in 1900 to 350 million. For sheer size and rapidity of growth, this must be one of the most spectacular success stories in history.[21]

Furthermore, the decline in church-going can be misinterpreted. Except when the practice was compulsory, as in the age of Queen Elizabeth I, the churches have rarely been full, save at important festivals; and what was after that time a mark of respectability is no longer so, partly because of the increase in fashionable scepticism and partly because respectability in itself is no longer respectable. The use of churches for more than one purpose, so long as they are worthy ones, is not to be condemned. Provided the annual liturgy is performed by an incumbent for whom it remains significant, there seems no reason why the adherents of other faiths, or the agnostics, or indeed all those who find downright humanism unsatisfactory, should not feel able to attend. The churches obviously need greater patronage to make them viable, and this invitation should be made public, especially where there is a large and often spiritually adrift immigrant population. This somewhat heterodox suggestion is made in the belief that the closing, and even the amalgamation, of too many churches will mean a cultural impoverishment from which the community might never recover. As institutions, churches, like temples and shrines, are unique: many people who were denied access to churches overseas might be glad to patronize a shrine, if they were sufficiently aware of what was going on to make the procedure significant. In such edifices, the music and the movement are doing that for which music and movement (dance) are primarily intended. If, as we have argued, all art is at root religious art, then art of all kinds is best employed, however indirectly, in the service of religion. We have become so used to listening to music and viewing art in concert halls and galleries as to have forgotten that these secular places are for the most part artificial and inappropriate, though it is clear that the practice must go on until our culture takes a new direction. Moreover, such cultural metamorphosis must come about largely by itself: attempts at cultural organization or adaptation, however well-meant, usually produce effects totally unexpected. The recognition that churches were open to all, even if participation in certain services were to be only partial, would do no harm to anybody and might be of supreme benefit to some, being psychically therapeutic, while preserving those unique and sometimes exquisite places from neglect and perhaps demolition.

There are at least two groups of person to whom such a suggestion might appear ludicrous, or even pernicious. There are those for whom religion is the 'opium of the people', etc., and secondly there are those who would see in this invitation to return to the churches so much solemn humbug. Religious people are sometimes inclined to condemn Marx's statement out of hand; but was he not right about at least *some* of the effects of religion – the Erastian tendencies in the English Church, the lengths to which superstition has sometimes gone in the Church of Rome, and the extravagance of much Evangelical fervour? But such abuses are the result of a religious consciousness which has failed to undergo the process of conversion of psychic to spiritual. Consequently, it has not provided a source for the developments of those other activities which, as Jung and Collingwood said, should spring from the religious impulse. Melanie Klein has argued that men never completely emerge from the phantasy world of the psyche. If this should mean that the intellectual and spiritual consciousness always live in a psychic matrix, such a remark is acceptable; but if it means that men remain for ever imprisoned in their phantasy world, how does it come about that we are able to raise this matter at all? To be immersed in phantasy is to fail to recognize it as such. On the other hand, most of us revert to the psychic world for a great part of the time, and therefore mistake phantasy for reality. It is the invitation or inducement to remain in such a condition that makes a people 'priest-ridden' or, for that matter, dictator-ridden. In our time, we have witnessed in Hitler a man who exercised power almost wholly at the psychic level; and the

Church has sometimes assumed a similar command over the psychic life of the faithful, or a particular section of it, as in the witch craze, or in the horrifying events recorded by Aldous Huxley in *The Devils of Loudon*. The act of transition from psychic to spiritual can be a difficult and painful one, but this is true of consciousness in general, which is hard to sustain and periodically a relief to renounce.

In the second objection, likewise, there is no little force. The practice of religion in the West, perhaps on account of the now waning cult of respectability, has acquired a specious air of solemnity. Like much that is solemn, this gives it the illusion of seriousness. In many Church services there is precious little joy, lightness of heart, or even atmosphere of charity. To watch a Catholic congregation leaping to its feet and trotting rapidly out at the conclusion of the Mass, as if it were liberated from a spiritual *corvée*, is a depressing experience. This spectacle is not to be found in some African churches, or in many negro churches in the United States, or in the Orthodox church; and it is in these directions that we may have to look for the spiritual renewal which, in spite of experiments, is not so perceptible in the West. Heaven save us, it will bear repeating, from the deliberate cult of fun, which some well-meaning clerics, faced with youth's indifference, have tried to encourage.

Similarly, there does not seem to be much hope in 'the new mysticism'.

No, the reason for dwelling at length upon the future of the churches is that here are institutions available in every town, suburb and village which are dedicated to the 'sacred'. To disband the churches will mean only the erection of community centres or institutions dedicated to the dissemination of what we can only call the secular-sacred. In view of the political secularization of a country still as religious-minded as France, there have grown up in recent years the Maisons de la Culture, where culture, regarded as an autonomous product, is viewed with as much solemnity as the religion it has sought to displace. As true culture is a by-product, however, such culture is largely synthetic and *ersatz*; and it easily becomes a vehicle for political propaganda ('liberation', revolution, etc.), as the French experience amply demonstrates. Indeed, wherever there is an official culture, as in the Soviet Union or Communist China, it is made a vehicle for political indoctrination. But we do not need to go as far as China or Russia for evidence of politicized culture: there is the depressing case of such a 'model' Western democracy as Sweden. Not long ago the Artistic Director of the Royal Dramatic Theatre in Stockholm observed:

> Education is turning out people who haven't learnt to fit into society. So that means I won't allow plays that glorify the individual. . . . It definitely cuts out Ibsen. *Brand* and *Peer Gynt* are two plays I do not want to see performed. . . . *Coriolanus* can be interpreted in a radical way. We put it on as an attack upon bourgeois values. . . . Among Scandinavian classics, I would not do Holberg. His morality is doubtful. He's aristocratic, and we've got to be democratic.

No wonder Sweden has been described as 'a spiritual desert'.[22]

Cultural Centres, Poets' Pubs, and such ventures as those of Arnold Wesker, a political as much as a literary figure, are evidence that the true springs of culture have been diverted elsewhere. Again, we must not condemn too readily: the audience at some such place might be put in contact with works of which it might otherwise have remained ignorant, and receive some psychic nourishment. In the same way, there is no absolute objection to pictures such as the Mona Lisa being transported to the other side of the earth, or of Japanese or Chinese or Egyptian art being exhibited in London. But how many of these exhibits were really intended as 'works of art' to begin with, and how many have, in Bullough's words, 'become' works of art in consequence of their divorce by time from a religious context? In the case of most traditional Japanese and Chinese (and Tibetan) art, for instance, the original impulse was almost entirely religious; for the royal personages whose burial garments or tombs were so exquisitely fashioned were themselves sacred figures, exercising the mandate of heaven. 'In the Far East what is called the "aesthetic emotion" still retains a religious dimension, even among intellectuals.'[23] The exhibitions to which the public crowd with such enthusiasm come mostly within the category of archaelogy. As such they provide the PN assimilable from all objects which stimulate the theme of mystery. The critics, being 'art critics', will treat them as 'art', and the public will read their often strained explanations as a somewhat irksome duty. But this conspiracy to cultivate an exclusively aesthetic sphere will not long convince the ordinary man, still less the ordinary woman, who endeavours to press through the aesthetic terminology to a vision of the sacred community which the artist or craftsman originally served. If the periods in question are studied profoundly, it will be realized that the 'post religious' art of Europe (for example) still retains its coherence as a by-product of the 'sacred'. Beauty has become the name of the new god, with portraits and landscapes and later 'abstract' designs as manifestations of that deity. The characters are not 'in search of an author'; the authors, artists and composers are in search of that sacred community to which they feel they rightly belong. Hence the old guilds have been supplanted by colonies of artists, working for a community which is in virtual disbandment; or, as they are sometimes now called, by Workshops, or by artists living alone in their 'cells', sometimes in great financial straits, who testify by their isolation to their wish to serve the god, and who await, as do all those who so serve, the coming of his kingdom. 'Human nature needs a holy community.'[24]

In the last of his novels, *Island* (1962), Aldous Huxley has some interesting things to say (Chapter 2) about the 'religious' nature of landscape painting as opposed to non-representational art in general. 'All I know,' concludes one character, 'is that in your abstractions I do not find the realities that reveal themselves here. . . . Which is why this fashionable abstract non-objective expressionism of yours is so fundamentally irreligious – and also, I may add, why even the best of it is so profoundly boring, so bottom-lessly trivial.'

Although most art historians today refuse to recognize the basi-cally sacred character of art, some of the more perceptive are clear in their own minds that art which can be called traditional is always dedicated to the service of the sacred.

> A traditional art is the creative expression of a society in which every form of creation – painting, sculpture, architecture, and even the slightest articles of everyday use – is fashioned not only for its utility, but as an appropriate symbolic revelation of the supernatural powers that are believed to govern the terrestrial order.[25]

The writer goes on to say, however, that in non-traditional periods

> artists will express themselves in realistic terms because their whole belief and experience are centred on the material world. The term, non-traditional art, is usually assigned to all work beginning with the Renaissance in Europe when the artist strove

to record the outward appearance of nature rather than the underlying spirit operating behind the facade of actuality.[26]

But is this really so? What artist – who was at the same time a good artist – has ever striven to represent merely 'the outward appearance of nature'? The great artists of nature, like the great portrait painters, have never rested content with copying nature from the outside, if that is what the writer means; and if at any time they conceived this to be their task – as for instance when they were commissioned to paint 'a good likeness' – they soon went beyond it and placed the likeness in a context, or relief, which served to bring out the spirituality (such as it was) in the countenance of the sitter. Who minds whether the *Mona Lisa* was a good likeness? As a matter of fact, we have no means of telling; and, if we had, it would be an historical rather than an aesthetic fact. The attraction of the *Mona Lisa* is precisely its high mystery, if not necessarily a mystery so ineffable as that which Walter Pater attributed to it. The feature most striking about the lady is not her famous smile but her hieratic pose. She *presides*; hence her authority, her sacred presence. Furthermore, to take an example from the book we have cited, in what sense could Whistler's painting of Old Battersea Bridge be called 'the outward appearance' of the object? The bridge is transformed into a construction almost supernatural in nature, and certainly numinous: it is by no means 'the valid expression of a period in which science replaces tradition'.[27] The statement on the same page that, in respect of traditional and non-traditional art, 'we cannot say one is better than the other' cannot be true; for non-traditional art as an autonomous creation does not exist – and could not come into existence – of itself. Art with a capital A is a figment of the imagination of the Critic with a capital C. In so far as the artist succeeds in setting to work at all, he gives evidence of the pull exercised, at first through the psychic medium, by the Logos.[28] This does not mean that the Logos paints directly *through* him, as some artists feel to be the case, but that it uses him, delegates him, to paint on its behalf, thus extending and deepening the sacred order. And it is this, rather than the 'increase in consciousness', which is the true goal of man's terrestrial activity.

The question how a culture which is largely subconscious in origin can be encouraged and maintained in health has therefore already been implicitly answered. We must cultivate Jacapone da Todi's 'ordered life in every state', drawing upon our psychic energy and replenishing it by seeking nutrition both from the 'cultural heritage' in the narrow sense of the fine arts, literature and music, and from that larger heritage or reservoir of PN, much of which is best assimilated in a subconscious manner. This larger heritage includes such aspects of nature as have been left undesecrated, and which is fed upon most satisfactorily by living in it as part of our ordinary surroundings; and it includes also the social heritage, which contains the nourishment of the past, the home with its associations with our upbringing, and the fellow beings, human and otherwise, with whom we enjoy communion. 'Man's greatness is always to recreate his life, to recreate what is given to him, to fashion that very thing which he undergoes'[29]: for from this fashioning and re-creation will spring up the cultural fount at which we need to drink. Culture is a means to renewal, replenishment. If a child draws a triangle with accuracy and care, he is 'living in the truth', which, as we have seen, means living at more than one level – the level of essences and values, which we descry through a direct intuition, and the level of the psyche where these essences and values are realized in their opaqueness but also in their concreteness. For while the child seeks to understand the triangle intellectually (which includes understanding why there cannot be a biangle), he is psychically nourished by the act of drawing skilfully and accurately, and by the satisfying contemplation of the finished product; and what is true of the elementary drawing of a triangle is the more true of higher creative work, where an audience is drawn into the creative act. In short, PN is reciprocally giving and taking; and that which is given and taken at this level provides the foundation, the humus, of all that is precariously constructed upon it.

The economics of PN

That every budget, be it family, institutional, or national, makes provision for expenditure on PN, is obvious. In fact, a local or national government which declined to make such provision would be considered lacking in public spirit. Although PN expenditure is the first to come under the axe when cuts are made – usually described as 'prudent' if a left-wing government is in power, and 'wicked' if the ministry is more to the right – they are also among the first to be considered for restoration. Even the philistine bestirs

himself when some familiar traditional 'cultural' heritage is under
threat. Granted, such heritage has on occasion to be concealed or
categorized as archaeology: too much emphasis on the arts, above all
the 'fine' arts, arouses supicion. On the other hand, those arts can
themselves lend a certain prestige, especially to politicians who wish
to distance themselves culturally from their fellows. Then there is the
Arts Council, at present (1984) in receipt of a government grant of
£100,000,000 – which is the subject of political skirmishes, but
which testifies by its subventions to the feeling that the government
ought to educate public taste.

Local authorities have always felt it desirable to budget for PN,
whether it be for the performing arts (where the use of the term
'workshop' seems effectively to silence opposition), the dance,
music, especially in its 'popular' forms, or the provision of parks and
sporting facilities. A significant portion of the rates is now allocated
under these heads. Some authorities even support writers in residence, or commission artists to paint gigantic frescoes, usually with a
social 'message'. No doubt they may in due course appoint official
jesters and clowns, though here expense could be saved by recruiting
personnel already on the pay-roll.

It is not only official organizations which budget for PN. The
National Trust, that admirable charity, is designed to extract from
ancient or disused buildings a residue of PN and make it publicly
available. For many years it has been the custom for certain enter-
prising firms, or newspapers enjoying a large circulation, to allocate
funds for the arts, including sport, which can be counted as a
performing art now that sportsmen have become prima donnas. The
Association for Business Sponsorship of the Arts (ABSA) has a
budget of £14,000,000 (1983). Financing sources of PN can add
greatly to a firm's prestige, and so feature prominently in the
Company Report. And the sums disbursed are allowable against tax
as a 'business expense'.

Finally, as mentioned earlier, the twentieth century has witnessed
the export at government expense of PN overseas. All major countries now have an organization designed to disseminate its culture –
or a carefully vetted selection of that culture – with a view to
supplementing, or on occasion replacing, its diplomatic efforts.
Originally viewed with scepticism by experts in international affairs,
the provision of this supplement is now perceived to be, in some
cases, more efficacious and enduring than the traditional methods –

some of them clandestine – of influencing foreigners. It may finally supplant economic aid. An example is provided by the Indian sub-continent. Although the British Raj as a political force is now a distant memory, the 'spirit' of the Pax Britannica – the ideas of freedom under the law, 'fair play', and other principles which, because they are indefinable, remain of crucial importance – has, if anything, gathered strength since the political independence of India and Pakistan. Modern India, using that word in a general sense, is a striking tribute to the potency of a certain kind of PN emanating from the UK, upon which the intelligentsia continues to draw. Nirad Chaudhuri's *Memoirs of an Unknown Indian* is a remarkable tribute to this legacy.

Needless to say, other countries, but particularly France, have achieved a comparable influence. Pay a visit to one of the ex-French colonies in Africa, and you will find the predominant atmosphere so French as to induce in the European a feeling of nostalgia: for if 'spiritually we are all semites,' culturally we are all francophile. The 'atmosphere' is precisely the PN distilled from long habituation with French culture. The inhabitants would as soon dispense with such influence as with their own indigenous traditions. Indeed, if con-fronted with the choice, they might settle for the first.

The policy whereby local and central government allocate funds for the provision of PN is likely to be reinforced. It is not impossible that experiments will be made to institute a special PN tax, though this might need to be concealed under some euphemistic title. To this subject, our last, we now turn.

The future of PN

George Orwell's nightmare vision in *1984* has not so far been realized, at least in the Western world, though the means to its realization have accumulated to a degree which some consider a threat to our liberties. There are those, like Nick Hentoff in *The Village Voice*, New York, who, 'with a kind of anguished glee', argue that surveillance devices at the disposal of the police, the FBI, and the US government generally, prove that in America Orwell's 1984 is already here.[30] This is the kind of hyperbole of which people of his radical persuasion are masters. It is curious that their horror at what they claim to be taking place in their own country does not extend to its ever-present reality in countries for which, short of wanting to take shelter there, they profess such admiration. What is disquieting in the Western democracies is not so much an advance towards totalitarianism, as the fact that, with standards of living far above the rest of the world, there is evidence of psychic enfeeblement afflicting both young and old.

Naturally, the plight of the young is the more poignant. If the only alternative to a 'soul-destroying' unemployment is employment almost as 'soul-destroying', then it may conceivably be preferable to have one's soul destroyed quietly and at leisure; and this seems to be the attitude of some of the young themselves. As for work, what kind of education, or incentive to help society, is shown in the case of the young boy from Grantham (birthplace of our first woman prime minister), who, asked what he wanted to do after school, replied that he looked foward to having 'a well-paid job'?

During the present century, longevity in the developed countries has increased by thirty per cent. The average life-span during the sixteenth century was thirty years. Therefore the proportion of old people, with a preponderance of women, is increasing to the extent that one of the most acute problems is to maintain the solvency of pension funds. The other problem is to achieve some sort of worthwhile life in the interval between retirement and postponed death – a problem which naturally has never risen before. To the ardent young scholar, the future would seem to promise unlimited opportunities for intellectual cultivation, in the company of like-minded *savants*. He imagines that intellectual concentration, if persisted in, must produce a sudden illumination or moment of vision bringing about the descent of the Logos, just as the practitioners of TM are persuaded, during their early efforts, that spiritual enlightenment or *satori* will assuredly be vouchsafed to them. But for most people, and even for those aspirants grown older and perhaps wiser, such expectations fade. It is the psyche that principally needs sustenance. This can be provided by the arts, the rites, the myths, the play, and even the taboos, and not least by compatible company. The grandchild is for many – to their surprise and gratification – a unique source of PN; for togetherness at more than one age-level, and often at the extremes, is a psychic need.

It is not necessary to be a futorologist to know that within the next few centuries the material and economic condition of the world will undergo unprecedented change. Sources of energy – above all, oil, upon which the developed world is still almost wholly dependent, but also plutonium – will be exhausted. The next certainty – apart from the fact that the unexpected will happen, as it always does – is that, whatever economic and social changes may take place, man's basic needs will remain the same. So far as human nature is concerned, we can expect no genetic mutation. The superman is as much a fantasy as perpetual motion. If the human race should colonize the farthest planets – which would entail the birth and death of several generations on the way – the resulting society would consist of men and women endowed with a *nature* no different from that of their earthly palaeolithic ancestors. If man is to survive, it will be as Man, not as another creature.

Consequently, there will remain a stability about psychic response and nourishment, even though the manner of its provision may alter.

In addition to his organic or ecological niche – which man can change, though not always to his advantage – everyone has what we may call a *psycho-niche*. This is where his ideals, loyalties and affections lie. When Keats spoke in one of his letters of the 'holiness of the heart's affections', he was referring to the supreme importance of the psycho-niche. A psycho-niche is one's inner nature, one's heart of hearts. A person who has not by adulthood established for himself a psycho-niche is not spiritually whole: he lacks *integrity*. The psycho-niche is therefore the apex of cultural formation. The prevalence of mental illness is due partly to such a lack of wholeness or balance, just as certain forms of anorexia among the young, especially girls, are due to loss of psychic as well as physical appetite.

Why we have described the better part of eduction as being an education in PN is because the end of education is to establish a psycho-niche: and why education is said to continue best after school is because the establishment or maintenance of a psycho-niche is a life-time's work. Naturally, a community educated in a common ethos has a communal psycho-niche. The ideal is the formation of creative centres. That is how European culture at least was built up. The old city-state, for instance, embodied a norm that later centres have not always been able to realize.

The crisis of culture in our time is due not merely to the existence of psychic poverty in the midst of material plenty, but to the disintegration of the communal psycho-niche, or the breakdown of the network whereby a regional or national or international culture was maintained.

This network of creative centres preceded the formation of nations and, though much dislocated, may in some cases survive them. Indeed, it is imperative that they should do so. The myths associated with such centres – e.g., Athens's link with the olive and Venice's 'marriage' to the sea, as reaffirmed in an annual ceremony – may prove more powerful than the national or, more accurately, nationalist myths, about which there was always something slightly unreal. 'My country right or wrong', though nominally professed, is a grossly immoral sentiment – a crude chauvinism which has nothing to do with true love of country. The question is therefore whether, with the formation of the World State, new kinds of myths will come into being. If the nationalist myths fall into desuetude, a psychic void is bound temporarily to yawn; but can we imagine the World State generating its own myths, or any myths at all? Perhaps the problem is robbed of some of its difficulty by the reflection that, among the myths that men have lived by, those associated with nationality are powerful only in appearance and not in reality; that the nation, having a life of only a few centuries, has moulded human nature less thoroughly than its champions have sometimes supposed; and that, as a form of human community, it may pass out of history more rapidly than it entered in. If therefore, the decline of nationalism leaves a psychic void, the existence of that void will have been revealed, rather than caused, by this change: for the ferocity of nationalism may be due to some extent to its being an *ersatz* generator of myth. What may survive national allegiance, in other words, will be regional allegiance, and the supersession of nationalist myth will no doubt reveal the potency and enduring nature of regional myth. The region is the true cultural unit. Europe was formed from a unity of regions, modulated into nationalities (which developed internecine strains), and may resume regional patterns in a larger union.

We referred earlier to differences in the appeal of PN to men and women. Such differences, which have been denied by some, were stressed by the Kinsey Institute, whose ideas on sexuality have for most people taken on a kind of orthodoxy. 'Contrary to our earlier thinking (1948:50), we now understand that there are basic psychological differences between the sexes.'[31] It looks, therefore, as if something pretty interesting happened to the staff of the Institute for Sexual Research, Indiana University, between the years 1950 and 1953.

In the light of this assertion, we would resume an earlier theme that women not merely live on and by PN more than men, but that they are to some extent its guardians. The advocates of women's total emancipation (whatever this might imply) can repudiate such custodianship only by eroding the femininity they are supposed to preserve. Demythologizing in that direction must come to a halt. The deliberate elimination of the female mystique may well have removed certain qualities or conventions which needed removing – an absurd submissiveness, for example. But by reducing the female appeal to purely sexual terms, it has laid women open to greater male exploitation, in the sphere where they are most vulnerable. The fact that emancipation in the extreme sense should have proceeded at the same tempo as the rising tide of pornography, including the pornography of violence, is not a coincidence: it is cause and effect.

After these words were written, the author, opening the pages of a useful compendium, *The Fontana Biographical Companion to Modern Thought* (1983), made an interesting, if rather alarming, discovery. Of the few dozen women whose biographies were included out of a total of two thousand, Marilyn Monroe was made out to be the most important. She was described as an 'ideal of sexual delight', a 'legend', who haunted not merely the popular mind but the imagination of writers and artists. If that were really so, then the emancipation of women could not have gone very far. What is apparently forgotten is that beauty – female beauty above all – is of its very nature psycho-organic; that the possession of PN can endow a woman with an attraction transcending, or taking the place of, plainness or even physical defect; and that, going further still (for the psychic can merge or modulate into the spiritual), Bernard Shaw was right, in referring to a performance by Eleanora Duse, to say that 'no physical charm is noble as well as beautiful unless it is the expression of a moral charm'.

This does not imply a reversion to the woman's-place-is-the-home type of attitude, though that is one of her places, for the home is largely her creation. It is compatible with everything that is desirable and necessary – and there is much that is desirable and necessary – in women's liberation. With many thousands of years ahead, a new form of family life will no doubt be worked out; the notion of the abolition of marriage and the adoption of a kind of communal life would, as experience has shown, merely reduce women to another form of servitude. But in so far as PN will itself play a crucial part in

193

Notes

Introduction

1 From the posthumous *Speculations* (1924), pp. 70-1.
2 'Philosophy of Science: A Personal Report', in *British Philosophy in the Mid-Century* (1957), p. 177.

Chapter 1   Psyche, religion and the new science

1 By Silvano Arieti (English translation 1967).
2 C. Judson Herrick, *The Evolution of Human Nature* (1961), p. 302.
3 To speak of Wittgenstein's 'school' is midleading: for an examination of Ryle's *Concept of Mind*, see page 11.
4 See also *Body and Mind in Western Thought* (1958), by Joan Wynn Reeves, who cites Onions extensively.
5 The point was earlier made in *Psyche: the Cult of Souls and Immortality among the Greeks*, by Erwin Rohde (English translation London, 1925), p. 30.
6 Cf. Aristotle's *De Anima*, Books II and III, translated with Introduction and Notes by D. W. Hamlyn (1968), p.12.
7 All quotations from Trevor-Roper (Lord Dacre).
8 *The Magic Circular*, February/March, 1973.
9 A. J. Toynbee, *An Historian's Approach to Religion* (1956), p.22.
10 *Le Songe de Descartes* (1932).
11 *A Critique of Analytical Philosophy* (1970), p. 49.
12 *The Concept of Mind*, Chapter 10, Psychology.
13 See Raymond Ruyer, *Néo-Finalisme* (1952), p. 81, also *La Gnose de Princeton* (1974), pp. 33-9, and, for an earlier interpretation, R. G. Collingwood, *The New Leviathan* (1942), II, 'The Relation between Body and Mind', pp. 8-11.

Chapter 2   Culture and the three nutritions

1   R. S. Peters, 'Emotion, Passivity and the Place of Freud's theory in Psychology', in *Brain and Behaviour*, vol. 4, edited by K. H. Pribram (1969).
2   *The Listener*, 30 May 1968.
3   H. Guntrip, *Personality Structure and Human Interaction* (1961), p. 222.
4   *Notes towards the Definition of Culture*, p. 27.
5   R. W. G. Hingston, *Problems of Instinct and Intelligence* (1928), p. 268.
6   W. M. Wheeler, *Social Life among the Insects* (undated), p. 282.
7   Suzanne H. Langer, *Philosophy in a New Key*, p. 37.
8   N. Tinbergen, *Social Behaviour in Animals* (1953), p. 2.
    Raymond Ruyer, *Les Nuisances Idéologiques* (Paris 1972). p. 187.
10   Cf. R. M. MacIver, *The Modern State* (1926), p. 326.
11   Cf. T. S. Eliot, *Notes towards the Definition of Culture*, p. 27.
12   George Orwell, *Coming up for Air* (1939), part II, ch. 2, pp. 48-9.
13   F. Fraser Darling, *New Highland Survey* (1955), p. 282.
14   *What I believe* (1884), English translation 1921, p. 312.
15   Ivan D. Illich, *Tools for Conviviality* (1973), p. 4.
16   The concept of psychic nutrition was outlined in Raymond Ruyer's article 'La Nature du Psychique' in the *Revue de Métaphysique et de la Morale* (Janvier-Mars, 1952), and in his *Dieu des Philosophes et Dieu des Sciences* (1971); but the writer of those works had communicated to the author a paper forming substantially Chapter 5 of the latter book. some years earlier. Full acknowledgement is hereby made, though the uses to which the argument is here put are in many respects quite different. In his *Principles of Art* (1938), R. G. Collingwood expounded a theory of magic whereby emotion was expressed and canalized into practical life, by contrast with amusement-art, whereby emotion was discharged in such a way as not interfere with that life. The author is likewise greatly indebted to this distinction; but he calls Collingwood's 'magical' emotions psychic nutrition, and the emotions aroused by amusement art, *ersatz* or pseudo psychic nutrition. For the concept of psychic energy, see C. G. Jung, *Collected works*, 8, 'On Psychic Energy'.
17   David Holbrook, *Human Hope and the Death Instinct* (1971), p. 179.
18   Quoted in *The Stricken Deer* (1965 edition), by Lord David Cecil, p. 162.
19   Cf. Carl O. Sauer, *The Morphology of Landscape*, University of California Press, 1939.
20   *Utopia*, Penguin edition, Book II, pp. 96, 98 (my italics).
21   *News of the World*, 14 May 1972.

22 Guntrip, op. cit., p. 129.
23 *Paleface.*
24 Desmond Morris, *Intimate Behaviour* (1971), p. 7.
25 Originally published in *England's Ideal* (1887).
26 In the collection *Do what you will* (1929).
27 Robert Attfield, 'Christian Attitudes to Nature', *Journal of the History of Ideas*, July–September 1983, p. 378

Chapter 3   Positive and negative nutrition

1 Richard Williams, *The Times*, 28 June 1982.
2 R. G. Collingwood, *The Principles of Art* (1938), pp. 321–44.
3 *The Times*, 11 July 1983.
4 *The Rise of the Common Player* (1962), p. 162.
5 Kenneth Rose, *Sunday Telegraph*, 30 January 1977.
6 Victor Hugo, 'Les Feuilles d'Automne'.
7 This point is well brought out in the chapter on Eros in C. S. Lewis's *The Four Loves* (1960), especially p. 109.
8 Letter in *New Society*, 5 February 1970.
9 *Taking it like a woman* (1983).
10 Byron, *'So, we'll go no more a-roving'.*
11 T. S. Eliot, *The Waste Land*, III.
12 *Sunday Times*, 11 March 1962.
13 Christopher Dowling, keeper of the Department of Education and Publications, Imperial War Museum, speaking of the *Radio Times* Colditz Escape Exhibition, 1974. In London, a war exhibition is dedicated 'to all fighting men'.
14 *International Herald Tribune*, 14 November 1973.
15 Cf. Jung. See page 160.
16 See, e.g., *The Exeter Book Riddles*, translated by Kevin Crossley-Holland (1969).
17 *Piers Plowman*, passus XV, 203-5, translated by Terence Tiller (1981).
18 T. S. Eliot, 'The Rock', VI.
19 Henry Chadwick, *Boethius, The Consolations of Music, Logic, Theology and Philosophy* (1981), p.101.
20 *The Letters of Marsilio Ficino*, vol. 1, pp. 40, 46, translated from the Latin by members of the Language Department of the School of Economic Science, London (1975).
21 See page 47.
22 *The Examination of Men's Wits* (1594).
23 'In Western societies the Jews and Italians have very low rates of alcoholism. In these two cultural groups alcohol consumption is an

integral part of socialization and of group rites rather than being individual and sporadic. On the other hand, in America, the Irish American ethnic group has always had a rate of alcoholism many times that of any other group. It is postulated that historical and social factors in Irish society, which have encouraged high rates of alcoholic consumption, particularly in men, when added to the deprivations found in the American environment, all combined to produce a societal group in which alcoholism would be common.' (Random J. Arthur, *An Introduction to Social Psychiatry*, 1971, p. 110.)

24 W. B. Yeats, 'The Stare's Nest by my Window'.
25 Christopher Booker, *Encounter*, September 1977, pp. 73-4.
26 See the author's 'Non-Science for the Citizen' (*Universities Quarterly*, Winter 1983); also *Soft City*, by Jonathan Raban (1974), concerning the Notting Hill Gate area of London and its arcane interests.
27 From an advertisement for the magazine *Fate and Fortune* in the *Daily Express*, 29 March 1974.
28 See Peter Worsley, *The Trumpet Shall Sound; a Study of 'Cargo Cults' in Melanesia (1957)*.
29 Harold Rosenberg, *Discovery the Present* (1974).

Chapter 4 The Nature of PN

1 The new 'little red book' is now the 'Selected Works' of Deng Xiaoping.
2 See 'Obsolete Youth', by Bruno Bettelheim, *Encounter*, September 1969, pp. 39, 41.
3 Archbishop Lawrence J. Shehan of Baltimore, commenting on the decision of the Supreme Court ruling against the New York State Board of Regents' prayer for schools (1962).
4 *Mysterium tremendum* was an expression made familiar in Otto's *Idea of the Holy* (1923), with its concept of 'the numinous'.
5 A more extreme case is the Revd Chad Varah, for whom 'Christian Lib is sexual lib' (see, e.g., *Forum*, vol. 6, no. 1).
6 Paul Fort's poem, 'Les Baleines', from which this line is taken, is a parable of the nature of PN.
7 *The Economist*, 1 October 1983.
8 Donald MacRae, 'In Praise of Literacy', *New Society*, 17 April 1969.
9 Max Picard's remarkable book *The World of Silence* (1954) is really a book about a particularly healing kind of PN.
10 Arnold Toynbee, *Cities on the Move* (1970), p. 174.
11 F. R. Cowell, *Culture in Private and Public Life* (1959), p. 186.
12 Ibid., p.171. Equivalent expenditure for tobacco was £1.32 (approx.). Cowell was of course using the old currency.

13 See the remarkable Preface to *Late Lyrics and Earlier* (1922).
14 See his essay 'On Going to Church'.
15 The film *Secret Rites* is an example.
16 The reader who is curious on this point might care to look at the author's *In Search of St Piran* (1981).
17 P. A. Talbot, *Southern Nigeria* (1923), p. 606.
18 See the remarkable letter addressed by Solzhenitsyn to Patriarch Pimen, leader of the Russian Orthodox Church (reprinted in *The Tablet*, 15 April 1972).

Chapter 5   Religion, culture and counter-culture

1 *The Essence of Philosophy*, quoted by F. R. Cowell, *Culture in Private and Public Life*, p.22.
2 *The Idea of History* (1946), p. 315.
3 See George Herbert's poem, 'The Elixir'.
4 *Notes towards the Definition of Culture*, p.19.
5 *Homo Ludens* (1949), p.211.
6 *The Aesthetic Education of Mankind* (1793), Letter 15.
7 *Notes Towards the Definition of Culture*, p.30.
8 *Beyond Politics* (1939), pp.20-1, my italics.
9 Ibid., p.28.
10 Ibid., p.53. See also an almost identical statement on p.57.
11 This has its political wing, the Komeito, or 'clean-government' party. See pp. 104, 105.
12 Dawson, op. cit., p.78.
13 E.g., the work of Ivan Illich, himself a former priest.
14 Jeff Nuttall, *Bomb Culture* (1970), p.9.
15 Ibid., p.22.
16 Ibid., p. 33.
17 Ibid., p. 37.
18 True, they later returned them; but was not this, at the time, a trendy thing to do, like the renunciation of titles?
19 *The Observer*, 9 February 1964.
20 Introduction to *The Martyrdom of Spain* (1938) by Alfred Mendizahal.
21 Hence Nuttall's description of the Soviet dissidents Daniel, Sinyavsky and others as being 'exactly on the same mental wavelength as the Underground elsewhere' is therefore a serious error.
22 Nuttall, op. cit., p. 202. Ginsberg adds: 'I am proposing these standards to you, respectable ministers, once and for all, that you endorse publically the private desire and knowledge of mankind in America, and so inspire the young.'

23 'Apology', *Late Lyrics and Earlier* (1923), p.xvi.
24 *The Defence of Poetry*, my italics.
25 George Herbert, 'The Elixir'.

Chapter 6   Psychical distance, the fine arts, amusement and 'magic'

1 Of the extensive literature which has grown up on the subject, George Dickie's 'Psychical Distance: In a Fog at Sea' *(British Journal of Aesthetics,* Winter 1973) is perhaps the most useful critical study.
2 'There is some evidence that Dylan wrote his poems and proceeded to cook them up into the necessary obscurity which he thought fashionable.' (Cyril Connolly, 'The Greatness of Dylan Thomas', *Sunday Times,* 30 May 1971.) The same was true of W. H. Auden. 'When Auden was younger, he was very lazy. If I didn't like a poem, he threw it away and wrote another. If I liked one line, he would keep it and work it into a new poem. In this way, whole poems were constructed which were simply anthologies of my favourite lines, entirely regardless of grammar or sense. This is the simple explanation of much of Auden's celebrated obscurity.' (Christopher Isherwood, 'Some Notes on Auden's Early Poetry.')
3 *Civilization,* p.101.
4 Frieda Fordham, *An Introduction to Jung's Psychology* (1953), p.27.
5 *The Principles of Art,* Chapter 4.
6 *The New Leviathan* (1943), p.76.
7 *The Principles of Art,* pp.66-7.
8 *Sunday Times,* 5 August 1973.
9 *Speculum Mentis* (1924), p.110.
10 Byron, 'The Prophecy of Dante' (Canto I).
11 Einstein on Shaw, at a dinner at the Savoy, 1930.

Chapter 7   Jung on psyche and religion

1 *New Horizons in Psychiatry* (1964), p.31.
2 *Freud and the Post-Freudians* (1961), p.43. For a contrary and more balanced view the reader is referred to David Stafford-Clark's *Psychiatry Today* (1963), especially pp.152-6.
3 David Holbrook, *Human Hope and the Death Instinct* (1971), p.67 *et al.*
4 *Two Essays on Analytical Psychology* (1942), p.116.
5 *The Practice of Psychotherapy* (1951), p.115.

6   Foreword to Frieda Fordham's *Introduction to Jung's Psychology* (1966), p.11.
7   *Über den Archetypus* (1936), p.263.
8   *The Politics of Experience* (1967), p.104.
9   Raymond Hostie, S.J., *Religion and the Psychology of Jung*, translated by G. R. Lamb (1957), p.60.
10 *The Psychology of the Unconscious* (1911), p.144.
11 *Memories, Dreams, Reflections* (1963), p.174.
12 *Two Essays on Analytic Psychology* (1926), p.74.
13 *Modern Man in Search of a Soul* (1933), p. 175.
14 *Psychology and Religion*, p.113.
15 *Individuation: a Study of the Depth Psychology of Carl Gustav Jung* (1955), p.189.
16 Ibid., p.186.
17 Mircea Eliade, *The Sacred and the Profane* (1959), p.34.
18 Sometimes called 'efficient' causality.

Chapter 8   The cultural prospect

1   From an article entitled 'Living with Sex' by Robert Shields, part 2, *The Observer*, 13 June 1965.
2   Fr Joseph Nuttin, in *Psychoanalysis and Personality* (1963), vol. 1, p.170.
3   *Memories, Dreams, Reflections* (1963).
4   Frieda Fordham, *Introduction to Jung's Psychology*, p.121.
5   See pp. 82-83.
6   *The Meaning of Love* (English translation 1945).
7   *Notes towards the Definition of Culture*, p.27.
8   Letter to Constance Malleson, 29 September 1916, *Autobiography*, vol. 2, p.75.
9   *Heaven and Hell*, p.28.
10 *Civilization* (1969), p.41.
11 Cf. Claude Lévi-Strauss, *Tristes Tropiques* (English translation 1973), for many examples.
12 *Memories, Dreams, Reflections*, p.343.
13 The following letter in *The Times* (20 August 1973) from Dr Mervyn Stockwood, then Bishop of Southwark, is a useful piece of evidence from the sphere of education:

   'Sir, – Today I received a memorandum from a group of London teachers, entitled *The Right to Learn*. In it occurs this sentence: "The presumption that the social background of London children now dictates a need for socialization before education can even begin, has now got such a grip that the ILEA is experimenting with operant techniques of behaviour modification."

What about "dialogue in depth" to "restructure" and "hospitalize" the London teachers' vocabulary?'

14 *Sunday Express,* 12 August 1973. Something of the depths to which 'art criticism' has sunk may be gauged from the statement of *The Times* art critic, Paul Overy, that Andy Warhol is 'the most serious artist to have emerged *anywhere* since the war' (12 March 1974, my italics).

15 'Research in the Humanities' (*Daedalus,* Spring, 1973, p.4). The suggestion that the word 'heritage' should be dropped in favour of 'entail' is an unfortunate one. The legal associations of entail are far too entrenched.

16 See, for instance, *Social Science as Sorcery,* by Stanislav Andrevski (1973).

17 Jerry Rubin, *Do It!*, p.256.

18 'There was a chord of the Oedipus legend in every Greek, which longed to be touched directly and respond in its own way. And thus it was with the German nation and Faust.' (Burckhardt, quoted Jung, *The Psychology of the Unconscious,* 1918, p. 490.)

19 *Introduction to a Science of Mythology,* by C. G. Jung and C. Kerényi, p.30.

20 Rubin, op. cit., p.256.

21 David Barrett, *Schism and Renewal in Africa* (1973), quoted in *The Times,* 19 July 1973.

22 Roland Huntford, *The New Totalitarians* (1971), pp.310-11 and 347.

23 Mircea Eliade, *The Sacred and the Profane* (1959), p.154.

24 Christopher Dawson, *Beyond Politics* (1939), p.131.

25 Benjamin Rowland, Jr, *Art in East and West* (1954), p.1.

26 Ibid., p.2.

27 Ibid., p.2.

28 Most creative artists are aware of the psychic stirring which heralds artistic production, and have expressed it metaphorically. T. S. Eliot speaks of the 'dark womb' from which a poem is born (critical note, *Collected Poems of Harold Munro,* 1933, p.iv).

29 Simone Weil, *Gravity and Grace* (1947), p.157.

30 John Wain, *Encounter,* September–October 1983, p.47. In fact, Orwell did not anticipate the total extinction of liberties until half-way through the twenty-first century.

31 *Sexual Behaviour of the Human Female,* by the staff of the Institute for Sexual Research, Indiana University, 1953, p.288.

Index

Index

Index

Plumb, J. H., 24, 39
Plutarch, 83
plutonium, 191
PN (*see* psychic nutrition)
Podgorny, President, 55
Poetics (Aristotle), 9
poetry, 42, 47, 85, 118, 139, 175, 176
Poetry and Truth (Goethe), 113
Politics (Aristotle), 84
Polynesia, 2
pop culture, 4, 42, 51, 97: music in, 46; and religion, 126; stars in, 54, 172
Pope, the, 80: inept salutation to, 109
Popery, 69
Popper, Sir Karl, 3
popular songs, 47, 81
pornography, 40, 93, 99, 146, 175: and female demythologizing, 193
Porphyry, 85
Port-Royal, 178
potlatch ceremonies, 97
Prayer Book (Anglican), 117
Presley, Elvis, 81
priesthood, 27, 182
Princess (Tennyson), 179
prisons, 49
proletariat, new academic, 176
prostitution, 90
protoplasm, 12
Proust, Marcel, 33
psyche, (*see also* psychic nutrition), 4, 46
psychiatry, 9, 117
psychic nutrition (PN), 33: and art, 34; conservatism of, 49, 68: crisis in, 42; cutting of appetite for, 94, 191; economics of, 187–9; and entertainment industry, 44; *ersatz* form of, 51, 111, 149; intoxication of, 44; Jungian view of, 156–65; negative form of, 51, 87–91, 194; opacity of, 85, 140, 153, 155, 163, 164; 'psychical distance' and, 141–7; psycho-niche and, 190; in relation to abundance, 97, 191; in relation to amusement, 92; and religion, 122, 155, 161–5; substitutes for, 51, 91–100; surfeit and starvation of, 43, 49; and thematism, 43
psychology, 5, 6, 7, 9, 10, 11: Freudian form of, 156–7, 159, 161; Jungian form of, 156–65, 166–7; psycho-synthesis, as culmination of, 165

psycho-niche (*see also* PN), 191
Psychology and Religion (Jung), 162
psycho-synthesis, 165
Psychotherapy East and West (Watts), 157
Ptolemy, 67
punk rock, 138, 148
puritanism, 99: Freudian form of, 157; revolutionaries characterized by, 128, 178
purpose (*see also* final causes), 22
Pythagoras, 43, 85

Queen, H. M. the, 40, 54–5, 132

Rabelais, François, 75
Racine, J. B., 70
radio, 48
Radnor, Lady, 57
rag-time (*see also* jazz), 47
Rain (Maugham), 72
Ramadan, 77, 89
rationalism, 3, 67, 122
rationality, 3, 9, 76, 123, 135, 138
Reade, Wynwood, 177
Red Square, 103
reductionism, 3, 11
relics, cult of, 171
Religio Medici (Browne), 16
religion (*see also* Church), 18, 139, 147, 153, 170, 171, 181, 182: demythologizing of, 96; in relation to drama, 35; as 'form of the spirit', 120–23; Mother Goddess and, 110, 126, 173
Renaissance, 185
Republic (Plato), 9
research, as occupation of academic proletariat, 176
'Resolution and Independence' (Wordsworth), 41
Rheims cathedral, 73
Richards, I. A., 67
Ricks, Christopher, 73
Riddles, 74
Rimbaud, Arthur, 173
rites (*see also* ritual), 123, 190: of passage, 3, 35
ritual, 32, 117: Christian form of, 52; and drama, 35, 51–3; PN fortifying, 150; thematic nature of, 35
Robinson, Bishop John, 108, 109
Robinson Crusoe, 79, 88

211

rockers, tribal uniform of, 131
Rogers, Samuel, 60, 67
Rolle, Richard, 76
Rolling Stones (*see also* Mick Jagger), 52
romantic literature, increased sale of, 75, 146
Romantic Revival, 37, 137
Rome, 8, 68: gladiatorial games in, 175; and Roman Empire, 46; Saturnalia and Lupercalia, 64
Romulus and Remus, 80
Ronsard, P. de, 24
Roszak, Theodore, 135–8
Rouge et le Noir, Le (Stendhal), 96
Rousseau, J–J., 137
routine, positive and negative aspects of, 88–90
Rubin, Jerry, 133, 178, 180
Ruskin, John, 76
Russell, Bertrand, 169–70, 176
Rutherford, Lord, 167
Ruyer, Raymond, 30, 196
Rycroft, Charles, 5
Ryle, Gilbert, 6, 11

Sabine women, rape of the, 68
sacred, the, 27, 118, 172, 183, 184–5, 186
sadism, 131, 134
Saint-Simon, Duc de, 70
Samadhi, condition of, 154
Sampson, Anthony, 44
Sanskrit, 78
Sartre, J–P., 15, 148
satori, 190
scatology (*see also* eroticism), 93
Scheler, Max, 25
Schiller, J. C. F., 9, 16, 83, 124
schools (*see also* education), 4, 127, 174–5
Schopenhauer, Arthur, 67, 75, 138
Schrödinger, E., 155
science, world view of, 3, 15, 135, 137, 139, 177
science fiction, 78
Scott, Reginald, 9
Scott, Sir Walter, 41
Scottish diaspora, 83
sea, the, 59–60
Secret of the Golden Flower (Wilhelm), 159
Secular City, The (Cox), 107–15
secularization, 107, 116, 117, 153: and

secularism, 107–8
security services, 177
self, the, 5, 13, 161, 162, 168
Sensations (Rimbaud), 173
sex (*see also* eroticism), 4, 7, 18, 28, 46, 72: appeal, 54, 57–8, 172–3, 193; denial of, 46; desacralization of, 108, 146; deviations of, 131, 135; education, 56; excitement, 72; Freudian and Jungian differing views on, 158; hypocrisy about, 135; intimacy, 75; 'joys of', 45; Kinsey Institute changed view of, 192; in marriage, 90; and puritanism, 99–100; revolution in, 75, 128, 130; and the scatological, 93; as substitute for PN, 54
Shakespeare, William, 24, 41, 67, 69, 75
shaman, the, communal need for, 117
'shared zoology', 23, 29, 114
Sharif, Omar, 53
Sharp, Cecil, 47
Shaw, G. B., 73, 116, 154–5, 193
Shelley, P. B., 140
Sherrington, Sir Charles, 11
shinkō-shūkyō (Japanese new religions), 104
Shinto (*see also* Japan, Buddhism), 104, 105, 109, 127
shrines, 181
sign-symbols (*see also* evocative signals), 25–6
silence as healing PN, 111–12, 122, 170
Sillitoe, Alan, 132
Simon Stylites, St, 80
sin, sense of, 8
Skinner, B. F., 11, 123
Slade School of Art, 174
sleep, 101
Smart, J. J. C., 11
smile, role of the, 71–2
social sciences, 177
socio-biology, 14
Socrates, 48, 76
Soka-Gakkai, 104, 105, 125
solitude, as positive source of PN, 90–1, 113
Solovyev, V., 167
Solzhenitsyn, Alexander, 104, 199
Sophocles, 69
soul, the, 6, 43, 84, 162
South Pacific, 79
Soviet Union, the, 20, 48, 49, 96–7, 135:

214